Transacti

is an exciting new method of problem solv-
ing that has become widely known through such best-selling books as GAMES PEOPLE PLAY, BORN TO WIN, and I'M OK—YOU'RE OK. Now, with SUCCESS THROUGH TRANSACTIONAL ANALYSIS, we have a book that shows you exactly how you are interacting with others, what secret goals and desires are driving you, and how to understand the actions of both your superiors and your subordinates.

Whether you are just starting out at the bottom of the ladder or are on the top of the heap, this eye-opening book can be the most important book that you have ever read!

Success Through Transactional Analysis

Jut Meininger

with a Foreword by
Robert L. Goulding, M.D.

A SIGNET BOOK
NEW AMERICAN LIBRARY
TIMES MIRROR

To Mom,
for those first few years
which made all the rest OK

Library of Congress Catalog Card Number: 72-90837

This is an authorized reprint of a hardcover edition published by Grosset & Dunlap, Inc. The hardcover edition was published simultaneously in Canada.

SIGNET TRADEMARK REG. U.S. PAT. OFF. AND FOREIGN COUNTRIES
REGISTERED TRADEMARK—MARCA REGISTRADA
HECHO EN CHICAGO, U.S.A.

SIGNET, SIGNET CLASSICS, MENTOR, PLUME AND MERIDIAN BOOKS *are published by The New American Library, Inc., 1301 Avenue of the Americas, New York, New York 10019*

FIRST PRINTING, MAY, 1974

5 6 7 8 9 10 11

PRINTED IN THE UNITED STATES OF AMERICA

Contents

Foreword
by Robert L. Goulding, M.D.

Although many transactional analysis therapists have consulted with business in one way or another, and many short articles have been written, *Success Through Transactional Analysis* is, so far as I know, the first book to take the main body of T.A. knowledge and apply it to business in a broad way. I have therefore read it with considerable interest.

In this book Jut Meininger gives simple, straight examples of his points in a way that makes good sense to the reader. He defines strokes, games, and scripts for a lay audience. I particularly like Chapter Seven, "Contracting for Change"; I especially like the last part of that chapter, which deals with "how to go about changing."

The essence of my brand of T.A. (and I believe that the author first got excited about T.A. after hearing some of my own experiences) is that each person is really in charge of himself, but he has been persuaded by most of the people around him that he is not. Our songs, our folklore, our literature repeatedly insist that the world "makes me feel bad, or good, or sad, or angry." The author attempts to let you, the reader, know that this is really not so; he gets to it often enough that you need to consider carefully how you, and you only, are responsible for your feelings as well as your behavior. Freudians will shudder at this, and talk about the unconscious; I won't deny my unconscious, but after all, whose unconscious is it? I cop out on myself if I say I am not responsible because, after all, my unconscious made me feel bad—this is the most sophisticated cop-out of all, but still a cop-out.

The author suggests some ways in which each of us can check out where we are, in terms of our interpersonal relationships, and how we can stay out of games with others. It is a bit naive to think that simply because we refuse to play, the other person will change. Usually he won't—the best we can hope for is that he will quit playing with those who refuse to engage in the Game and find someone else to play with.

I hope that the reader will enjoy this book and will use it to start being aware of how he structures his time, how he gets and gives strokes, what kinds of games he plays, how he perpetuates his bad feelings (rackets) by both playing and fantasizing, and how he just might quit feeling bad and start being autonomous. As a start, close your eyes. Think about your life and how you are living it. Where will you be in five years, ten years, twenty years, if you don't change? If you don't like your answer, better change. If you do, stay with it!

Preface

No one sets out to falter on the road to success. No one starts work each morning saying, "Today, I'll make the same mistakes I've always made, and, whenever possible, I'll get bogged down by the same old problems." To the contrary. Many of us begin each new day planning to set the world on fire. We say to ourselves, "Today, I'll learn from the mistakes of my past. No more doubts. No hesitations. No more fumbling." Then, like clockwork, the phone starts ringing, people do not do what they are supposed to do, and events start slipping out of control. The old problems crop up all over again. Suddenly, despite our best intentions, we are right back where we started, not knowing what went wrong or what to do about it.

It is not hard to get caught up on this merry-go-round of mediocrity. Try as we may, most of us never get off. None of us likes it. Often, we would give anything to change. But it is not that simple when we have run out of ideas and do not know where to turn.

Fortunately, clinical research has recently given us the tools to break out of this mold. New theories and techniques, not complicated by technical mumbo jumbo of the past, are already being used by lay people in a variety of ways. The results have been impressive. The theories cut through many layers of complicated Freudian concepts, and the techniques they have led to are both remarkably efficient and capable of being used by normal, everyday people, in normal, everyday situations.

This book deals with practical applications of one new theory in particular—the theory of Transactional Analysis. Its purpose is to expose people in organizations to the extraordinary possibilities that Transactional Analysis offers for solving their basic problems. While many corporate executives admit that the vast majority of their problems are "people" problems, most will also admit that they have no systematic way of dealing with such problems, other than the rule of thumb methods they have picked up over the years. This book puts an end to that difficulty. It not only contains background material on the theory of Transactional Analysis, but also included dozens of concrete examples of how T.A. techniques can be used to cut through an enormous range of people problems, as well as many other ordinarily complex business issues. It can help both rookie salesman and chief executive alike understand and solve a wide variety of their most difficult day-to-day problems with an unusual degree of skill and effectiveness.

Acknowledgments

My sincerest thanks to Gene Kerfoot, Ph.D., a fine therapist who graciously let me watch and learn from him for several years; to Boyd Lester, M.D., who taught me that skill in helping people was not just a special magic of psychiatrists, but something I could learn for myself by working hard to increase my awareness of myself and others; to Jim Allen, M.D., who lent encouragement at important moments; to Jerry Marshall, president, Liberty National Bank, who had the courage to let me work with his senior management while I was still learning; to Larry Savage, executive vice president, Standard Life and Accident Insurance Company, for his generous and ongoing cooperation; to Dan Batchelor, general counsel, Oklahoma City Urban Renewel Authority, for his friendship; his insights, and his confidence; to Karen Adams, Mary Ann Coates, Barbara Collins, Dolores Cornelison, Kathy Cornelison, Lois Fagin, Andy Haswell, Martha Haswell, Bill Stephens, and my wife Elissa, all of whom did special things at special times to help; and most of all to the many professional and personal lives who contributed either directly or indirectly to the ideas presented in this book, and for whom clarity is by now a way of life.

1. The Magic of Transactional Analysis

How to Have the Right Advice—Always

The techniques of Transactional Analysis can be mastered by just about anyone interested in mastering them. Those who do master these techniques often appear to have magical powers of insight. They seem to have a knack for cutting to the core of a problem, frequently clarifying and resolving complex issues with a simple phrase or two.

Bill, sales manager for a large insurance company, sat at the office coffee bar one morning, frustration etched across his face. "I'm simply at my wit's end," he said dejectedly to his friend Sam, another manager. "My men are really taking advantage of me, but I'm scared stiff of cracking down for fear they'll leave to join another company."

Acutely aware of his friend's concern, Sam began to offer every suggestion he could think of, but to no avail. None of his advice seemed to work. He had about run out of ideas when Bill remarked with a note of finality, "Things are really getting pretty bad. It's gotten so I just don't know *what* to do!" At that moment Fred, their sales vice president, who had overheard their conversation, joined them.

"Bill," Fred said quietly. "Would you really like to know what to do in this situation?"

Bill looked up, startled. "Yes, sir, I would."

"Well," Fred continued, hesitating ever so briefly, "What do you *want* to do?"

Bill was taken by surprise. He had not expected that sort of question. He thought for a moment, then said emphatically, "I want to let my men know that if they keep on this way, we'll *all* be out of a job."

"Okay," Fred answered. "How could you go about that?"

Bill was quiet, his face knotted in thought. "Well, I guess I could just go ahead and *tell* them," he replied tentatively.

"Good," Fred answered. He waited a moment longer. Then, in a serious, but relaxed manner, he asked, "Can you tell them just like you told me?"

Both managers sat in silence for several minutes. Finally, Bill seemed to resolve the issue in his own mind. He took a deep breath and answered, "Yes, I can."

"Fine," Fred replied, satisfied that Bill meant what he said.

Only after Fred had left did it occur to either Bill or Sam that Fred had not uttered a single word of advice. He had only asked questions. Yet somehow, within a few minutes, he had been able to help Bill think through his difficulty and come to his own conclusion about how to solve the problem.

This story illustrates a very simple, yet far-reaching insight: established patterns of advice-giving, patterns of the you-ask-me-I'll-tell-you variety, can often be severely limited in their effectiveness. Sometimes, they do not work at all. (Usually when we need them most.) Strange as it may seem, the best answers to many of our most perplexing problems are often already tucked away in the far recesses of our own heads! We sometimes have trouble getting to them, and then, typically, we go around asking others for help. Very often, what we are looking for (even if we cannot express it in so many words) is not advice, but help in thinking the problem through for ourselves. Advice-giving, in fact, often undercuts this process.

Rather than give someone advice and have him reject it (or have him use it and find out that while it may work for *you*, it does not work for him), it is often more appropriate to help him develop his own autonomy, his ability to think for himself, by asking questions. (This is particularly true in management situations, where the purpose is to develop people who think for themselves.) Questions, instead of answers, may at first tend to throw him. They may surprise him or frustrate him. But questions which help a person cut to the core of his problem will help him come, eventually, to the best possible solution to his problem. Such a solution will be *his* solution. It will, in a sense, prepare him to deal with the situation standing on his own two feet, based on what he believes is realistic for *him,* not on what someone else might do in his place. It will, above all, be a solution which he himself is willing to live with.

In helping someone think through a problem, some questions are more helpful than others. In the case of Bill and his wayward salesmen, the most useful questions were those which 1) helped Bill identify exactly what it was he *wanted* to do (he had become too mixed up and worried to see this by himself) and 2) helped him figure out how he could go about accomplishing it.

Janet, a hardworking, extremely competent secretary, had always been a soft touch for anyone with work to be done. Lately, people had been taking advantage of her, and the work was stacking higher and higher. Janet had become very depressed and her resentment toward everyone in the office had mounted. Tears of anger rolled down Janet's cheeks as she turned to her friend Martha and blurted out, "I just don't know why Mr. Jones gives me all this work to do! He has his own secretary, but he still gives all this work to *me!*"

Martha, wanting to be helpful, yet knowing the pitfalls of giving advice, replied instead by asking questions. "What sort of work does he give you?" "Is his secretary too busy?" "How long has it been going on?" she asked. But even though Janet kept answering the questions, they could sense they were not getting any closer to the heart of the problem.

Just then the personnel manager happened by. Seeing Janet's distress, he asked, "What's the problem, Janet?"

"Oh, nothing much," she replied. "It's just that Mr. Jones has given me all this extra work to do."

"How is that a problem?" he continued.

"Well, I've got too much work already. I really can't handle any more," Janet replied heatedly.

"What would happen if you told that to Mr. Jones?" the personnel manager asked.

"Oh, I couldn't do that," Janet said. "He wouldn't understand."

The personnel manager looked off for a moment, as if collecting his thoughts, then turned to Janet and with a gentle voice asked, "Can you tell him that so he *would* understand?"

For an instant Janet was speechless, but the more she thought about it, the more she knew she *could* tell Mr. Jones in a way that he *would* understand. A look of relief came over her face as she answered, "Yes, I think I can. I'll just have to be calm about it, but let him know I mean what I say."

"Good," the personnel manager murmured pleasantly as he started to leave. "Let me know how it works out."

A successful line of questioning will often help a person crystalize a problem in his own mind. It will help him identify where he is stuck and, hopefully, isolate what confuses him. It is the only valid way to get a truly accurate statement of the difficulty and to pinpoint the real source of conflict. Asking questions is usually far more efficient than either trying to guess what the real problem might be (which could typically go on all day) or assuming that the problem is really what the person says it is (which it usually isn't).

One basic mistake most people make in trying to help others is in assuming that when someone is bothered, he has usually isolated the source of his difficulty. Not so! In fact, one reason many people never get to solve their problems is that they never actually define their problems clearly. They have a million and one things buzzing around in their heads and often have real trouble sorting them out. (It happens to the best of us at one time or another.) Helping someone clarify his problem before trying to solve it is perhaps the most important step in helping him think things through for himself. Once the problem is identified, additional questions can then help him come to grips with the best way of solving it. *

What Repetitive Behavior Patterns Reveal—The Notion of Life Scripts

Another way T.A. helps us deal more effectively with others is by giving us special insight into what other people are all about. Sometimes a brief glimpse into someone's past, or a knowledge of his habits, can be enough to help us size someone up with unusual speed and accuracy.

Dan and Jerry, two vice presidents of a large midwestern manufacturing company, were discussing Oscar, one of Dan's subordinates. "I don't know what's wrong with Oscar," Dan was saying. "He has great ideas, but never does anything with them. He doesn't finish anything he starts. If he doesn't change soon, I'll have to let him go."

Jerry, who understood some basic T.A., smiled. "Do you really think he's going to change?" he asked quietly.

"I sure do," Dan answered. "That is, if he wants to keep his job! Why do you ask?"

"Well," Jerry continued, "even if he finishes up a few projects just to keep his job, my guess is it won't last. It sounds

*See Chapter Ten for some extremely effective examples.

like his life script* doesn't really call for him to complete things."

"What do you mean by that?" Dan asked.

"From what you tell me, Dan," Jerry replied, "I get the feeling that the unconscious payoff for Oscar, even if he isn't aware of it, is only in starting things, or working on them—not in finishing them. In fact, I'll bet he probably goes out of his way just to *avoid* finishing them."

Dan thought for a moment. It was a new idea for him. A look of recognition suddenly flashed across his face. "You know, I think you're right!" he exclaimed. "I've been trying to get with Oscar for the past two weeks to wrap up this last project he's been working on, but all he seems to do is make up ways to put me off!"

"And does he also keep two or three other projects up in the air at the same time, so that when he *does* finish one, it won't be like the end of the world?" Jerry asked.

"Two or three!" Dan replied. "It's more like five or six! He's always cooking up some new idea. I never can get him to concentrate on one thing at a time!" He hesitated a moment, then continued, "And what's more," he said, "whenever I want a status report, Oscar suddenly starts playing hard to get. He's either out of the office, or out of town. Sometime I really have to start tracking him down!"

"And I'll bet, when you do," Jerry continued, "you probably have to give him a real push to tackle the next part of whatever project he's on!"

"Boy! Do I ever!" Dan answered. "I'm at my wit's end. But, tell me, don't you really think Oscar can change? Isn't there some hope for him?"

"Well, it's not that he can't change. In fact, I think he can, if he wants to, and if he actually knows what he is doing to himself," Jerry answered. "It's just that he probably doesn't *know* what he is doing at this point, and even when it's brought to his attention, he'll need to make his own decision to change. Not just to keep his job, or even to please you, but because the personal payoff for completing things, the emotional payoff to himself, has become greater than his present payoff to himself for just working on them."

Dan quietly absorbed what Jerry had said. He was obviously intrigued with this new insight. His face slowly began to

*More about life scripts, or the unconscious life plans we follow, in Chapter Four.

light up. He said, "You know I think you've really got something! But what can I do about it?"

Jerry answered, "Well, for one thing, you can help Oscar become more aware of what he seems to be doing. Then, after having spent some time with him, you'll be able to make explicit with him whether or not he's interested in changing. If he really isn't, at this time in his life, you can either readjust his job in terms of the reality of how he goes about things, or if that isn't possible, you can help him relocate."

At this point, Dan and Jerry walked off—Dan excitedly engaged in trying to grasp exactly how to handle his next meeting with Oscar, and Jerry anxiously trying to help his friend overcome his nagging problem.

One of the secrets of gaining quick insight into people is in being able to observe clearly the reality of what they do with their lives. In particular, the facts related to their *repetitive* behavior patterns—how they handle themselves, how they deal with people, how they structure time—in essence, what they actually *do*, day in, day out. A person's life, viewed through the eyes of a T.A. specialist, can be seen as a series of ongoing decisions which that person continuously makes about what to do, starting from his earliest years. Many of his current decisions will be predicated on those he first made when he was very young–decisions about what is important to him, decisions about how he sees himself, and decisions about his relationships with other people. He will, in a very real sense, *build* on his early decisions. If his early decisions were realistic and appropriate to his later life, he will have a firm foundation to build on. If they were not, he will have difficulty. Unfortunately, many of our early decisions are made unconsciously, or when we are too young to assess decisions adequately, or when we simply have too little data available to arrive at reasoned conclusions. The odds that all these decisions will be realistic or appropriate to later life, when both the context we live in and the demands upon us will have changed dramatically, are not very high.

While the circumstances surrounding such early decisions may have long been forgotten, their implications can be seen all around us, every day. The reasons why the shy, antisocial person avoids people may well be buried in his past, but the *fact* of his avoidance is observable in everyday life. The sources of the compulsive loser's self-defeating behavior may well be unknown, but the pattern of his failure is easily documented. How these early decisions came to be made, how they can be brought into conscious awareness, and how they can be changed, is the subject of much of this book.

Self-Defeating Patterns of Conversation —The Concept of Games

Hardly a day goes by when most of us do not have some situation we wish we had handled better, some difficulty we had hoped to see through more clearly. Coming to grips with these problems, however, is frequently much more of a task than it seemed at first glance. Those of us who try soon find out how exhausting it can be. It is easy to become frustrated in a world where many things seem unexplainable, many problems impossible to understand.

Harold, manager of information services for an international oil company, always had trouble dealing with his boss, Frank. Frank had the annoying habit of constantly making spur of the moment, unreasoned demands upon Harold. Out of a clear blue sky, Frank would phone, saying, "Harold, come into my officc right away, and bring the such-and-such report with you!" Whenever this happened, Harold would obediently march in with the report, only to be confronted by a barrage of "Why isn't it finished?" Why don't you have it out by now?" "You never have things ready when I need them!" At this point, Harold, who was usually so busy he could barely hold his head above water, would respond, "I haven't had time!" "I have a thousand *other* things to do!" "I can't do *everything* at once!" The two would then become hopelessly locked in a power struggle—a struggle which Frank (being the boss) would inevitably win, and from which Harold would inevitably emerge feeling more frustrated and resentful than ever. This scene had repeated itself over and over again. It was a constant emotional drain on Harold and always made him feel bad. Sometimes it would take him days to recover. Finally, Harold became fed up and vowed to do something about it. He turned to Transactional Analysis.

In a very short time Harold learned how, long ago, he and Frank had first established their self-defeating patterns of conversation. He learned how Frank had always felt pressured and how he, Harold, had always reacted to Frank defensively, responding to the sharpness and urgency in Frank's voice, while never really trying to understand Frank. Harold also learned how to avoid getting caught in these self-defeating dialogues with Frank, how to focus instead on what was actually going on between them and to express himself in a way to really reach Frank.

Sometime later, after much rehearsal and review, Harold finally felt prepared to deal with Frank. He once again sat waiting for the inevitable phone call. This time he was ready! Suddenly the phone rang! "Harold, come in here right away, and bring the such-and-such report," Frank's voice boomed on the other end.

As Harold entered Frank's office, the familiar words began to assault him. "Why isn't this ready?" "What's holding it up?" "Why hasn't it been finished?" But Harold was prepared. He was not seduced by the urgency in Frank's voice, the tone of his demands. He did not reply, "I haven't had time!" "I haven't been able to get to it!" or any of the other self-defeating words Frank had come to expect from him. (In fact, he found it rather easy to avoid such responses!) Instead, he saw in Frank all the anxiety which Frank created within himself. He saw how Frank responded to pressures, both real and imaginary, by building up tension inside himself and by passing that tension on to others. He *understood* Frank, and in reacting, he avoided saying all the sentences Frank had so long been accustomed to hearing. He said instead, "Frank, these situations have been uncomfortable for me for quite a while, and I get the impression that sometimes they may be frustrating for you, also. Now to be honest, I didn't know that there was a deadline on this report, let alone that it was today. I really don't recall our speaking about it. In the absence of any such information, I've assigned other things a higher priority."

Frank was speechless. Harold had never spoken to him like this before. Furthermore, it made sense. He was soon willing to accept Harold's suggestion for assigning completion dates to each of their projects. Harold had, at last, put an end to his humiliating arguments with Frank and had opened the door to a new and more satisfying relationship between them.

Harold's approach was based on his new understanding that many established patterns of conversation are so automatic, so second nature to us, that we often fall into them without having the faintest idea what we are doing. *Without knowing it*, we can easily get caught in a self-defeating dialogue which spirals forever downward, accomplishing little more than structuring our time in a way that makes both parties feel bad. These dialogues can repeat themselves time and time again. All we need is someone else to fill in the other half of the lines. (We already know *our* half.) In the language of T.A., these repetitive, self-defeating dialogues are called *games*.

The game Harold had inadvertently played with Frank always started when Frank asked, "Why isn't this finished?" "What's holding it up?" or "Why isn't it out?" Frank was saying the same sort of thing he had always heard his parents say to him when he was young (and bosses always say to subordinates). It translates "What's wrong with you?" The expected answer is, of course, "Nothing's wrong with me!" which everyone learns to say in childhood, and which was implied in Harold's typical reply, "I haven't had time," or "I can't do everything at once!" Once Harold had answered, however, he had been hooked, and the game became a replay of the famous power struggle, "What's wrong with you?" "Nothing's wrong with me!" "Yes, there is!" "No, there *isn't!*" "YES, THERE IS!" (This is a variation of a more commonly played game called NIGYSOB, or, in its long form, "Now I've Got You, You Son of a Bitch," which we'll hear more about later.)

The way out of such a situation—the way to avoid playing someone else's game—is found (as Harold discovered) by analyzing the intent of the words that pass back and forth and by avoiding the use of the transactionally expected response (the automatic response you are accustomed to giving and the other person expects to hear).*

One reason we often find it hard to work through difficult situations with other people is that we fail to acknowledge the extent of our own participation in transactions with them. We ignore the possibility that the course of our future transactions with someone can be changed by altering the pattern of our own behavior. Our inclination is to wait, hoping for something in the other person to change. Failing this, we typically try to manipulate him in some way so as to get him to change, only to find it more and more impossible as he becomes more and more rigid. Sometimes the only sure way to change what happens between us and someone else is simply to find out what goes wrong and to change what *we* do. T.A. can help

*What to say instead is discussed in greater depth in Chapter Five.

us understand the effect our behavior has on other people, examine the effect of their behavior on us, and then help us alter our actions and reactions in a manner consistent with our conscious intentions.

Unraveling the Mysteries of Impulsive Responses

Analyzing our transactions with people, and altering our responses, takes practice. Sometimes it's easy; but often it isn't. The biggest problem is one of perspective. Sometimes our automatic responses to situations can be so automatic, so much a part of us, that we never think to question them. At other times, when we finally get around to questioning them, the damage has already been done. It happens over and over, in an endless variety of situations. Time and time again we look back and say, "Gee, I did it again, didn't I? That's the fourth secretary I've lost this year!" (Third sales prospect I insulted this week; hundredth time I clutched under pressure; millionth time I let my boss intimidate me.)

Often the words which come out of our mouths are triggered by the feelings which have come over us—our internal reactions to the circumstances at hand. We hear "What's wrong with you?" and immediately feel resentment and the compelling need to defend ourselves. We instantaneously reply, "Nothing's wrong with me!" (or its equivalent), and by the time we realize that "nothing" was the transactionally expected response, *the response the other person was looking for*, we have already put our foot in our mouth, have been hooked into playing the other person's game. The downward spiral has begun! Once started, it is almost impossible to stop. In the past, when confronted with one of our self-defeating impulsive reactions ("I just don't know what came over me!"), we typically might have bit our tongue and shrugged it off, believing such things beyond both our capacity to understand and our ability to control. Recently, however, it has been discovered that we may still sometimes succeed in such situations if we first determine 1) *what we're feeling*, 2) *what it is were reacting to*, and 3) *what we are doing to make, or keep, ourselves feeling the way we do*. The words, in an impulsive reaction, are often tied to what we are feeling; and by using new techniques to deal with those feelings (the real source of the difficulty), the words we speak in response may change almost by themselves.

Ted, assistant manager of a wholesale drug firm, was a creative young man with many bright new ideas. His problem was that his manager, Ken, was a self-centered, pushy person who rarely listened to his subordinates. Whenever Ted brought up a new idea or a different way of doing things, Ken would interrupt him with, "We don't have time for that now!" "We've got to get this done!" "We'll do it my way!" Ted, seeing no other alternative, would say, "Okay," and would reluctantly resign himself to the situation; but he would go away smoldering inside. Sometimes he would decide to do things Ken's way just out of spite, as if to say, "Okay, we'll do it your way, but I'll show you it isn't the right way." None of this, however, was getting Ted anywhere, and one day he resolved to do something about it.

Ted decided to analyze the transactions between Ken and himself and change whatever self-defeating words he had been using—words that caused him always to give in and accept what Ken told him to do, right or wrong. But the more he tried, the harder it became. The words always seemed to be out of his mouth before he could do anything about them. After half a dozen attempts, Ted could tell he wasn't getting anywhere, and he decided to cut to the core of the problem.

The next time he confronted Ken with a new idea, and Ken responded in the same old forceful, yet negative way, Ted tried to determine exactly *what he himself was feeling.* While he was standing in front of Ken, he forced himself to identify what was happening inside himself! Although it wasn't easy, Ted could recognize that somehow he felt small and insignificant next to Ken. He was also suddenly aware of an unsettled feeling in the pit of his stomach—as if he were afraid of something but didn't know what. Satisfied for the moment that he had adequately identified what he was feeling, Ted continued with his experiment by asking himself *what he was reacting to.* Almost immediately, he discovered that it seemed to have something to do with the look in Ken's eyes, and possibly the sound of Ken's voice.

He then asked himself the final question: *What was he doing to make or keep himself feeling this way?* And as he mentally detached himself from his surroundings, Ted noticed that for some reason he kept looking directly into Ken's eyes. He also noticed that whenever he looked away, he felt a little better; but when he went back to looking into Ken's eyes, the queasiness would come upon him again. Suddenly, a startling revelation occurred to Ted! *The way he made himself feel so insignificant was by looking directly into Ken's eyes!* Whenever he looked away, the feeling disappeared! He could, he determined, control the way he felt by just deciding where to look!

The more Ted watched himself over the weeks that followed, the more he became convinced that he "saw" things in people's eyes and that he responded by feeling small and insignificant whenever anyone looked at him with the same air of authority that Ken used. They just had to *look* at him in that way and he would wilt. He discovered, in fact, that he always let people like Ken control the way he felt just by their looking at him or sometimes speaking to him in a certain way. He also discovered that it had been going on for as long as he could remember. (Ted was appalled at the implication that all his ups and downs in life, his good feelings and bad, might have actually depended on how other people looked or spoke.)

As he slowly learned these things about himself, it occurred to Ted that, somehow, he *gave* people this power over him. Some people, like his boss, seemed to have a basic need to control others out of their own insecurity, as if they were panicked by what might happen if they lost control. In reacting as he did—by accepting the way they looked at him as some sort of absolute power over him—Ted actually was giving them this control. They never *took* control. He *gave* it to them. The more he thought about it, the more he wanted to change that pattern. He was tired of feeling small and insignificant.

Finally Ted's day came. He and Ken were discussing a new project, when Ken said, "We'll do this my way," in his typically forceful way. Ted was ready. He ignored the authority in Ken's voice, the implication that the interview was over. In replying, he looked directly into Ken's eyes, denying the power he had once given them, and focused instead on how difficult it would be for Ken to control him now that he knew what was really going on.

As he did this, the old feeling of insignificance, the old fear of whatever it was, did not appear! (Ted used to say it was fear of being fired; but it wasn't. It was really much more than that. It was fear of something behind those eyes!) Ken was still trying to control Ted with his voice and his eyes, but it did not work. Ted felt relaxed! He could think! He wasn't all tied up in knots! He no longer felt *compelled* to answer, "Okay," (the transactionally expected response) when Ken said, "We'll do it *my* way!" He could see the trap that Ken was unconsciously laying for both of them, the trap of looking at things as Ken's way versus all other ways. Ted could also see that even though Ken was, through force of habit, trying to push his way, he had not really thought it through carefully. Ted did not talk about the issue of Ken's way. He concentrated, instead, on obtaining Ken's understanding of the goal they were both trying to achieve; he quietly began speaking about how this goal could be accomplished more effectively. He captured Ken's attention in a way he never had before, and in less than five minutes he had won Ken over to his way of thinking.

Unusual as this story may seem, it illustrates an important new discovery—that contrary to what we have believed for generations, people can not only control their behavior (which we have always known), but can, in a very real sense, control their feelings (which we have always doubted). We all have certain unique, internalized behavior patterns which we unconsciously use to dictate what we feel in any given situation. These repetitive behavior patterns, and the feelings associated with them, almost always seem to go hand in hand.

There are endless examples of this link between what we *do* and what we *feel*. The way Ted made himself feel insignificant is just one of them. Some people make themselves feel both angry and fearful (at different times) by doing such things as constricting their breathing or by tensing certain of their muscles. Others make themselves feel anxious or guilty by fantasizing about all the catastrophic consequences (none of which will ever come to pass) of their past actions.*

Whatever we do, the feelings which come upon us every now and then trigger certain verbal responses, and these frequently lead to games. Sometimes games can be avoided merely by changing the words we are so accustomed to saying. At other times, if the words seem to come upon us too quickly, we can still stop the game, if we want, by dealing directly with the feeling itself. Rather than being victimized by the feelings which come over us, we can learn to

*Chapter Six outlines much more about how these patterns work and what to do about them.

master these feelings in a straightforward manner, free of complicated introspection and self-analysis. If we pinpoint what we are feeling, what we are reacting to, and what we are doing to make ourselves feel that way, we can often cut directly to the source of the problem.

But before we can systematically use T.A. to deal with the full range of problems it is designed to handle—problems not only of dealing with people, but of sorting out information, establishing priorities, and making decisions that really pay off—it will be helpful to get more of a feel for the theory behind it all. Even a sketchy understanding of this theory can provide the framework in which to fit any one of a myriad of other day-to-day problems and the perspective with which to deal with them on a more enlightened basis.

2. Getting a Feel for People

When we speak of Transactional Analysis, we generally speak of two things. One is the *process* of analyzing transactions between people (he said this, I said that, and what did it all mean). The other is the *theory** of Transactional Analysis, which covers a much wider range of related material, some of which has been illustrated in Chapter One. Selected aspects of the theory which pertain to transactions and relationships in business and organizations have been chosen as the subject of the next few chapters. Familiarity with them will be helpful in learning to employ the techniques described later in the book.

How Our Brains Store Experiences— The Tape Recorder Principle

The very first step in learning about T.A. is to become familiar with some of the sound neurological facts on which it is based. Some fascinating experiments conducted by Dr. Wilder Penfield, a Canadian neurosurgeon, have particular significance. These experiments, conducted in the early 1950s, had nothing at all to do with psychology. Dr. Penfield was doing work in the study of epilepsy. His experiments involved the use of a weak electric current to stimulate selected areas of the brain of a patient under local anesthesia. The electric current was transmitted through a small probe. In each case the patient was fully conscious and able to talk.

*T.A. originated in the late 1950s and early 1960s as the brainchild of Dr. Eric Berne. Thousands of professionals across the country have since been converted to Berne's way of thinking. Many of these people have contributed to, and expanded upon, Berne's original theories. The process is still going on.

One of Penfield's unexpected, but remarkable, discoveries was that the electric probe *forced* the patient to suddenly remember things—things he had once been aware of but had long since forgotten! And each time Penfield touched a different part of the brain, a different memory was evoked! The experiments were handled exhaustively. Repeated stimulations of the same areas produced the same recollections. To test his findings, Penfield occasionally told his patients they were being stimulated, but did not apply the electrode. When this was done, they remembered nothing. When the electrode was again applied, the memory was complete in every detail! In addition, not only did they remember the facts related to a particular event, but they were actually able to *feel* the same as they had when the event first occurred. It was as if they were reliving the experience! In Penfield's own words, "Recollection evoked from the temporal cortex retains the detailed character of the original experience. When it is then introduced into the patient's consciousness, the experience seems to be in the present, possibly because it forces itself so irresistibly upon his attention. Only when it is over can he recognize it as a vivid memory of the past."[1]

Occasionally, we can find ourselves involuntarily reliving a past experience in our everyday life without the help of an electric probe. Usually, the feeling is more vivid than the facts. When Barbara, a young secretary who was trapped in a burning house as a little girl, awakes screaming in the middle of the night from a dream that her house is on fire, she is reliving the terror she first felt as a youngster. A different situation (her dream of a fire) evoked the old terror. Only later, when she thinks about it, can she remember the facts associated with the original event.

Sometimes when we relive an experience, the facts related to it are so vague that we cannot remember them at all. For example, many babies born in Germany during World War II grew into adults who cringe at the sound of even remote thunder. These adults are reliving the terror of their childhood whenever such loud noises occur. They may no longer remember the bombers flying overhead or the look on the faces of the people around them—but they can still feel the terror! They relive the feeling without remembering the exact event.

All the evidence in Penfield's work points to one inescapable conclusion: Much of what we have been consciously aware of in our life has been recorded in detail and stored in our brain, and is available for replay in the present! It is available as a series of clear, single recollections, and not as a hazy mixture of memories. It can be evoked involuntarily; and not only will precise events be recalled, but we will again feel the emotions which were associated with those events, and we will be aware of the original interpretations we placed on them.

It can also be concluded that our brains act like two-track stereo tape recorders, with one track for events and the other for the feelings associated with those events. Both tracks record simultaneously. But during involuntary playback, the feeling tape may preempt the fact tape. We may relive without remembering! It can also be concluded that the recorder is on all the time from the day we're born, whenever we're consciously aware of things.

How the Experts See Us—The Parent, the Adult, and the Child

Pioneers in Transactional Analysis have classified the "tapes" people collect; and by observing the manner in which we put them to use in everyday life, they have come up with a simplified new language to describe what we are like. They start out by saying that we all have three observably distinct parts in our make-up. All of our behavior can be related to these three parts, and we switch back and forth between them constantly. They are referred to in T.A. language as "ego states," and they have been named the Parent, Adult, and Child.*

The Parent

The Parent, described by Dr. Thomas Harris in his bestselling book, *I'm OK—You're OK,* "is a huge collection of recordings in the brain of unquestioned or imposed external events perceived by a person in his early years, a period which we have designated roughly as the first five years of

*These are not, by the way, the same as the id, ego, and superego. The Parent, Adult, and Child are each an observable reality, identified by changes in such things as posture, voice inflection, and attitude.

life."[2] The name Parent was selected because most of the important "tapes" are produced when a young person observes and listens to the older people in his life. These tapes include all the do's and don'ts he hears, all the rules of living he is taught which will make life easier for him as he grows up. They include all the "how to's"—how to hold a fork, how to button a shirt, how to tie a shoelace.

The Parent has two very useful functions. First, it contains recordings of how mothers and fathers behave, and enables a person to eventually act effectively as the mother or father of his own children (an essential ingredient for the survival of the human race). Second, it enables us to respond immediately to a wide variety of situations in our daily lives without having to recalculate what is happening each time the same problem comes up. Knives are usually sharp. It is *always* wise to approach them with caution. Fires are dangerous. *Beware!* A fall can break your ribs. (Falling several times and finding it painful, we don't have to check it out constantly.) The Parent provides a set of automatic responses for dealing with repetitive situations, thereby saving us a great deal of time and energy. It would be impossible to live comfortably without the Parent.

There is only one problem. Much of the data in the Parent is taken in "raw" and is put on tape in that condition, without editing. As Harris explains, "The situation of the little child, his dependency, and his inability to construct meanings with words made it impossible for him to modify, correct, or explain. Therefore, if the parents were hostile and constantly battling each other, a fight was recorded with the terror produced by seeing the two persons on whom the child depended for survival about to destroy each other. There was no way of including in this recording the fact that the father was inebriated because his business had just gone down the drain or that the mother was at her wits' end because she had just found she was pregnant again."[3]

Parent data recorded under extremely emotional circumstances may have particularly lasting impact. So may instructions accompanied by booming voices and stern looks and emphasized by words of finality like "never" and "always." (Never hit a lady. Never trust a communist. Always believe your friends. Always obey your father. Never leave anything on your plate.) Harris points out, "During the period of his actual dependency upon his parents for security, however tenuous this security may be, it is likely that [a young person] will accept his parents' [attitudes about things]. *For a little child, it may be safer to believe a lie than to believe his own eyes and ears.*"[4]

The important thing is that whether or not the material in the Parent is good or bad, true or false, realistic or unrealistic, it is recorded as truth obtained from the source of all knowledge (parents). Whether it will help or hinder a person as he grows older will depend on its appropriateness to future situations.

Any two people (husband and wife, boss and subordinate) may have parent tapes with much in common, yet their tapes can also differ in many ways. For example, some of us may have tapes on the major issues of life, like sex, religion, and politics (never kiss a stranger or go out with married men, never believe a Baptist, and above all, never trust a Democrat). Some may have tapes on minor issues (who does the dishes, who makes the bed, who cuts the grass, who buys the groceries). If two people have conflicting tapes on any of those issues, serious arguments may develop, sometimes ruining good relationships.

Many people grow up with tapes on both major and minor issues, and some grow up with tapes on neither. Occasionally, if our parents disagree on something and we receive conflicting information, that information cancels itself out. Later in life, we may draw a blank. It all depends on what we were told and what we were in a position to observe for ourselves. If we were not exposed to things, we did not record them.

Once information gets on tape, however, it becomes a permanent recording, available for replay any time in the future (as Penfield was able to verify with his electric probe). Since the recorder is on all the time, experts have come to believe that a child has been exposed to most of the important rules in his life before he leaves home to start school. While new information may be introduced after that time, much of it is apparently used either to reinforce what has already been recorded or to update it.

The process of updating Parent information is one to which we will devote much more time later in this book.* Even though all our recordings are permanent and cannot be

*The single most startling revelation to every businessman I have discussed this with has been the sheer volume of nonupdated Parent data even the most thoughtful and reflective of them are saddled with. So don't worry if you discover the same thing about yourself. Just join the crowd.

erased, *old tapes may be turned off and replaced by new ones.* Tapes which prove to be out of date can be turned off and replaced by tapes with more current or more appropriate information.

Some people have more trouble doing this than others. Those who were both encouraged and permitted to make decisions for themselves when they were young may develop considerable skill. But a person whose early lessons were imposed upon him by stern commands accompanied by fearful looks and booming voices, who was not given permission to question, to investigate things for himself, and to make up his own mind about them, will often find it very difficult to examine his old ways. He may hold on to them long after they have lost their value.

One final word about the Parent. When someone is actually in his Parent ego state—when he is acting automatically on the basis of old tapes, he will often be acting *just like his mother or father* (or any other significant older person in his early life). He will not only use the same words that they used, but he will often sit, stand, frown, and carry himself as they did.* His own Parent is very much the embodiment of how he experienced his parents.

The Child

When our mental tape recorder is recording events on one track (the Parent), it is recording the feelings associated with those events on another track. It is recording joy, surprise, amazement, and all the wonderful feelings associated with our first discoveries about life. It is also recording terror, agony, and all the fearful feelings we experience. This body of recordings is called the Child. It is the source of our emotional responses.

The Child is, in many ways, the most rewarding and enjoyable part of our personality, as it can give to our lives the same things that a real child gives to family life—things like spontaneity, openness, and charm. Our Child knows how to have fun. It is exhibited in people in two forms: the *natural* Child and the *adapted* Child.

Our natural Child is exactly what it sounds like. It is that part of us which acts as a child naturally would. In it are found genetic recordings of all our primary biological urges.

*Chapter Three explains additional ways of spotting the Parent.

When Beth, a housewife of thirty-seven, cocks her head coyly to one side and smiles flirtatiously at her husband as he walks in the door, she is exhibiting her natural Child. When Bill, her husband, jumps up and down on the living room sofa while watching the football game, he is doing the same thing. In the natural Child are also found creativity, intuition, curiosity, and the urge to explore, to feel, to touch. It is our natural Child that feels crushed by disappointments and overjoyed by successes. It is our natural Child that loves.

The *adapted* Child, as Berne explains, "is one who modifies his behavior under Parental influence. He behaves as father (or mother) wanted him to behave: compliantly or precociously, for example. Or he adapts himself by withdrawing or whining."[5] He may also adapt with vindictive, rebellious behavior.

Some people exhibit more of their Child as they go through life than others. The father who can really have fun playing with his kids, whether he is thirty-five or fifty-five, has some tapes of good experiences to fall back on—experiences which he himself had when he was a youngster. They are a part of his natural Child. The housewife who acts like a little girl when her mother comes to visit, who hides her cigarettes and won't take a drink, has some tapes recorded in her adapted Child which tell how to act when mother is around. (The adapted Child rarely enjoys life as much as the natural Child.)

Some people record few "fun" tapes at all when they are young. Especially people from dull households (where there isn't any fun and where little is rewarded), from families where there is a lot of tension and bickering, or from families where there is a premium on acting grown up. These people often seem to have difficulty having fun later in life. They never quite get the hang of enjoying themselves, of relaxing and luxuriating in the sheer joy of being alive.

It is our Child that also gets us into trouble. Our Child wants to have its cake and eat it too. It wants the whole cake for itself. It is greedy, vain, and spiteful. It wants to beguile and seduce the world. It wants to get its way, *now*. It wants to go off to Las Vegas and never come back.

The Adult

John and Betty, a young couple married only a few years, have a baby-boy named Scott. Scott has just turned eleven months old, and John and Betty get great joy out of seeing Scott maneuver around his crib. It is fascinating to watch him as he begins to learn how to manipulate himself and his surroundings in an intelligent manner. Scott has figured out, for example, that if he extends his hand so many inches to his left, he can accurately make contact with his favorite toy without any difficulty whatsoever. He is so overjoyed at his accomplishment that he will do it whenever anybody appears to be watching. (He is quite a showoff.)

Every mother has witnessed the time when her child begins to do this sort of thing. It is the first real evidence that the highly touted computer-like brain in his possession is beginning to operate. In technical terms, she has witnessed the emergence of his *Adult.** (The name *Adult*, as you can see, has nothing to do with being grown up in the chronological sense.)

The Adult is the computer-like part of our personality. Its function is to process data. (How far to the nearest rattle? How far to the edge of the crib?) After processing the data, it computes probabilities and makes decisions based on the facts at hand. (What are the chances of falling out of the crib if you roll over when you are three inches from the edge? How fast should you walk across the street to avoid being hit by the oncoming car?) The Adult, as well as the Parent, is necessary for survival.

The Adult takes data from the Parent, the Child, and from its own observations of reality. It then makes decisions based on all the available information. In doing so, it in a sense mediates between the Parent and Child. John wants to seduce Mary (Child). John knows that it would be wrong (Parent). John decides that under the circumstances it would be inappropriate and risky and defers the action, at least for the time being (Adult).

The Adult does not judge. It deals strictly with fact. It knows no right or wrong. (But it *is* aware of what the *Parent* understands to be right or wrong.) In mediating between the Parent and Child, it examines Parent data and Child data to determine which, if either, is realistically applicable to the present. Although playing may be fun, there are times when playing may be dangerous. Although punishment may often

*This is the first visual evidence of the emergence of his Adult. When his Adult really starts functioning is anybody's guess, since an eleven-month-old can't speak for himself.

appear necessary, there are times when punishing oneself, or others, can be pointless.

The Adult appears to be slow to develop in most young people, and frequently has a hard time catching up later in life. Few children are encouraged to really think for themselves, and the Child and Parent continue to operate on primary circuits as "automatic" responses, as we get older. Tapes may replay spontaneously, and the damage is often done before we realize that we can plug in our Adult.

In determining how well someone's Adult actually functions, it is important to examine the process by which he arrives at decisions, not the decisions themselves. The quality of the data processing system cannot be determined by the accuracy or appropriateness of the decisions it makes, but only by the *manner in which the computer uses the data available to it.* A young person with practice in thinking for himself may develop a highly sophisticated computer capability; yet his decisions may still be impractical due to the limitations of his experience (or, in computer terms—his available data input). On the other hand, an older person with much more available data input may turn out equally poor decisions simply because his computer does not function well, or because he doesn't even use it. The best test of a person's computer capability, therefore, is to look not at the decisions he makes, but at the method he uses to arrive at them. The person who *processes* data best has the best potential. (One reason some young men vault past executives many years their senior on their way up the corporate ladder is that their computers simply work well, regardless of their years. They are particularly skilled in handling messages from their Parent and Child.) It is much easier to feed more information into a system that is already operating smoothly and efficiently (give more facts to someone who thinks well) than it is to reprogram a poorly functioning computer (teach him how to think).

In dealing with people, it is useful to recognize when they are in their Parent, Adult, or Child. While it is sometimes hard to distinguish between the Parent and the Child (an angry Parent and a defiant Child often act alike), it is particularly useful to recognize when someone is *not* in his Adult. A common mistake many people make is to assume that by the time someone has gone through college and spent five or ten years (or twenty or thirty years) in the business world, he automatically operates in his Adult. In fact, some people almost never do. They may be nearly frozen in their Parent. Many Parent and Child statements given in a well modulated tone of voice can be mistaken as Adult, causing all manner of difficulties.* Contrary to what we might like to believe, all three elements of our personality are very much in evidence on any given day, and being able to identify them in other people can be of considerable value in dealing with those people.

The Key to How We See Life—The Principle of Stroking

John and Betty, whose young son, Scott, provided our example of how the Adult emerges in a young person, also have a young beagle puppy named Boots. Whenever Boots wants to get some attention, he puts his ears as far back as he can, wags his tail as cutely as possible, and quietly comes over and leans against his young owners. Boots' urge for attention is most satisfied when John and Betty pick him up, pet him, scratch the back of his neck, and gently stroke him from head to tail. If that isn't possible, then at the very least they must bend down and pet him affectionately on the top of his head. Boots always makes it very clear that what he wants is physical contact, and he isn't satisfied until he gets it.

Human beings appear to have this same strong need for physical contact during the first few years of life. As Harris points out, "Within moments [of being born] the infant is introduced to a rescuer, another human being who picks him up, wraps him in warm coverings, supports him, and begins the comforting act of 'stroking.' This is the point of Psychological Birth. This is the first incoming data that life 'out there' isn't all bad. It is a reconciliation, a reinstatement of closeness. It turns on his will to live. Stroking, or repetitious body contact, is essential to his survival. Without it he will die, if not physically, then psychologically. Physical death from a condition known as marasmus once was a frequent occurrence in foundling homes where there was a deprivation of this early stroking. There was no physical cause to explain these deaths except the absence of essential stimulation."[6]

As soon as a child is old enough to walk by himself, he

*See Chapter Three to learn how to recognize if someone is in his Adult.

loses the best opportunities he ever had to obtain physical stroking—he no longer has to be picked up. For several years longer, however, many children think to extend their arms out imploringly to older people, looking for physical contact. Even as we grow older, although we don't go through life constantly embracing people, one of the most comforting things we can do to someone is to hold him close. The best way to console a person, to show that we really care, is to hug him, put our arms around him, or let him cry on our shoulder.

Stroking, then, in its most direct form, is the recognition of one living being by another through touching or bodily contact. If we don't receive it early in life, we die. But as a child becomes separated from his mother and begins to walk about for himself, he can no longer expect constant physical stroking. He learns to look for, and to accept, other less direct substitutes—substitutes which still provide the necessary recognition and feeling of closeness and belonging. Physical contact is now more likely to be reserved for very special occasions.

A young person's search for an acceptable substitute consumes many minutes of his day. The warm, comforting feeling he is looking for is very elusive. It is one of the best feelings we ever have, and trying to duplicate it is an imposing task. Nothing is ever as good as direct physical stroking. In turning elsewhere, we have little choice but to settle for *psychological* stroking—verbal and nonverbal signs of acceptance, recognition, and warmth that fall short of bodily contact. The kind of psychological alternative a young person learns to accept as *the* substitute in his life has much to do with his later understanding of what life is all about.*

Some Common Stroking Patterns

There are two major categories of psychological strokes—positive strokes and negative strokes. In its simplest form, a positive stroke is a warm smile, affectionate tone of voice, or friendly gesture. It is a clear, obvious, warm sign of acceptance. A negative stroke is a kick or similar negative recogni-

*One of the most fascinating recent discoveries is the extent to which stroking can contribute to a person's "life script," or unconscious life plan, which he blindly acts out, year after year. This will be explained in more detail in Chapter Four.

tion. (Not much by way of acceptance, but far better than no recognition at all.) Positive strokes result in good feelings, negative strokes in bad feelings.

Positive Strokes—Given Unconditionally

Fortunate, indeed, is the little person who starts out on his quest for strokes in an atmosphere of love and understanding—an atmosphere where people are warm, and where they accept him just because he is there—an atmosphere in which positive strokes are given unconditionally.

This is an atmosphere where a young person can learn to feel good about himself just because he is himself. Here no one says, "I'll only stroke you if you do what I want," or "I'll only stroke you if you make me feel good enough to stroke you." Strokes are given freely, without reservation. He doesn't have to deserve them. They are simply *there*, and the psychological warmth he feels is much like the physical warmth he felt during his first few months of life.

An unconditional positive stroke is the unconditional acceptance of another human being *because he is a human being* and for no other reason. Simple as it may sound, parents often have trouble giving such strokes. Either they are all wrapped up in themselves or they don't know how. Many have strong Parent tapes which say they should make judgments about people (and kids) before deciding how to act towards them. Others have tapes which tell them to respect only those people who embody certain qualities or who have been able to achieve certain enviable goals. To them, some people are worthy of more respect than others. Or, perhaps more appropriately, it is not the people, but only the qualities and achievements that are worth respecting.

Even parents who dearly love their children and who *try* to give good strokes consistently often dilute the effect of their efforts by withholding them until certain conditions are met. ("We'll love you, if. . . .") Giving strokes unconditionally means giving a person respect regardless of his behavior. When we act judgmentally, we prevent ourselves from doing this. Children, in their unending search for strokes, need to be loved, not judged. They need to know that they will not be rejected by their only real source of stroking just because they act human. On the contrary, they need to be accepted just because they *are* human.*

Little Kent Thomas and Jimmy Johnson both got caught

stealing several bushels of apples from a farm not far from their homes. Kent's parents were embarrassed and greatly disturbed. Kent was spanked soundly and told that because he had been so bad, he would not be allowed to play with Jimmy any more. To avoid further embarrassment, Mr. Thomas quickly mailed the farmer a check for Kent's share of the pilfered apples.

Jimmy's parents, on the other hand, were not greatly disturbed. They told Jimmy that while they still loved him, that did not mean he could avoid the realistic consequences of his own actions. (Swiping something from someone usually makes that person want to recover his loss.) They suggested that he might go back to the farmer, apologize for what he had done, and offer to work off the cost of the apples since he was the one who had stolen them. His parents also pointed out that while he did not *have* to do so, if he did so at once, he might be able to work something out before things got any worse than they were.

The net result was that Jimmy learned his parents still loved him (and would continue to be a source of strokes) even though he got in trouble now and then. He also learned that he alone was in charge of his behavior, and he hustled over to square things at the farm. Kent, on the other hand, ended up confused. He still has bad feelings about himself (only *bad* boys get in trouble) and he concluded that his parents don't really love him, or at best, that they only love him *sometimes* (when he is good). Lacking any supportive information, he is planning to try to prove he is bad all over again the very first chance he gets.

Unconditional positive stroking gives a young person a feeling that he counts for something and that other people count for something, too (since they give him strokes). It helps him feel good about himself—not ambivalent. It gives him confidence to deal with the outside world, to succeed. It is what helps a young man grow into a good executive who instinctively has a feel for how to go about doing things and who isn't afraid of failure.

But the message that he gets when he is young must be loud and clear. And it must be fairly consistent. His parents must describe their good feelings about him in many ways:

*All this is not to say that a good spanking (negative stroke) every now and then is bad. It is the general pattern of stroking that counts. Spankings will rarely damage a youngster raised in a family where love abounds.

by looks, tone of voice, by including him in activities, and by saying they care for him in as many ways as possible. It is the most important thing in the world to him. Anything less does not produce anywhere near as healthy an attitude or as good a result.

Positive Strokes—Given Conditionally (We'll Stroke You, If. . . .)

While *un*conditional strokes are, by definition, given unconditionally, a wide variety of conditions may be imposed before *conditional* strokes may be granted. We will touch on three of the more common ways this is done, and briefly explore their implications. Each produces a person who grows up *believing* life to be a certain way, a way different from that perceived by those accustomed to other kinds of stroking.

1) Performance-oriented Strokes

Parents who withhold strokes until a child performs a certain act, produces a certain (good) result, or achieves a particular goal, might be spoken of as *performance-oriented*. Their relationship with their children is *judgmental*. They establish rules for their children to live by and proceed to extend or withhold strokes in accordance with their own personal judgment as to how well the rules are being followed, how well the child performs.

Little Freddy Mitchell* has learned his lessons so well that at the age of twelve he already acts like a puppet on a string. All Freddy's really big moments in life, the times when he gets his best strokes, come with his really big achievements (good report cards, winning little league baseball games, getting first chair in the school band). Nothing much ever happens in between.

Freddy's parents have carefully laid down the rules for him to live by. They go something like this: "Get good grades in school, and you will be rewarded. If you don't make A's, at least be sure you study hard to avoid our disapproval. If you work hard at everything you do, you will be the best and

*The illustrative cases in this chapter (Freddy Mitchell and others) are used to point out typical long-term implications of common patterns of stroking. These are general implications only. For any one person, behavior in later life will depend on his own early life experience.

we'll be proud of you. Don't engage in group activities unless you can outshine everyone, because the best strokes come when you can steal all the glory for youself. (Why share the strokes?) Don't ever waste time. Idleness is the devil's workshop. If you discipline yourself adequately, you will always be able to master everything you tackle. In a pinch, if you aren't worthy of receiving really good strokes, you can avoid our disapproval through obedience and diligent effort."

Freddy is now set for life. There is nothing uncertain or inconsistent about his rules, and the pattern of stroking has been unremitting. He has an internal Parent filled with tapes on how to get strokes forever. His own Parent tapes will be able to take over for his mother and father and guide his performances long after his real parents have gone.* Work hard! Achieve! He will make his way through life feeling good about himself when he has performed well and feeling dejected when he has not. He will most likely have trouble relating to other people, because the best strokes come only from his own individual performances. People raised on other types of strokes will mystify him. He may well be considered a loner. He will feel guilty when he fails to discipline himself. He will have difficulty respecting others who do not work as hard as he does and will be quick to criticize. If he goes into the business world, he may grow into a tyrant. He may become successful by most practical standards, but he may also have nagging doubts about his inability to understand many things that are going on around him. He will always be certain that *his* way is the right way, however; and when he encounters resistance to his ideas, he will consistently act as if he is convinced that the rest of the world is wrong. He will be ruled by his Parent, which he will often believe to be his Adult. As a businessman this may well become his downfall, because when the chips are down, it will prevent him from making truly objective decisions.

2) Accommodation-oriented Strokes

Little Clark Harrison has a different problem. His parents are just as convinced as Freddy's that you cannot simply give a child unconditional strokes. They are sure there must be rules for him to follow so that he can "earn" his strokes, but the trouble is *they are not sure what the rules are!* Therefore,

*Parents often ask how they can raise their kids to work hard and achieve success while avoiding the pitfalls of conditional stroking. The answer is to always give unconditional strokes but also provide conditional strokes for good performances, when they occur.

while they have been successful at withholding strokes (it really isn't very hard), they have not been able to give Clark very much to go on as he pursues his instinctive search for security. (It isn't their fault, poor souls. They are always asking for advice from all of their friends. They are just very insecure people themselves.)

Needless to say, young Clark is batting his brains out trying to find the damned rules. He has become a very anxious lad. The only thing he has been able to figure out is that he gets a nice reaction from his parents when *he* strokes *them;* when he does things they think are cute, or funny, or amusing. He has become very sensitive to the attitudes and wishes of the people around him. He has learned to quickly accommodate his own thoughts to those of others, to acquiesce, to be agreeable, to be solicitous. This isn't very much for a young person to hang his hat on, but it is better than nothing, and it is all Clark has.

Clark is set for life, too. He feels good about himself when he is accepted by people, and he becomes depressed when he is rejected. He has learned that being accepted by people is a very tricky thing, indeed. (You have to get a feel for what others are thinking, what they expect of you, and then conform quickly.) He often acts the part of the clown at social gatherings, trying to avoid rejection by getting people to laugh. Either that or he tries to unobtrusively join in conversations by agreeing with everybody on unimportant issues. When it's his turn to bring up a subject, he makes certain that it's not controversial. He is always nervous. He approaches each situation he faces as a new test. He keeps himself on the brink of being rejected, and if he cannot keep finding new solutions, as situation after situation is hurled at him, he believes he will fall off. He may well go through life being thought of as a nice guy, but he will never have learned how to actively stroke someone else (unless something is in it for *him*), and his niceness will have no positive appeal. He will be nice, but harmless.

3) Conformity and Compromise-oriented Strokes

Another youngster, Bobby Fredericks, is a little better off than Clark. While his parents are absolutely certain that they have some good rules (they have always worked well in the past), they are not fanatical about enforcing them. They know how to give positive strokes and are careful not to withhold them. Bobby is convinced that his parents love him, that he is accepted. His life is secure.

The fascinating thing about Bobby's upbringing, however, is that while his parents do not stint on giving strokes, they have been careful to let Bobby know that if he does something to cause them shame, they might be compelled to withhold strokes. Thus, while they have not given him rules on how to get strokes (they give them freely), they have given him rules on *how to keep them!* The rules are of a more general nature than are "performance" rules. Bobby has more leeway than Freddy, for instance. Bobby's rules are more often guidelines, with a strong emphasis on what *not* to do.

They go something like this: "We will aways love you so long as you don't disgrace us. But you will find that there is no *reason* to disgrace us, as there is ample precedent around to use in developing your own sense of values. Our family traditions provide standards of the highest order for you to draw on. When in doubt, always look to those established practices which experience has shown to be best, and watch what the people you respect are doing. When things get rough, there will always be a middle ground, and it is always wise to seek a compromise. When people disagree, you can expect them always to be willing to bargain. In addition, majority positions are usually the safest. Just be careful not to rock the boat and bring shame and disgrace down upon those who love you most."

In a sense, Bobby has been provided with the ultimate in traditional Parent data. The only way he can possibly lose his source of strokes is to have an original thought. Why risk it? Everything has been laid out for him, and he feels good most of the time. Panic only sets in when he has to go out on a limb, and he has learned to avoid such situations. His Parent tapes will carry him comfortably through life so long as he stays away from the deep water. He has all the guidelines he will ever need. He just won't think for himself.

Negative Strokes

Some parents pay almost no attention to their kids at all. When this happens, and a child receives very few unconditional or conditional positive strokes, he can become very concerned. He will often go to great lengths to get *some* sort of recognition. In fact, when things really get bad, just about *any* acknowledgment of his existence will do. Typically, he will try to call attention to himself by getting into some sort of trouble—by doing something "bad." If he succeeds, he will receive a scolding—a *negative stroke.** Recognition in this negative way tells a person that people care enough to yell at him, at least. A negative stroke tells a person that he exists. It is better than no stroking at all. (In fact, it is infinitely better than no stroking at all, which is why some kids will go to such extremes to get it.)

This type of situation occurs every now and then in the life of every young person. But for some it provides virtually the only means of ever being noticed. There simply is no other way. Their parents have let them know there isn't anything they can do to get positive strokes. When kids come to accept this pattern of stroking as a way of life, they soon look for bigger and better strokes. It's only a matter of time before they graduate to swiping hubcaps, and then to swiping motorcycles. From there it's only a hop, skip, and a jump to the really big time.

Some Practical Implications of the Principle of Stroking

All people, then, start out life by seeking something to replace the constant physical stroking they lose shortly after birth. Our need for recognition, or psychological stroking, governs much of our activity early in life. The particular kind of stroking we learn to accept as the substitute is preordained, however: it is the kind our parents are familiar with, the kind they can give us.** It sets up patterns in the way we act which we carry through life, patterns that become such a part of us that we seldom recall having been without them, patterns that provide each of us with a view of life which we believe to be the way life is.

It is important to realize that these patterns were spawned by some of our earliest, never-to-be-questioned Parent data.

*Negative strokes, as well as positive strokes, may be conditional (I'll spank you *if* you do that once more) and unconditional (a spanking, an insult, a kick, an arrest). The distinction is one of limited importance in this book, however; a life devoted to obtaining negative strokes will most likely produce a criminal.

**The most common situation occurs when parents mix up their strokes, depending on the situation or on how they feel (you have to feel good to give unconditional positive strokes). Most people grow up having had exposure to more than one kind of stroking, although one in particular will often provide the dominant influence in their lives.

They are among our very first tapes, tapes about the way life *is,* the *only* way life is: I must perform well to be accepted. Or I must conform and avoid sticking my neck out to be accepted (or to retain my accepted status).

Once understood, these patterns are easily observed in everyday life. In business, they govern much of our day-to-day activity. Many of them are clearly unrealistic and serve only to get in our way. Some are extremely deceptive, such as those of the performance-oriented person. He may do very well in business under certain conditions (where he can develop great skill in an individual area of expertise, where he can perform well by himself). He may become an outstanding lawyer or supersalesman, and his performance may well disguise his basic inabilities either to understand people (other than perhaps to manipulate them) or to make truly objective decisions. If he becomes an executive, his company may never find this out until he achieves considerable power and then proceeds to make some colossal blunders.

Once we can pinpoint these patterns, the challenge is to bring new techniques to bear in dealing with them. Perhaps the most exciting development of all has been the increased awareness of *man's capacity to change.* Although most of us go through life convinced that many of the archaic notions we carry around in our Parent are our own well-thought-out ideas, convinced that the way we each get our strokes is the only way strokes can be obtained, the fact is that we in truth do *not* have to be branded for life by our past. Although our tapes are with us for life, we may, if we choose, turn off those tapes we deem obsolete, useless, or inappropriate to the reality of the present.*

We may, in a very real sense, *reprogram* ourselves. We can learn to watch ourselves and become aware of what we do to stroke ourselves. We can also learn to observe what we do to get strokes from others. And when we feel it might be appropriate to our new wishes for the future, we can consciously take time out to stroke ourselves in ways different from our accustomed stroking patterns of the past.

In managing and supervising others, we can make a conscious effort to give people positive unconditional strokes at all times as well as conditional strokes for good performances. We can actively avoid giving any kinds of negative strokes.

*How to go about this for oneself is the subject of Chapters Six and Seven. How to help others go about it is the subject of Chapters Nine and Ten.

3. Catching Up with the Experts

The Impact of Our First Opinions of Ourselves—The Concept of Life Positions

Of all the aspects of early childhood that influence our later lives, none is more significant than the very earliest opinion we form of ourselves and of others around us. This opinion is derived largely from the kind of stroking we first experience and the kind we learn to give others around us. It is much stronger than the more ordinary opinions we might form later. It is more in the nature of a fixed, unthinking, and unchangeable emotional stance. Research into the behavior of very young children has shown that an understanding of relationships between events—such as cause and effect—begins in the early months of life and is acquired by the end of the second year. At this age a child reaches a state of equilibrium and establishes a central emotional position which he will be inclined to return to for the rest of his life. Harris says that he "believe[s] this state of equilibrium, evident at the end of the second year or during the third year, is the product of the child's conclusion about himself and others: *his life position*."[1]

There are, in T.A. terms, four such life positions:

I'm not OK—You're OK
I'm not OK—You're not OK (neither of us is OK)
I'm OK—You're not OK
I'm OK—You're OK (we both are!)

The first, I'm not OK—You're OK, appears to be by far the most common. A young person reaches it by putting on tape all the discouraging facts he hears about himself and recording them as truth. "You're sloppy," "You're lazy,"

"You're too slow," "You can't do anything right."* These attitudes are often reinforced by the way people treat him. As such data goes on tape, the young person computes, "*I'm* lazy," "*I'm* too slow," "*I* can't do anything right." If he wasn't that way before, he soon begins to become so.

As if this were not enough, many a youngster confirms this depressive self-image through his own independent observations of how things go in his life. By the time he is two years old, much of the data he has accumulated about himself appears to support the conclusion that he is simply "not OK." He has tripped over his own feet, spilled milk all over his clothes, put his shoes on backwards, and hit his nose with his spoon, so many times that there is *no way* (in his mind) he can do things right. This opinion is confirmed by all the "Don't do that's" and "No's" he's been subjected to, as well as by his self-inflicted pain as he stumbles into things, falls down, and hurts himself.

While he is recording all this not OK data about himself, a young person is also recording the feelings associated with it—all the anger, frustration, and inadequacy. These feelings are said to be recorded in his "not OK Child." When we see the same person later in life acting as if he is incapable of whatever it is at the time, we can be sure that he is replaying not OK Child tapes, that he is *in* his not OK Child.

Fortunately, for the average child, the conclusion that he is not OK is tempered by the fact that his parents love him and comfort him, and are a source of stroking. Also, although he is at their mercy, he sees his parents and all the other big people around him as supremely capable of doing all the things he cannot do (they are the ones who are always correcting him). He will typically form the opinion that *they're OK*, thus settling on the position, I'm not OK—You're OK.

This particular life position appears not only to be the one which most children initially reach, but also the one which *most people continue to maintain throughout life*. It is a reasonable enough position at the age of two. For a two-year old, such a decision can be the result of a lifetime of observation. For a thirty-year-old, it may merely be an obsolete burden. The tragedy is that many people never reassess this early conclusion about themselves. They make the decision and stick with it for life.

Some children, however, *do* reassess things and eventually

*All negative strokes, as the reader may have noted.

change their I'm not OK—You're OK position. This usually occurs if the information a youngster receives as he grows older is substantially different from his earlier data. It can make things better for him, or it can make things worse. Perhaps the worst that can happen to a youngster is to lose his stroking. This typically occurs at the point in his life when he learns to walk and does not need to be picked up any longer. He may be left to his own devices, abandoned by a mother with other things on her mind. Or his mother may just be a cold, unstroking person. In any event, if this state of abandonment continues without relief for a year or so, a young person may come to decide—in the depths of his loneliness and despair—that other people are not as OK as he had thought. In fact, they're really not OK, because, after all, they don't provide strokes. He may then settle on the second life position. I'm not OK—You're not OK. *Nobody* is OK. (And everything we do is futile.) This can lead ultimately to suicide, because life is rarely worth living under such conditions.

The third life position, I'm OK—You're not OK, is produced by a life experience that is so traumatic, either physically or psychologically, it causes the little person to completely reverse his earlier stance. As Harris points out, "A child who is brutalized long enough by the parents he initially felt were OK will switch positions . . . to I'M OK—YOU'RE NOT OK. . . . It is as if he senses, I'll be all right if you leave me alone. I'm OK by myself. . . . Such a little person has experienced brutality, but he has also experienced survival. What has happened can happen again. I did survive. I will survive. . . . For this child . . . [his] position is a life saving decision."[2] When reached under these conditions, as a result of the worst kind of negative strokes—kicks and beatings, it may well be (depending on the person's Parent data, or his interest in self-preservation), a criminal position. (If other people aren't OK, it has to be all right to steal from them or to kill them.) It is also a paranoid position. (I am right and the rest of the world is wrong. I am right and the rest of the world is against me.)

The last life position, I'm OK—You're OK, is the only really constructive position. A youngster may arrive at it almost automatically if he grows up in certain ideal circumstances—circumstances in which he always receives positive unconditional strokes and receives, as well, conditional strokes for growing at his own pace (as he learns to walk, talk, pronounce words correctly, and the like). Few kids get such ideal treatment, however. When this doesn't happen, a youngster may still reach an I'm OK—You're OK position as the result of a *conscious* decision, made after his earlier unconscious decision (I'm not OK—You're OK). He may reassess his own "OKness" if, for example, he is repeatedly exposed to situations where he can prove to himself that he *is* in fact OK, that he can do things well, that he can succeed. If this information outweighs his earlier data, a little person may begin to change his position. He may decide, "I was wrong. Lo and behold, I *am* OK!"

A very special kind of conditional stroking is helpful in preparing a young person for a successful career in business. He really needs to be able to see life as a series of continuing successes, not failures. He needs to be provided with tasks which challenge him, but which are nonetheless within the range of his capabilities. If a particular job is too big, he may become discouraged unless it is broken down into a series of smaller tasks of more manageable proportions, each with a limited objective. Too many discouragements will only confirm his not OK feelings.

For example, dressing can be a formidable task for a little person. But if he takes it step by step, with lacing shoes, buttoning buttons, and putting on a jacket, each learned as a separate project, dressing can be seen as a series of accomplishments instead of an insurmountable problem. The important thing for the little person is how he perceives himself and his capacity for success. In a sense, it is a matter of defining what he does as being successful. If he gets to see himself as pretty much always doing things "right," and if the big people around him reflect the same sentiment, he'll become convinced that he is, in fact, OK, that he can accomplish things.

These, then, are the four basic life positions. While we all, at one time or another, probably have some exposure to each of them—there are times when we all feel not OK, times when we don't think too much of the people around us, either—each of us tends to settle on one of these basic positions as a *dominant* position in his life. This will be the position to which we will return time and time again, and it will exert a major force in our life—influencing our actions perhaps 60 or 70 per cent of the time.

One more point remains to be covered. It has to do with the manner in which the vast majority of people who believe themselves to be not OK typically try to relieve themselves of this not OK burden. The process begins early in childhood when a youngster, "knowing" himself to be not OK, comes to the realization "I can be OK, if. . . ." He learns that he can develop a sort of *conditional* OKness by responding to various kinds of conditional strokes. It is a formula which provides varying degrees of temporary relief. For the performance-oriented child it reads, "I can be OK if I perform well." For the accommodation-oriented, "I can be OK if I succeed in accommodating myself to my surroundings," and so on. Many people who have settled on I'm not OK—You're OK have seen such half-OKness as the only possible alternative in their lives. Yet the big drawback to this kind of early decision is that it never really makes a person OK.

Another method often used to relieve the burden of the not OK Child is to develop a kind of *relative* OKness by deciding, "I can be OK, so long as I'm more OK than you." (This is the source of the famous childhood game—Mine is Better Than Yours.) Once a little person has made this decision, he may switch his life position to a less pathological form of the (criminal) position, I'm OK—You're not OK. When this happens, it may, or may not, be a permanent switch—the basic position often seems to remain I'm not OK—but it is a switch which he makes whenever an opportunity arises later in life to relieve his not OK burden, whenever he thinks he has half a chance of convincing somebody else that *that somebody else* is the one who's *really* not OK: "Look at you, *you're* not OK" (and that makes me feel better).

By its very nature this is an extremely judgmental position. It seems to dominate the lives of many judges, district attorneys, ministers, and "bosses." It is also very parental. When a person is in its grip, he will be inclined to come on as a very stern Parent, indeed. "I'm OK, *you're* the one who's not, so you better do what I say" (or "I'll send you to jail," or "You'll go to Hell," or "I'll fire you").

Before the development of Transactional Analysis there seemed to be little hope for ever changing one's (basic) life position. This attitude, however, has been vastly altered over the last decade. One of the cornerstones of T.A. techniques is the belief that *any* of our early life positions can be changed—in much the same way it was originally arrived at—by a decision. This process is referred to as a *redecision*—the bringing into conscious awareness the data reflected in the original decision, the updating of that information, and the making of a new decision! Many of the techniques developed to help "sick" people accomplish this in clinical situations can be mastered by any reasonably capable supervisor or manager to help his own employees overcome their more moderate not OKnesses in business situations.*

Childhood Decisions Which Affect Our Later Lives

So far, we have seen how our entire lives can be governed by unexamined Parent data and by early attitudes formed and conclusions reached at a preconscious level far back in our youth—long before we really knew what we were doing. Unfortunately, these are not the only sources of negative childhood influences. Very often a youngster can go on making *conscious* negative decisions as he grows older which have an equally devastating effect on his later life. These conscious decisions can have an even more direct relationship to his business career than those described earlier.

Tommy, age seven, had become absolutely disgusted with his mother. Every time he decided something for himself—what clothes to wear, how to arrange his room, how to spend his allowance—mother never agreed. She always took over and made him do it *her way*, regardless. One Sunday morning, as Tommy proudly started downstairs, ready to go to Sunday School in a nifty new suit he had just gotten for his birthday, Mother stopped him abruptly.

"Tommy!" she snapped, "Go change that suit immediately! You can't wear it today. I ironed your regular suit for today. Save your new suit for Easter!"

Tommy wheeled around and ran back upstairs in a silent rage. "Who does she think she is!" he muttered to himself. "I'll show *her*!" he said, hastily jerking off his new suit and slamming it to the floor. "I won't *ever* bother thinking for myself anymore! It doesn't pay. I'll just ask her approval before I do anything! Phooey on her!" That was the moment! Tommy had decided, with good reason, never again to think for himself. It was a decision which would stick with him for a long, long, time.

*See Chapters Nine and Ten for details.

Tommy's case is not unusual. Youngsters typically start making hard-and-fast decisions about life before they've barely begun to grow up. Some of these decisions are well within a young person's awareness at the time he makes them. This process begins to appear increasingly observable in a youngster's life as he reaches the ages of six or seven. As Berne puts it, "At this point he begins to settle on certain compromises which will affect his relationships with people in later life. These solutions require making decisions, taking positions which justify the decisions, and warding off influences which threaten the positions."[8]

Charlie, age six, was a very imaginative little fellow. He was always exploring and trying out new ideas. Unfortunately, Charlie had a mother, father, and three older sisters who never took him seriously. They always laughed at him and teased him. They called him "silly" and "stupid" and made him feel ill at ease.

One day, on his way home from school, Charlie stopped at the five and ten cent store to buy his teacher a bottle of perfume for her birthday. It cost thirty-nine cents. "How wonderful," Charlie said to himself. "No one else will ever think to give her perfume!" As he arrived home with his gift clutched in his little hand, two of his sisters met him on the back porch.

"Charlie," giggled one of them. "What's that you're holding. It looks like perfume." (Giggling again.)

"None of your business!" Charlie replied, walking straight ahead into the kitchen where his mother was preparing dinner.

But the girls were not to be denied. "Mother," one of them yelled into the house, "Charlie bought himself some perfume." (Laughing hilariously at this point.)

His mother turned to him and, spying the bottle of perfume, asked, "Charlie, what are you doing with that?"

Charlie thought to himself, "They're laughing because they don't know it's for my teacher's birthday. Once I tell them, they'll stop laughing." To his mother, he said proudly, "I'm going to give this to Miss Larsen for her birthday."

His mother took the bottle from him, looked at the thirty-nine cents tag, and broke out in gales of laughter. "Oh, Charlie," she exclaimed, barely able to contain herself, "this will never do!" Bang! Charlie's world deflated like a balloon bursting. All he could hear was laughter. *Laughter!* LAUGHTER! He ran, sobbing, to his room. "All right for them," he said to himself, with an air of finality. "Let them laugh. It's for the last time. I just won't think up any new ideas on my own ever again!"

That was it for Charlie. Never again would he have an original idea. When he grew up and went to work, he would become the one who never contributed anything—because he learned long ago that it never paid.

Many decisions we make based on our early life experiences are of the "never again" variety, like Tommy's and Charlie's. They occur when a young person is pushed past the limit of his endurance and throws up his hands in despair, as if to say, "That's the last straw!" Such a decision, inflexible as it is, can go on to become a central influence in our lives.

An interesting way to view such decisions is to include a reference to the circumstances in which they were initially made. As Berne says, "The full statement of a decision should include its origin."[4] For Tommy, such a statement would read, "Never again will I make a decision for myself—because Mommy took over once too often." For Charlie, "Never again will I have an original thought—because I was laughed at too many times."

Many others can be seen in everyday life:

> Never again will I speak out—because no one at home ever listened to me.
>
> Never again will I be honest—because I was always punished for telling the truth.
>
> Never again will I work hard—because I never got credit for anything I did.
>
> Never again will I risk feeling anything (and I'll put all my energies into work, instead) because when I did risk feeling, I got hurt.

Often, if a person works at it, he may trace current difficulties back to the actual time and place when, many years back, he made such a decision in a state of utter exasperation. Sometimes, while the exact circumstances may be unknown, much of the information can be inferred from his current behavior.

There are other kinds of decisions people make in childhood. Like the "never again" decisions, they gain clarity when seen in conjunction with their origins. Some are general in nature, such as:

I can't make it (in life)—because Mother doesn't want me to leave her.

or,

I can't be myself—because Father wants me to be (like) him.

These may occasionally cause a person really serious difficulties. "I can't make it," for instance, seen as a decision forced on a young person by the fearful Child that exists in his mother (who doesn't want him to leave her and therefore convinces him of his "inadequacies") may conflict with Parent data from the same mother which says "work hard." Such a young person may well grow up always working hard but never achieving success, without ever figuring out why.

Other decisions may be less pathological, yet equally influential. Every day we can see people around us sticking to them.

I don't have to make my own decisions—because everything was always laid out for me.

The world revolves around *me*, not other people—because Mother was always there when I needed her.

I'm not a responsible person—because my older brother was always in charge.

People should always do what I say—because Mother always made the other kids obey me.

Once I make a decision, I stick to it—because I was never allowed to change my mind.

I can get my way if I hold out long enough—because Daddy always gave in.

All these decisions, and many others like them, are outgrowths of the life experience of a young person. Once he makes such a decision, *it becomes a part of him*. Often it can be seen as an extension of his life position. For example, a person who believes himself to be not OK is likely to decide that he can never make decisions or that he is not a responsible person. He will probably *not* conclude that the world revolves around him or that he can always get his own way (he's not OK enough for that).

How to See People More Clearly

One way to see a person more clearly is to become aware of how he gets his strokes, what his dominant life position seems to be, and what his Parent, Adult, and Child are like.* There are many physical and verbal clues through which people reveal these things, and familiarity with them can be extremely useful.

How People Get Their Strokes

People usually go through life looking for strokes in the same way they did when they were very young. They also stroke *themselves* in the same old ways. Thus one of the most useful questions to ask about a person is, *What does he do to feel good about himself?* Some people appear to do very little, while others seem to spend most of their waking hours congratulating themselves, building themselves up, and looking for the approval, attention, or recognition of others.

In one office, Gene, a better-than-average salesman, likes to gather the younger, less experienced men around him every week or so to tell them the details of his conquests of the previous week. Then, as the appreciative "Oh's," "Ah's," and "Wow's," of his audience start rolling in, he slowly collects all his strokes. Gene has set things up so that the adulation of the younger salesmen in the office will convince him, at least temporarily, that he is OK. It is as if he were still a youngster believing himself to be not OK and casting about for some relief from his awful burden. For Gene, this procedure is enough to keep him going another week. Without it, without the chance to say, "Look how good I am," and to hear the reply, "Gee, you really are good," from as many people as possible, he ends up in the doldrums for days on end.

On the other hand, Phil, the best salesman in the office, doesn't seem to need strokes from other people at all. But he does need to keep busy. His Parent tells him to work hard, and he dutifully obeys. He doesn't socialize, nor does he ap-

*The management techniques discussed later in this book rely heavily on this approach.

pear to need companionship. He's his own man, and seems to get all the stroking he needs internally, from his own Parent. *So long as he works hard.* When he doesn't work hard, he can sometimes be seen grumbling to himself, just as if his internal Parent were beating on his Child. Phil, unfortunately, is a driven man.

Sally, the boss's secretary, is also performance oriented. Like Phil, she, too, needs strokes from a Parent. But her own Parent doesn't seem to be strong enough, so she looks directly to her boss for approval. Whenever he compliments her, tells her what a good job she's done or what a wonderful girl she is, she beams with pride and feels good all over. But when he scolds her for not doing her best, she feels ashamed and depressed—just as she did when she was a little girl. Her own feelings tend to duplicate what her boss feels about her. As one might imagine, Sally really tries very hard to make him happy.

Emma, one of the administrative clerks, is a forty-year-old unmarried woman who is known as a chronic complainer. Nothing is "right" in her life, and her major occupation seems to be letting people know it. She rarely stops until she reaches the point when someone in the office says, "Oh, Emma, will you stop complaining!" Having received her negative stroke, her "recognition" for the day, Emma will remain quiet until quitting time. But each day is a new day for Emma. Tomorrow, she will start all over again. She is *very* insecure.

Other people in the office use still other methods to get their strokes. Fred, the assistant manager, likes to do favors for people, then wait around to be thanked and receive his praise for being such a "thoughtful" person. Mary, the administrative supervisor, likes to speak out at staff meetings, volunteering answers to questions, so that everyone will know she has done her homework. Bill, the newest salesman, likes to tell jokes, keeping everyone happy and accommodating himself to other people as much as possible.

These, and many other patterns of stroking, can be seen in just about any office situation. Understanding them can be a very rewarding process, particularly insofar as one can begin to see the little child in persons, and begin to picture the possible circumstances which may originally have triggered present behavior patterns. Most people, when they are looking for strokes, are at least temporarily acting out the insecurity of their not OK Child. It is as if they were asking, "Tell me I'm really OK."

Clues to Their Life Position

Because most people have at one time or another had some experience with all the basic life positions, and because their dominant position accounts for the way they feel most but rarely all of the time, expecting complete accuracy in pinpointing life positions can often lead to frustration. It can nonetheless be extremely rewarding just to be able to get a general feel for "where" a person is in the way he leads his life. The most important clues are those which reveal how he feels about himself (that is, is *he* OK with himself?) and the way he feels about others (are *they* OK with him?).

One of the first questions to ask about a person is, *Can he take compliments gracefully?* Or does he always deny them, saying, "Oh, anybody could have done it." or, "Don't be silly, it wasn't anything." Does he get flustered by compliments, change the subject, look away, or look down at his feet? Or does he take the other approach, and exaggerate or boast about his accomplishment? In general, people who are really OK can accept a compliment, return it, or go on to another subject without any difficulty. People who are feeling not OK always seem to have great difficulty accepting a good, honest positive stroke. *They need to deny that it is a stroke, or avoid dealing with it, in order to maintain the integrity of their life position.* They know they're not OK. There's no sense going through that all over again. They have to politely let you know that you are wrong, or they are in very deep water.

Another good question to ask about someone is, *Can he stroke other people?* Does he give compliments easily? (Genuine compliments, that is, not exaggerated compliments produced by a not OK Child, such as "Oh, you're just so wonderful at everything!" which carry with them the implied message, "And I'm so terrible!") Can he listen to other people, accept their point of view, even if it differs significantly from his own, and then *still* stroke them? Or does he become uptight, pushy, tightlipped, and try to tell them they're not OK? Or, on the other hand, does he just withdraw, become not OK, and refuse to deal with them? Can he treat people with respect? Or does he mistrust or disregard others?

In general, a person who feels basically not OK will find it very difficult to stroke others. Since he cannot *accept* strokes, he finds it extremely hard to give strokes to others. He may very well believe other people to be OK, but since *he* isn't (in his mind), how can he compliment them, offer his respect and openly accept *them,* when *he's* the one who's desperately trying to become accepted? At the other extreme, people who believe themselves to be OK but don't think that others are, have the same difficulty in stroking other people. (The way they see it, you don't stroke people who aren't worthy of it.)

Other clues to the life position may be seen in how a person handles himself physically. Does he appear confident, relaxed, and comfortable? Or does he slouch, bow his head, and slump over? Or, on the other hand, does he strut, "puffed up," with his chin out, as if he's looking for a fight? Does he smile easily and often? (Be careful here. Appearances provide good clues, but people often erect façades. How a person acts in his "off" moments will provide the best data.) Is he a compulsive person, an anxious, nervous person? Is he tense? At conferences, does he want to be heard and always "butt in," or is he the other extreme—hard to open up? Is he insecure or secure? What is the *emphasis* of his approach to life? Is it relaxed and positive, or is it negative?

Another good clue to someone's life position is the *extent to which he has to do things to feel good about himself.* Is he *down* one day, and *up* the next? Is each moment a different moment, and does he need to depend on what's *happening* before knowing if he is OK?

Once you become alert to these things, you'll be able to pick up many more clues on your own. It is a big step toward real understanding of people. You will soon learn how to stroke people the way they really want and you will soon become aware of all the opportunities you used to miss.

Spotting Parent, Adult, and Child in People

People usually lack real awareness of how their behavior looks to others. We reveal our Parent, Adult, and Child, however, in many ways that are easily identifiable. A small child, for instance, in learning to play "house" (which is essentially playing "Parent"—mother or father), imitates the frown, the stern look, the gestures and words of "big people." Other clues to the Parent are the pointing index finger.

("You better do what I say!"), the arms folded across the chest ("Just what do you think you're doing!"), and resigned sighing ("How many times must I tell you?"). Many judgmental words * provide additional clues to the Parent, insofar as they are automatic, archaic responses, and not Adult evaluations. ("You should," "You ought to," "This is right," "That is wrong," and so on.) Typical Parental activities include moralizing, taking care of people, nurturing, punishing, criticizing, sympathizing, judging, and giving orders. Any words that fit these activities are good clues.

The best clue to the Parent, however, is *tone of voice.* When a person speaks and physically acts the part, his tone of voice (together with the speed of his response) will often indicate that he feels like a parent.** When it does, it provides the most reliable evidence of all.

Child clues are just as easy to spot. Words like "Wow!" "Golly," "I wish," "I want," are typical of children. When we are in our Child, we are usually smiling, laughing, crying, having tantrums, getting into trouble, having fun, and doing all the other things we did as youngsters. We will also be using characteristic facial expressions. Tone of voice, here also, is the best possible clue.

The Adult is a little more difficult to pinpoint visually. It is not, as many people might think, evidenced by a complete lack of expression (the stone face). All that a stone face indicates is that a person either has difficulty with his facial muscles or does not want you to know what he is thinking. The Adult face is a straightforward face. The Adult lets the Child show itself when it is curious or excited. When the Adult is *listening*, it is characterized by continual movement, with an eyeblink every three to five seconds. The Adult face is relaxed, but active. Verbally, the Adult is inclined to speak of probabilities, avoid words like "never" and "always," and use phrases like "It is my opinion," "Based on what I've observed," "Possibly," "Probably," and "So far, the facts seem

*A typical judgmental activity we almost all engage in at once time or another is putting the blame on *other* people so that we can feel better. It is a very common speech pattern. Think about it!

**Actually, the definition of Parent and Child contained in Chapter Two (the "event" and "feeling" tapes that we have in our heads) is not entirely complete. An experienced observer will notice that the tapes really seem to be mixed. When we're in our Parent, we're not only responding by automatically playing an old "event" tape; we often actually *feel* like a parent does—as if we experienced how Mother and Father once felt.

to indicate." People will usually be in their Adult when they are processing data together, exchanging facts, asking questions, solving problems, and discussing things rationally.

More important than being able to spot a person's Parent, Adult, and Child* is being able to assess the information involved—particularly the data in the Parent, the manner and situations in which the Adult functions, and the way the Child has learned to play. Through understanding the content of the Parent, Adult, and Child, you may also come to understand what is *not* there. These are the key things to know about a person. Fitting them into the other facts you know about him will give you a fairly good over-all picture of what he is like and enable you to select much more appropriate techniques in dealing with him.

Interpreting Everyday Conversations

In the language of Transactional Analysis, each exchange between two people is called a "transaction." Since everyone has three distinct elements to his personality (Parent, Adult, and Child), it is great fun, and useful, to analyze transactions in terms of which "part" of one person (which ego state) is speaking with which "part" of the other person. With very little practice, this can become a fascinating and enlightening pursuit.

Both Fred and Bill arrived at the conference room at 2:50 P.M. Neither had ever met the other, but both could see that, so far, they were the only ones to show up for the 3:00 P.M. meeting. They walked inside the conference room and sat down on opposite sides of the large meeting table. The conversation started like this.

BILL *shifts his chair back from the table, slouching down in it with a disgusted look on his face. His eyes meet Fred's momentarily. Then he glances at his watch. He shakes his head and sighs a resigned sigh.*

*Incidentally, all the clues in the world will never make you 100 per cent accurate. An angry Parent or a defiant Child are particularly hard to distinguish from each other. But, whether or not you're right 100 per cent of the time will rarely be important. A good hunch is usually worth going on.

FRED *shakes his head back. Looks up at the clock on the wall, which now says 2:55* P.M.*, and shifts his chair.*

BILL: For the life of me, I've never been to one of these meetings that started on time.

FRED: Looks like we hit the jackpot this time.

BILL: Boy! You sure said a mouthful.

FRED: I can think of a lot better ways to spend my time than sitting here doing nothing.

BILL: You'd think they'd at least have someone here out of courtesy.

FRED: Wouldn't you?

The conversation continued along this line. These transactions are Parent-Parent. No factual data of any sort has been exchanged. Fred and Bill are just finding fault and complaining, as they both heard older people do when they were young. It is a favorite Parent pastime. It usually ends up by putting the blame on somebody and acknowledging that nothing can be done. Both participants can then sit back in a resigned, knowing manner, confident that the subject has been thoroughly aired. It is a very comfortable pastime, and it could clearly go on for a long time. Such "comfortable" transactions are called *complementary*.

If Bill and Fred had not been able to converse on a Parent-Parent basis, the conversation might well have been much less comfortable. When Bill said, "For the life of me, I've never been to one of these meetings that started on time," Fred might have made an Adult response. He might have said, "The meetings usually start on time here," or "We still have five minutes," or "I don't attend many meetings, myself," or simply smiled in acknowledgment. If he had, however, the conversation could quite possibly have drawn to a halt before it even got started.

Parent-Parent Transactions

Here are some examples of Parent statements designed to elicit Parent responses. While possible Adult and Child responses are also shown, it can be seen that the Parent responses are by far the most comfortable. An Adult or Child response might simply stop all further communication.

TWO CLERKS, TALKING ABOUT THEIR NEW BOSS: "They say he drinks a lot."
PARENT: "I knew it was something like that."

Possible alternate responses:
ADULT: "Does he?"
CHILD: "Let's keep spreading the rumor!"

AN OLDTIMER, SPEAKING TO A YOUNGER ASSOCIATE: "Time was when you could *count on* getting a raise every year."
PARENT: "Those days are gone forever."

Possible alternate responses:
ADULT: "Raises based on productivity do seem more realistic."
CHILD: "Gee! Sure wish I'd been around then."

A COUPLE OF OFFICE WORKERS, DISCUSSING SOME FELLOW EMPLOYEES: "They caught Betty and Jack behind the files."
PARENT: "Wouldn't you know?"

Possible alternate responses:
ADULT: "They've apparently been seeing a lot of each other."
CHILD: "Lucky guy!"

TWO SUPERVISORS REVIEWING EVENTS AT THE WATER COOLER: "Poor Bill got transferred again."
PARENT: "It happens every time."

Possible alternate responses:
ADULT: "I know."
CHILD: "I get his old office!"

THE SWITCHBOARD LADY, TALKING TO HER BEST FRIEND: "Can you imagine? They hired the boss's son!"
PARENT: "Never fails."

Possible alternate responses:
ADULT: "Can he do a good job?"
CHILD: "We'll make life miserable for him."

When a person responds to such statements in a way other than that intended by the speaker (in this case, Parent), the speaker is said to have "hooked" another part of the listener's personality (in this case, his Adult or Child). The transaction is then called a *crossed* transaction. Communication usually stops.

Adult-Adult Transactions

Here are some complementary Adult transactions, with alternate Parent and Child responses:

ONE SUPERVISOR TO ANOTHER: "Is the report ready?"
ADULT: "Yes."

Possible alternate responses:
PARENT: "What a foolish question. Of *course* it is."
CHILD: "Quit bothering me."

TWO BUSINESSMEN, PASSING IN THE ELEVATOR: "When is the meeting?"
ADULT: "Tomorrow at 1:30."

Possible alternate responses:
PARENT: "Same time it always is. You ought to know that."
CHILD: "Don't ask me. Nobody ever tells me anything."

SECRETARY, QUESTIONING HER BUSY BOSS: "Where's the Acme file?"
ADULT: "In the drawer."

Possible alternate responses:
PARENT: "If you put things where they belonged, you'd know!"
CHILD: "I hope they threw it out."

ONE ENGINEER TO ANOTHER: "I have to finish the report tonight."
ADULT: "Okay."

Possible alternate responses:
PARENT: "Must you always wait till the last minute?"
CHILD: "Too bad for you. The rest of us are having a party."

ONE SALESMAN TO THE NEXT: (THIS IS SAID AS A STATEMENT OF FACT, WITHOUT USING TONE OF VOICE OR FACIAL EXPRESSION—SUCH AS A LEER, TO TURN THE STATEMENT INTO A PARENT OR CHILD PHRASE.) "They just hired a new secretary."
ADULT: "What's her name?"

Possible alternate responses:
PARENT: "As if they didn't already have enough girls."
CHILD: "What are her boobs like?"

Some of the most common crossed transactions result when an Adult statement hooks someone's Parent or Child. People can end up glaring at each other.

Child-Child Transactions

SALESMAN, LOOKING DOWN SECRETARY'S DRESS: "How about a date tonight?"
CHILD: (Unbuttoning top button blouse.) "How soon can you make it?"

Possible alternate responses:
PARENT: "Fresh!" (Slapping his face.)
ADULT: "Sorry."

TWO SALESMEN, AT LUNCH: "I always cheat on my expense account."
CHILD: "Me too!"

Possible alternate responses:
PARENT: "I'll have to report you."
ADULT: "How do you do it?"

ONE TROUBLE-MAKING SECRETARY TO THE NEXT: "I dare you to tell off your boss."
CHILD: "You're on!"

Possible alternate responses:
PARENT: "I wouldn't *dream* of doing such a thing."
ADULT: "This wouldn't be a good time."

TWO SALES MANAGERS, CATCHING UP ON THINGS AT A CONVENTION: (Gleefully) "Jimmy's after your job."
CHILD: "I'll fix *him!*"

Possible alternate responses:
PARENT: "Shame on you, saying such things about people."
ADULT: "What makes you think that?"

ONE YOUNG [MALE] COLLEGE TRAINEE, TO HIS BUDDY: "Suzy doesn't wear a bra!" (With great enthusiasm)
CHILD: "Boy does she bounce!"

Possible alternate responses:
PARENT: "Disgraceful!"
ADULT: "Are you concerned?"

Parent-Child Transactions

Parent-Parent, Adult-Adult, and Child-Child transactions are not the only ones that can be complementary. For instance, a Parent-Child transaction will be complementary when the Parent of the speaker addresses the Child of the listener, and the Child of the listener replies in the expected childlike manner. These transactions are often seen in business. Communication, for what it is worth, continues endlessly.

ONE CLERK, TO THE NEXT: "You don't *deserve* a raise!"
CHILD: "I know, I just can't do anything right."

Possible alternate responses:
PARENT: "Who asked *you?*"
ADULT: "I'm not sure that I agree."

A PUSHY SUPERVISOR, TO SUBORDINATE: "I want to see better work from you!"
CHILD: "I'm sorry I haven't been doing well enough."

Possible alternate responses:
PARENT: "Then why don't you keep your eyes open!"
ADULT: "I'll do my best."

AN ACCUSING-TYPE SECRETARY, TO HER FRIEND: "So! You left without permission!"
CHILD: "I'm so ashamed."

Possible alternate responses:
PARENT: "What's it to *you?*"
ADULT: "Yes."

BOSS, IN A BOOMING VOICE, TO NEAREST EMPLOYEE: "I need that report immediately!"

CHILD: "Please let me get it for you."

Possible alternate responses:

PARENT: "Then go get it yourself! You've got two feet!"

ADULT: "Which report are you referring to?"

ONE MANAGER, TO ANOTHER, IN A MORALIZING VOICE: "Laziness breeds mediocrity, you know."

CHILD: "I know. I'll keep trying harder."

Possible alternate responses:

PARENT: "Who are *you* to say?"

ADULT: "Where did you hear that?"

From a business point of view, awareness of how a person is "coming on" can go far toward helping relate to him in a comfortable manner. Developing facility at engaging in complementary transactions can be a big help in stroking other people. The implicit message in such transactions is that *you believe the other person is OK*, even if he's coming on Parent or Child, because you can come on Parent or Child in the same way. You understand him. You are like him. He can trust you.

In addition, being aware of how we ourselves are coming on can help us avoid being inadvertently hooked by someone else. For example, a person is more likely to have his Parent or Child hooked when he is tired than when he is alert. When he is tired, his Adult computer is in a sense run down and cannot work as well as it otherwise might. When he is under pressure, key circuits may be blocked. He is more likely to rely on automatic responses contained in his Parent and Child tapes. Awareness of how and when this occurs in our own lives can save us a lot of grief. When we know we're tired or under pressure, and when we *hear* our Parent or Child, we can assume responsibility for our part of a crossed transaction. We can take steps to avoid the endless downward spiral.

4. Extending Your Perspective

Hidden Meanings in How We Spend Our Time

Do you know how you structure your time? Do you know the effect other people have on how you fill in the minutes of your day? Do you know when and how you tend to withdraw from people, or keep them at a distance? Do you know when you stop people from getting to know you by "sparring" with them and playing games, or, on the other hand, when you press forward and *demand* their continued involvement at a high level of intensity? Whenever you do these things, are you aware of your alternatives?

Once our habits have become entrenched, it is easy to lose track of our other options. We're often unaware of what we're doing, and why. But each of us does have preferred ways of spending our day. How a person does this can reveal much more about him than one might think at first glance.

Time structuring first poses a problem for us early in life as we learn to coordinate what we're doing with what other people around us are doing. It can remain a problem for a long time. Essentially, it involves the recurring question of *how to get through the next moment (or hour) most comfortably*. When any two people get together, unless they already know each other, each is going to be faced with this question. Pressure will continue to mount until a decision is made.* As one person described it, "I just couldn't stand there with my hands in my pockets, shuffling my feet and staring at the ground forever." If two people are fortunate enough to already know each other when they get together, they will

*How many times have you met somebody new, drawn a blank after several stabs at starting a conversation, and ended up with nothing to say? Got a little awkward, didn't it? Particularly if you just couldn't turn around and get out of there quickly?

typically sidestep the possibility of arousing any anxiety by immediately turning to whatever it is they know they can be comfortable at. They will typically talk about what happened when they saw each other last, discuss mutual acquaintances (and what happened when they last saw them), and bring up anything under the sun that they know they have in common. From there, they may find new areas of mutual interest to explore and look for other transactions which will be complementary. But they will rarely get this far unless they have first found a comfortable base from which to start.

Our patterns of time structuring are established by the way we handle these situations when we are very young. In a sense, our need to structure time stems from our need to get strokes. Since we need strokes, we need people to give them to us. And because we need people, we have to find ways of being comfortable with them. The tension which can arise from the question, "What do I say next?" in a social situation stems from a person's need to assure himself of stroking possibilities. The real question in social situations is, "What can this other person and I do to start stroking each other as soon as possible?"

There are, in T.A. terms, six ways we can choose to structure our time. They are *withdrawal, rituals, activities, pastimes, games,* and *intimacy.** Here is what they involve.

Withdrawal

Many people become accustomed to withdrawing when they are quite young. They may, for example, seek relief from the constant demands of other people around them. (When Mother and Father consistently require his attention, a young person often needs to be alone.) They may feel awkward around other people and try to avoid the feeling by keeping to themselves. Or they may just get used to not having any people around, and being alone may become comfortable for them. Whatever the reason, when a person grows up and later finds himself making a decision to withdraw, he is acting out an old pattern of *deciding not to deal with people.* He may carry out this decision by physically removing himself from people (getting up and leaving the room) or by

*Sexual intimacy, which the word "intimacy" often brings to mind, is only one form of intimacy, and in fact is often not intimate at all in the T.A. sense of the word. (It can be a game.) Intimacy here means "openness" or "honesty."

daydreaming. It may sometimes be accompanied by such phrases as "Let me alone," or "I just want to be by myself." While "alone time" is important for many people, it is significant that some prefer to spend more time by themselves than others. For a person who has difficulty dealing with people, it is often the *safest* possibility, but at the same time it eliminates any chance he may have of getting strokes from others, and the need for stroking may well be his most basic human need.

Rituals

Rituals provide us with the opportunity of remaining largely withdrawn from people, but of still being with them in a very limited sense. As Harris says, "A ritual is a socially programmed use of time where everybody agrees to do the same thing. It is safe, there is no commitment to or involvement with another person, the outcome is predictable, and it can be pleasant insofar as you are 'in step' or doing the right thing."[1]

For centuries, many of society's significant rituals have been passed down from generation to generation. (The data goes from the Parent of the mother or father directly onto the Parent tapes of the child.) Church rituals and funeral rituals provide excellent examples. People can attend these functions and "do their thing" without even having to glance at the people in the next pew. There are also greeting rituals and departure rituals where everyone knows in advance pretty much what to say and do: "Hello," "How are you," shake hands, nod; "So long," "It's been a pleasure," "Nice meeting you," shake hands, nod.

In business, whether or not a situation is ritualistic will often depend on the Parent of the boss, or person in charge, and on his willingness to follow the traditions of the organization as a whole. In many companies, functions like board meetings, orientation programs, staff meetings (to set production goals, submit progress reports, distribute policy bulletins, etc.) and many other situations may *become* rituals, if the same things always happen and if they are programmed in advance by whoever is in charge.

Activities

Another safe way we can structure time is to *do something*. Lighting cigarettes, smoking, pouring drinks, and similar activities permit us to fill time in socially accepted ways when other possibilities don't appear too promising. Berne points out that "individuals who are not comfortable or adept with rituals sometimes evade them by substituting [activities]. They can be found, for example, among people who like to help the hostess with preparing or serving food and drink at parties."[2] When we are engaged in an activity (when we are "busy" at something), there is usually no need for intimate involvement with another person. Finding something to do is a method often used to relieve the anxiety of "what to say next." Activities can provide an excellent excuse for not dealing with a person without actually turning him off.

In a business setting, the most common activity is known as *work*. Work may be creative, productive, and satisfying in and of itself, but it does limit the need for developing transactions with others. Even though two or more people may be working closely together on a project, they may never get to know each other except in relation to the work at hand. Many people in business learn to deal with each other only through the limited transactions they have evolved from "working together," and are at a complete loss when confronted by the same people in a different setting. It is also significant if a person—particularly a very hard worker—appears to use his work to avoid intimacy with others. While he may well have many good tapes on how to work, his behavior raises the question of how skilled he is at other methods of structuring his time.

Pastimes

Don, an account executive for a small ad agency, was standing in the lobby of a downtown office building, waiting for an elevator. While he was waiting, Tom, an accountant he knew vaguely, walked up and stood next to him, apparently waiting for the same elevator. He nodded to Tom. Tom nodded back. Then each looked away, as if deeply engaged in thought.

About a minute of silence passed and the elevator had not

yet arrived. Tom started pacing back and forth, his mind still on other things. But Don was beginning to feel uncomfortable.

Don broke the silence. "Seems like the weather's started warming up."

"I think winter's just about over," Tom replied.

"Reminds me of a couple years back. We'd just put our skis away for good, and then had the worst storm of the winter."

"Oh? You ski?"

They then proceeded to talk about skiing all the way to the twenty-third floor. It was both a pleasant and relaxing ride.

Pastimes, as their name implies, are comfortable ways in which two or more people may pass the time by talking to each other. If the people are strangers, or just barely acquainted, the available pastimes are limited to semiritualistic discussions of commonplace things like the weather, current events, or families (wife, husband, mother-in-law).

A skilled player will use these as openings to keep a relationship going until the conversation can be expanded to include more promising pastimes like "General Motors" (man-talk about cars), "Kitchen," or "Grocery" (girl-talk about cooking, food prices), "Martini" (I know a better way), or "It's the Society We Live In" (moralizing about society or the world).

As Harris puts it, "People who cannot engage in pastimes at will are not socially facile. Pastimes can be thought of as being a type of social probing where one seeks information about new acquaintances in an unthreatening, noncommittal way."[3] When a pastime is in progress, the people involved will each be assessing the future potential of the other players. They will use this information to decide whether or not to continue, broaden, or terminate the relationship. Skill at pastimes vastly influences one's ability to meet people and make new friends.*

The dialogue during a pastime is largely Parent-Parent, although some reality information usually needs to be included if the relationship is to be broadened. Many transactions in a business setting can be identified as pastimes. Some examples are "It's the Company We Work In" (a variation of "It's the Society We Live In"), "Morning After" (the night before),

*Many salesmen I know, for whom this skill is critical, severely limit their potential by sticking to a handful of pastimes with which they have become familiar, adamantly refusing to learn new ones.

"Who Won" (the latest ball game), "Why Don't They" (change things around here), "If It Weren't For Him" (I'd be much better off), "Did You Hear" (the latest gossip), "What Became Of" (good old Bill), and "Ever Been" (to New York, L.A., Chicago).

Games

Once rituals and pastimes have been exhausted, people interested in broadening their relationship with each other will usually turn to games. Just as our pastimes often determine which people we meet, the games we play greatly influence the course of our future relationships with those people. As Berne says, in describing the value of games, "Because there is so little opportunity for intimacy in daily life, and because some forms of intimacy (especially if intense) are psychologically impossible for most people, the bulk of the time in serious social life [and business life] is taken up with playing games."[4]

A game, in its T.A. sense, is a sequence of transactions with a definite pattern and a set of unspoken rules and regulations. It is different from our normal understanding of the word, however, in that it is not necessarily either enjoyable or interesting. Games are differentiated from other groups of transactions by two chief factors. The transactions themselves are *ulterior* (with a *surface* meaning as well as a *secret* meaning), and, there is always a *payoff*. The payoff, usually identified as a feeling (either a good feeling or a bad feeling), signifies the end of the game.

Freddy, age five, and Billy, age six, were sitting together in Freddy's backyard late one day. It was getting dark, and they were getting tired. They'd been playing all afternoon with their dump trucks. Loading and unloading. Loading and unloading. It had been fun, but it had been hard work.

Freddy sat back to survey their accomplishments. He was not only tired and dirty, but was beginning to feel hungry. He was also depressed, because Billy, slightly older and larger than himself, seemed to have stood up much better under the strain.

As Freddy contemplated the situation, it occurred to him that although he didn't feel too good at the moment, he really *did* have a neat dump truck. He decided to point this out to Billy. "My dump truck is better than yours," he remarked.

Billy, knowing this to be true, but hearing in Freddy's statement the secret message, *"I* am better than *you*" (and that makes me feel better), couldn't accept it. "Oh, no it's not!" he replied.

Stunned by such a lack of appreciation for the facts, Freddy went on to insist, "Oh, yes it *is!*"

The conversation continued, "No, it's *not!*" "Yes, it *IS!*" "NO, *IT'S NOT!*" And, at this point (as we might expect), Billy shoved Freddy down into one of the dirt piles, and Freddy started crying. The game was over!

"Mine Is Better Than Yours" is one of the very first games children learn to play. It can be seen in many forms:

"My dad can beat your dad."
"My house is bigger than your house."
"My doll is prettier than your doll."
"My job is better than your job."

Children and grownups alike often turn to it when they are feeling really bad. On the surface, it seems to be an attempt to achieve a small degree of relative OKness, but, underneath it all, it is designed to backfire. When the game is pushed to its limit, the person who started it almost always ends up by confirming to himself that he is not OK. This is his real payoff.

Frank and Tom, two run-of-the-mill salesmen, were hanging around the office one afternoon having a cup of coffee. Tom was bemoaning his lack of success at his trade. The conversation went like this.

TOM: I just can't seem to make it in this business. It's been five years, and I'm no better off than when I started. I'm just no good at it.

FRANK: Why don't you try taking some sales courses? There are lots around.

TOM: Yes, but they all cost too much money. I can't afford it right now.

FRANK: Well, why not at least buy some books? You ought to be able to get something out of them.

TOM: Yes, but I've never been able to learn from books. I'm a lousy reader and I just can't concentrate.

FRANK: Well, Dick's really the best salesman in the office. Maybe if you ask him, he'll take you on some calls with him. Then you can watch the way *he* does it.

TOM: Yes, but I've tried that already. What works for him doesn't seem to work for me. I've got a different personality.

FRANK: Maybe if you tried taking a tape recorder on your interviews you could listen to them afterwards and find out some things you're doing wrong.

TOM: Yes, I've thought about that, but it would really make me uncomfortable, and I couldn't ever explain it to my customers.

FRANK: Well, I know one thing. If you spent less time talking about it, and more time *doing* something, you'd be *bound* to improve.

TOM: Yes, but I'm already putting in as many hours as I can. I get tired easily, and after that, I'm absolutely worthless.

FRANK: Tom, to tell you the truth, with *your* attitude I think you'd be better off out of the business. Have you thought about trying something else?

TOM: Yes, but that's just the problem. There's nothing else I can do. *I'm really no good at anything.*

And there it is, the typical salesman's dilemma. Tom starts out by complaining he's no good at selling and ends up acknowledging he is simply no good at anything. Now he can really feel sorry for himself.

This game of "Why Don't You . . . Yes, But" is typical of all games. It has an obvious purpose (in this case, an Adult request for information and assistance) as well as a secret purpose (in this case, reassurance for the Child). It also has a payoff—a feeling of despair. (The Child proves, once again, that there is no hope. He is, as he knew all along, simply not OK.) As with all games, this dialogue failed to accomplish very much at its obvious Adult level. All of Frank's advice went unheeded.

Games are always preprogrammed. Each move is carefully

followed by a transactionally expected response—a response provided by the next player that challenges, or answers the first player in a way which permits the first player to still remain in the game. Without this sort of unconscious help, the first player would often be at a loss as to what to say or do next. To play games, therefore, both players must unconsciously know all the moves in the game, and they must help each other continue to play.*

Intimacy

One reason our not OK Child avoids intimacy so actively is that intimacy is the one form of time structuring based on the life position I'm OK—You're OK. If both parties to a transaction accept this position, then defensive time structuring is unnecessary. Tension and anxiety disappear as factors in deciding what to do next, and two people can become open and honest with each other.

People with the capacity for intimacy have a sense of concern for others. They care for people. They also accept people as they are. They treat other people as OK, regardless of how those people may see themselves. They have no internal need to manipulate others to achieve their own (ulterior) goals, nor do they place limitations on their relationships with others by avoiding openness and honesty.

People with the capacity for intimacy are not on the defensive, constantly erecting walls to protect themselves. They are willing to risk becoming emotionally involved with other people. They feel good about themselves, and when they meet others who operate from the same I'm OK—You're OK stance, they develop unconditional relationships based on mutual respect, relationships of true intimacy.

While many business situations are traditionally game oriented (selling, advertising, negotiating), and often need to be for the continued success of the organization, there are other situations where game playing is severely detrimental to the health of the organization. Lack of an I'm OK—You're OK relationship between people can sometimes cause great harm. Take, for instance, the insecure boss who plays "Let's You and Me Compete" with his subordinates. Since he's *competing* with them in his own eyes (instead of *managing* them),

*Although the exact words in a move may vary, its impact and meaning will always be known to both players.

he can effectively keep them from growing and maturing. He can keep them from becoming competent enough to actually threaten his own job security. He can stifle creativity and frustrate personal development until the very survival of his own organization is at stake.

On the other hand, consider a Board of Directors that meets to decide an important point of company policy. Suppose that, instead of developing an atmosphere of openness and candor, where the Adult of each member can be brought to bear on the problem, they develop an atmosphere of mistrust, where the Child of each member becomes involved in a competing game with other members, or a conciliatory game with the Chairman. Anything can happen! And that important point of company policy which the Board originally met to decide may well get short shrift.

Secret Contracts We Subconsciously Make with People

Bob Turner, the hard-driving president of a small electronics firm, has just agreed to hire Joe Finney as a staff assistant. As they go over the details of the employment contract, Bob leans back expansively in his deep cushioned leather chair, takes a long puff on his cigar, and says, "Joe, you've got a good future with this company. I go to a lot of trouble to find the right man for this kind of job. Once I hire him, I expect him to make the most of it."

Joe shifts in his chair. He's not quite sure what that message means, but wants to make a good impression. "Thank you, Mr. Turner. I'll try, sir," he replies.

Bob takes the cigar out of his mouth and points it in the air. "Trying isn't enough around here, Joe. I won't tolerate less than a one hundred per cent effort!"

Joe feels slightly uneasy, but he wants to make Bob happy. He answers. "I know sir. That's what I meant to say. A one hundred per cent effort."

At that, Bob seems to relax a bit, but continues to stare intently at Joe. "Good. That's one of the things you might as well get used to. It's important to start off on the right foot. The company always comes first in my mind, and I expect an all-out effort at all times. Understand?"

"Yes, sir," Joe replies.

Now Bob breaks out in a smile, but for some reason his eyes don't change. They remain fixed on Joe. "I like you Joe. Keep your nose clean, stay out of trouble, and we'll get along just fine."

"I will, Mr. Turner. I really appreciate this opportunity."

"One more point. We like things the way they are around here, so be sure not to rock the boat. If you have any problems, you bring them directly to me, you hear?"

"Yes, sir. I sure will."

"Good!" (Bob stands up and hands Joe the pen to sign the contract.)

Joe takes the pen, and signs it, saying, "Thank you sir. I hope I can live up to your expectations."

They shake hands, and Joe leaves the room.

This dialogue has several intriguing aspects. On the surface it appears to be an exchange of facts about how the company is run. But it is really much more than that. Bob and Joe have sealed an agreement, all right, but none of the words that pass between them has anything to do with the employment contract they sign. They have apparently gotten together to sign a written contract dealing with such things as salary, length of service, and the general terms of employment. But by the time they shake hands, Joe may have gotten more than he bargained for. He has also agreed to another kind of contract—a *relationship* contract, between Bob's Parent and his own accommodating Child. That was what the talking was all about. Bob's Parent was very carefully giving Joe the rules, telling him how things were going to be between them. It was up to Joe to either accept or reject the relationship contract. (In this case, shaking hands was the signal that he had accepted it.)

But there is more to the story than this. There is yet another contract involved, and it is the one which provided the underlying basis for the arrangement. It is the *secret* contract between Bob's Child and Joe's Child. Among other things, it says, in effect, "I will abide by the rules." It contains the provision, "I will neither alter our agreement nor disturb the equilibrium of our relationship." When one player changes the rules, or undercuts the payoff of their game, it is the Child of the other player who cries "Foul!"

Whenever a person engages with another in a prolonged set of complementary transactions, certain contracts may be said to exist. There is, first, the *formal* contract between the two Adults. This may be an official document, such as an employment contract. Or, in less structured situations such as games, it may be a simple agreement to be polite and courteous at the social level of the game.

Next, there is the *relationship* contract. This contract is made between the Parent, the Adult, or the Child of one person, and the Parent, the Adult, or the Child of the other. Its terms are not openly stated. They will usually be determined by the kind of transactions the two people fall into when they first meet. This contract will typically contain the details of one or more games the participants have agreed to play.

Often the roles selected for this contract will be quite rigid. As with Bob and Joe, one person may play stern Parent, the other accommodating Child, and nothing else may happen between them. Sometimes, however, the roles will be flexible. The same person may be both a stern Parent ("You're going to get it now!") and a benevolent, nurturing Parent ("Come, put your head on my shoulder and tell me all about it"), depending on the occasion. The Child he plays to may be accommodating ("Whatever you say, sir,") or hurt ("They took advantage of me"), or any other typical Child state.

Sometimes the players may switch roles! As when the boss's secretary, who normally plays Child, consoles him when he feels bad. (Then *he* becomes Child, and she nurturing Parent.) Or when she scolds him for coming in late or gets annoyed at him. (Then she becomes stern Parent.) Often, these are sensible, practical arrangements which provide people with comfortable ways of structuring their time with each other. Other times they may not be so comfortable, even though they are still familiar (a person wouldn't normally be able to play a role he didn't have some familiarity with).

Relationship contracts, common as they may be, will rarely be taken seriously unless accompanied by a secret contract between the two Children. It is the secret contract which contains the key provisions. While the relationship contract outlines how two people will deal with each other, the secret contract spells out what will happen if they do not comply. The first provides guidelines. The second, penalties.

An interesting example of a relationship contract and a secret contract both made by the two Children of the players can be seen in secret duels of aggression between the Child of one executive and the Child of another. Often the terms of these contracts are set up by the organization the two men work for, and there is a third party to the contract—the Parent of their boss.

The big problem with secret contracts is that they guarantee intimacy will not occur. A relationship of I'm OK—You're OK between participants becomes impossible, because secret contracts, by definition, are underhanded. They are never openly stated. They force the participants to be dishonest with each other.

In the case of Bob and Joe, Joe has agreed to tell Bob whatever he wants to hear. ("Yes, sir. A one hundred per cent effort, sir. That's what I meant, sir.") He will have to acquiesce, and ultimately lie, in order to keep his part of the bargain. Bob, for his part, has set himself up to be cut off from any useful input from Joe. It is a contract written in fear. (Joe won't be honest with Bob for fear of being fired. Bob fears that if he starts being honest with people like Joe, his whole organization will begin to collapse.) Their Children, each in the grip of its own special terror, quickly sign the secret pact.

A secret contract is a dead end, both ways. Neither player can win. If they continue their charade in an "I'm OK—but you're not" context, they may maintain their equilibrium, but each knows he is perpetrating a fraud. If either breaks the contract, it will be the signal for a game of "Uproar."* The injured Child, aware that he has been doublecrossed, or "stabbed in the back," will then seek his revenge. Secret contracts between Children are signed in blood—forever.

How We Act Out Our Life Scripts

It was a bright, sunny morning, but Ed Giles was already an hour late as he walked into his office. He had slept only a few hours the night before, and the events of the evening were still very much on his mind. He sighed wistfully as he thought of them. It had been a hard night, but it had been fun.

He had arrived home, read the paper, and eaten dinner as usual, while his wife chattered on about something he couldn't remember. (Ed doesn't like small talk.) After dinner he had puttered around the house for a while and finished up

*See Chapter Five.

some chores. His buddies had dropped by around eight, as they often do, and they had played poker, drunk beer, and talked about old times into the wee hours of the morning. It had been exciting! That was the way to enjoy life! "Those fellows really understand me," Ed thought to himself as he passed by his secretary's desk. "We really have a lot in common." But this morning Ed was paying the penalty. He was really tired.

Sue, his secretary, smiled as he walked by. Ed managed to force a faint smile in return. Sue looked quite pretty today, but, as usual, Ed didn't notice. He rarely paid attention to such things.

"Good morning, Mr. Giles," she said cheerfully.

"Morning, Sue," he answered. "What did you think of that report I finished for the boss, yesterday?"

"It was just great, Mr. Giles. Up to your usual standard!"

Ed smiled inwardly, a smile of satisfaction. Sue always made him feel good. He glanced around to make sure everyone was busy, and continued on to his office. He was hardly inside a minute, when Betty, a cute young file clerk, stuck her head in the door. "Gee, that's a nice tie you have on this morning, Mr. Giles!"

"Morning, Betty," he answered, without looking up. Ed waited a moment until Betty had left, then called out, "Sue! See that these people don't bother me this morning. I have work to do."

Now he could relax again! He sat down and leaned back in his chair. He really didn't have any work to do, but he couldn't bear talking to people this morning. His mind drifted off. The silence was quickly shattered by the jangle of the telephone. It was his boss. "Ed. That report you did for me yesterday needs some more work on it."

For a moment Ed was stunned. He had reread the report yesterday afternoon, and it looked pretty good. Even Sue had said it was good, not over five minutes ago! "Yes, sir," he replied obediently. "Anything in particular you might suggest?"

"Try putting in more statistics and tighten the whole thing up a bit. You know, Ed, I'm surprised at you, sending me a report that is only half finished."

"Yes, sir. I'll get right on it." Ed answered, putting the phone down in a hurry. "Here we go again," Ed thought to himself, "Why does he always pick on me? Why can't he be more like Sue and some of the others around here? They appreciate me."

And that was how this day began for Ed Giles. Nothing out of the ordinary. Nothing that couldn't be seen every day in thousands of other offices around the country. But just this brief glimpse, this moment in a person's life, can reveal much more about him than the average person would ever believe possible. All the things we have learned about people can now be tied together to give us a clear-cut, incisive picture of what someone like Ed Giles is really like.

For instance, we can see that Ed has trouble stroking people. He never notices how his secretary looks, let alone tells her about it. When he is complimented on his tie, he doesn't think about returning the compliment. His wife chatters at the dinner table, but since he doesn't like small talk, we could guess that his contribution to the conversation is probably of the "Yes, dear; No, dear" variety. Not much stroking involved there!

Ed seems to see himself as not OK (his not OK Child says that his boss "picks" on him), and he structures his time to be alone quite often. He sticks to activities (putters around the house and does "chores"), rituals (the poker game with his beer drinking buddies, where most of the comments and the stories could most likely be anticipated), or straight withdrawal ("See that these people don't bother me"). It looks like he works hard to avoid intimacy and is most relaxed in ritualistic situations. The games he chooses will be those most likely to support this way of life.

He does seem to see other people as being OK, and he actively seeks strokes ("What did you think of that report, Sue?"), but since the report referred to wasn't actually as good as we might have expected (from what his boss said), we can guess that he may not be able to accept honest strokes, and may set things up to be told what he wants to hear. We have seen evidence of conflicting Parent data—he comes in late, but then checks to see if everyone else is busy, and we also know that he easily plays Child to his boss's Parent ("Any suggestions?" "Yes, sir!").

In looking at things this way, we can see that Ed's early stroking experiences, life position, and special ways of structuring time have significantly shaped his life. But the really fascinating question remains to be asked. In reading this story about Ed, have you stopped to wonder, *Why do all the people in Ed's life seem to go along with his way of doing things?* Why, for instance, does his wife keep on chattering away when she most likely knows her words are not registering? Why do his buddies still go for the beer and poker routine, and still join in for the stories about the good old days, when there are many other enjoyable ways of spending an evening? Why do Ed's employees agree to give him strokes when he won't stroke them back? Why doesn't anybody engage him in pastimes (the "small talk" he dislikes) or force some reality or intimacy into the closed world he lives in? The people around Ed seem almost handpicked to let him live his life the way his Child decided many years back—a life of I'm not OK—You're OK. A life of looking for strokes but never giving them. A life centered on withdrawal, activities, and rituals and the avoiding of intimacy at all costs.

As you may have suspected, in stating the question, the answer has already been revealed. *The people are handpicked!* Handpicked by Ed's Child to fill roles in the life script his Child has written for him.

A life script is a tool used by the Child to maintain the integrity of its life position. Early in life the Child takes all the information it has received—all the data about giving and receiving strokes, about how to structure time, and about the life position it has settled on—it takes all the early decisions it has made and decides, once and for all, that *that is the way life is.* The Child then goes about setting things up so that life always comes out the way its decision has preordained. It becomes a self-fulfilling prophecy.

After writing its life script,* the Child then assumes the role of a casting director. The Child goes through life seeking out those persons who best fit the roles called for by the script. Candidates are turned away when they refuse to give the appropriate transactional responses to the Child's overtures. As Berne says, "Provocative maneuvers are designed to reveal which of the transactionally eligible candidates will play the required games. Among the eligible candidates, the final choice falls on the one who seems most likely to go through with the whole script. That is, partners are drawn together by the intuitive assumption that their scripts are complementary."[5]

In Ed's case, his Child has surrounded him with people who, over a period of time, have volunteered all the required responses. In addition, it has established an elaborate network

*Written into the script, also, are a virtually endless number of unconscious, everyday habits—little ways of doing things that we settled on long ago and never changed.

of secret contracts to make sure that things continue to work out properly. Ed's wife was chosen because, among other things, she will accept an activity-oriented person around the house. While Ed putters around and does his chores, she will most likely busy herself elsewhere with her own activities. When she talks at the dinner table, she is content to speak *at* Ed, and not *to* him. One-way communication is apparently satisfactory for her Child. It is a good way of avoiding the reality of intimacy (if no one ever hears what you say, they cannot interrupt your private world), and it fits well into the nonintimate requirements of Ed's script.

Ed's contracts with his poker buddies are equally clear-cut. The unspoken conditions they have all accepted limit their transactions to the comfortable rituals related to drinking beer and discussing "old times." This way, they may go on believing that they all have a lot in common, and that they really "understand" each other. The tenuous nature of the agreement will be revealed, however, when one of them violates his secret contract with the others. He will be quickly, and unceremoniously, expelled from the group. (Undoubtedly accompanied by all the appropriate fanfare and comments like, "I don't know what's come over old Charlie. He seems to have changed so much lately.")

In the office, Ed's Child may well have achieved its greatest success. Total equilibrium has been reached with Ed himself being none the wiser. His Child has wrapped up secret contracts with everyone available, and Ed now has complete freedom to act out his not OK script in peace. His subordinates will stroke him without looking for strokes in return. His contract with his secretary will provide him with anything he wants to hear. He doesn't even have to write a good report to be told by her that it's good. He can, in fact, write a report, have her tell him it's good (and "convince" himself that it is), and still set things up so that his boss can call to remind him that it really *isn't* good, after all. In a roundabout, but extremely effective manner, Ed can end up by confirming what he wanted to hear all along. That he's really *not* OK. Only a properly selected boss will be good enough to do that on cue.

Typical Life Scripts in Business

There are as many different life scripts in the world as there are people. The Child in every one of us has unconsciously written one. It is, in fact, a very natural thing to do. As each young person learns about life, he becomes familiar, and perhaps comfortable, with his own special group of transactions—a group unique to him that has developed out of his own personal life experience. These transactions originate almost exclusively with members of his immediate family. Since they are the most familiar, he continues to favor these transactions as he grows older. He soon learns that people outside his family will also engage in them with him, and he begins to seek out those who will do the best job. In a very real sense, he is selecting new people to fill the roles "immortalized" in his life by such famous players as his mother, father, brothers, and sisters. (Hence the many Parent-Child relationships among grown people in the business world.)

It is the very naturalness of this evolutionary process which causes people their greatest difficulties. By the time a person is grown up and finds himself still acting out old games, his Child has had years to build up elaborate justifications for these games. Unaware of how it happened, many a person can find himself at the mercy of his fearful Child for the rest of his life. He may become too afraid to change. (It is safer just to act out the script.) The biggest fear is that without the repetitive pastimes, rituals, and games of the past (which do, in truth, make up a significant portion of one's tape bank) there will be nothing—a person will cease to exist (at least as he had come to know himself).* For many of us it is a tragically high price to pay. The obsolete transactions we find ourselves clinging to are often worse than useless.

While many elements of a young person's early life experience may influence his life script (he may not finish writing it until he is around seven or eight, or even later), his early stroking experience will be particularly significant. How he learns to get his strokes will influence both his life position

*It is because of this that replacing old tapes is best done one tape at a time—not all at once. This process is discussed in detail in Chapter Ten.

and the way he structures time (he will want to maximize his strokes in whatever way he knows how). It will determine which people he chooses to associate with (his friends will be those who stroke him, and whom he can stroke in return), as well as the kinds of secret contracts he makes with them. Because of this, it can be helpful to classify a few of the more common "business scripts" in terms of the type of stroking from which they evolve.*

Performance-Oriented Script

Fred Mitchell, whom we first met as a youngster in Chapter Two, was raised on strokes for performing well, according to rules set down by his parents. Their standards are now his, and Fred's major interest in life is "doing a good job." Nothing depresses him more than failing at something. His Child has written a life script of conditional OKness centered around work and other productive activities. When he is not engaged in an activity, he usually withdraws, either to plan his next move or to take time out and rest. He has not become at all skilled at normal pastimes, which he considers a waste of time, but he has developed some provocative maneuvers to determine which of the people he meets are willing to play achievement-oriented games with him. (Games like "Look How Good I'm Doing," or "I'm Staying Late," or "May the Best Man Win.") He tolerates rituals, but only engages in them when he absolutely has to. The roles in his script have strong Parent lines. He selects people either to play his mother and father (stroking him when he performs well), or to play Child to his own Parent (so he can give them rules, correct them when they have gone astray, and punish them when they have been bad).

Fred's management techniques are centered around his personalized concept of life. People receive little attention from him. He exerts much greater effort in organizing work than in organizing people so that they can work well. He believes, "You either have it or you don't," and has little feel for developing the potential of people in his organization. He prefers to hire those who already know their job, but criticizes them often and keeps pointing out ways they can improve.

*In real life, no youngster is consistently exposed to just one variety of strokes. Actual life scripts will reflect a mixture of several types of stroking. The examples shown here are therefore meant to be general illustrations only.

He calls it "evaluation." He doesn't believe much in training (except for passing along policies and rules), because he "knows" that things like supervisory talent cannot be learned, and training in human relations makes people soft.

Since Fred's personal activity is very goal oriented, he finds it easy to set goals for others. He makes the decisions. They carry them out. It is here that his Parent-Child contracts become most clearly defined. Subordinates are the same as children to Fred. They don't like work (Fred never did when he was young), so they have to be watched constantly. They cannot organize their own time (Fred's parents always did it for him and he never learned he could do it for himself), so someone (Fred) has to do it for them. They make mistakes (due to incompetence, foolishness, or not being careful), and when they do, they should be penalized. (Fred remembers all the times he himself was spanked.) When problems or disagreements arise among his employees, Fred's job is to suppress them. Or, at best, give them lip service. (As every stern Parent knows, personal feelings of a Child should not interfere with the more important goals of big people. Above all, their feelings must not be permitted to get in the way of their own performance.)

Fred has one big problem. A crisis is brewing and he has secret contracts with everyone which prevent them from leveling with him. There is an undercurrent of unrest in his organization. Sloppiness and shoddy workmanship are on the rise. He is certain that morale problems stem from "soft" leadership, and he is working his heart out trying to "set a good example." He makes sure that everyone has plenty to do (so that they don't have time to gripe or get into trouble), and he goes over their instructions with them time and time again to eliminate any possibility of misunderstanding. But somehow, in spite of all his efforts, resentment is still brewing. Most of Fred's subordinates signed their contracts under duress (some people will do anything for money), and their Children are getting together and rebelling against his Parent. The creativity he has so conscientiously suppressed (Children are to be seen and not heard) is being used to defeat the system, and he is powerless to cope with it. Fred is at his wit's end, but his script does not provide a way out. Instead, it has prepared him to stick to his guns, to try harder and to demand more and more of his subordinates, until he eventually goes down with the ship. (The signal that the ship has sunk occurs when his employees finally walk out, his department is dissolved, the company loses its market to a competitor, or he himself is replaced.)

Accommodation-Oriented Script

Clark Harrison, whom we also met in Chapter Two, learned to get strokes when he was young by stroking other people first. Hopefully, they would like him and stroke back. If he couldn't figure out how to stroke them, he was at least very careful not to annoy them. Clark has written a life script centered around *being nice to people.* The roles call for players who will go along with him in avoiding pressure, controversy, or any other disruptive activity. Their lines often contain dialogue between one person's accommodating Child and another's nuturing Parent.

As a manager, Clark never pushes people. Harassment is not in his bag of tricks. In fact, he goes out of his way to see that working conditions are as comfortable as possible—often at the expense of performance or production. (When he was very young, he learned that people would never stroke him if he antagonized them, and they didn't have the time if they were too busy.) Performance is actually a secondary goal to Clark. He really doesn't understand it. He knows that people are happiest when they are all part of one big happy family. (And if he can make everybody happy, he is most likely to get his best strokes.) When Clark hires someone, his chief criterion is that he "fits in," and he always gives the newcomer plenty of time to get acquainted. He will avoid performance reviews. (They are uncomfortable.) He prefers to believe that people will correct themselves when left to their own devices.

With his boss, Clark is extremely courteous and accommodating. He acts as a buffer for his subordinates and smoothes over any difficulties which may arise. (He actually suppresses them, because they hurt too much.) Unfortunately, while trying to play down problems below him, he often prevents critical issues from surfacing.

Like Fred, Clark has little feel for developing the potential of people in his organization. He believes that, given a pleasant environment, people will develop themselves. He himself is not involved in the process. (He is too busy looking for strokes.) When pinned down, Clark will expect his subordinates to do what is needed out of loyalty to him. (He secretly knows it is an idle hope. That is rarely part of their contract.)

And this is Clark's greatest difficulty. All the people around him know that he really isn't very much interested in them. (But their secret contracts say they cannot tell him.) Clark is out to get his own strokes, and he is so wrapped up in the process that he doesn't have an ounce of energy left for anyone else. While looking for loyalty, Clark sets himself up to be victimized. His script, like many others, is repetitive. There is no way out. He manages to lose at the end of almost every scene. Clark provides living proof of the old adage, "Nice guys finish last."

Conformity and Compromise-Oriented Script

Bob Fredericks, also from Chapter Two, has a script that is deceptively subtle. Bob has gotten good strokes all his life, and, as you may recall, his big lessons in childhood were on how to keep them coming. (Don't disgrace your parents. Stick to the tried and true. Don't go out on a limb. Find a middle ground.) Bob's Child has written a clever script around these rules. He has managed to stay out of the limelight and avoid controversy for years. He has also managed to lead a life of OKness. From all outward appearances, he's the perfect manager.

He keeps his options open and never plunges into things head first. He plans things well and is good at research. He knows how to keep people from feuding and how to help reconcile their differences. He operates democratically and, whenever possible, yields to the majority. He always understands both sides of an issue. He hires people based on their record, but gives them the chance to grow with their job. He sets goals, but knows that a target is something to be shot at and not necessarily hit every time. He rarely punishes, but still makes sure that employees know what is expected of them.

Bob's greatest asset in life is that he has internalized the stroking pattern of his mother and father. *But it is also his greatest difficulty.* His own Parent, satisfactory under normal conditions, also makes sure that he never goes out on a limb or risks being different under any conditions. He absolutely panics inside himself at the mere thought of taking a risk. It is as if an enormous invisible wall stands between Bob and the possibility of ever taking a chance on something. He goes up to the wall and stops dead. He always has. He always will. That is what the script says to do.

And it is going to cause Bob's downfall. In opting for the status quo, he has failed to establish a climate for creativity and experimentation in his organization. His company is beginning to slip behind its competitors, but Bob has not given his people the freedom to take risks. They are not trying new ideas and finding better ways of doing things. They don't have to. A key provision of all Bob's secret contracts is that his Child cannot tolerate risk, at any price. The tragedy is that Bob acts competent. His script calls for watching the company fall further and further behind the times, while all the while people in the sidelines ask, "When's Bob going to do something?" The answer is preordained: *Never.*

People can be seen acting out these life scripts all around us. Many of them don't fail. If they find jobs that suit their script, they can become quite successful. Performance people can be found heading up sales organization, technical staffs, and frequently their own companies—particularly if immediate performance is required for the survival of the company, and people will tolerate the bad feelings performance-oriented persons generate. (Or, sometimes a small company becomes a larger one, because of the efforts of a single performance-oriented leader. After having built the company, he may still be around.) Accommodation people often find themselves niches running personnel departments, sales promotion departments, editing house organs, or filling similar nonpressure positions. Conformity people usually end up running banks, insurance companies, and other businesses where change comes very slowly.

5. Using Game Theory in Business

How We Choose the Games We Play

Everyone has his favorite games—games he will play at the drop of a hat—games so comfortable and so familiar to him that he rarely needs to be coaxed into playing them. This familiarity begins early in childhood, as a young person starts to learn how to get strokes and becomes accustomed to the various feelings these strokes produce. (Positive strokes produce good feelings—happiness, elation, self-satisfaction. Negative strokes produce bad feelings—disappointment, sorrow, despair.) Those feelings which begin to recur more and more frequently in his life, whether good or bad, soon develop a very special significance for him. They make his existence more meaningful. He begins to identify them with life itself. This is what life feels like to him! This is *it!* In a sense, they justify his existence; for to feel is to be alive. And as a young person begins to equate certain specific feelings with his own existence, these feelings become central elements of his life script.

If a person's life has generally gone well, his script is likely to consist largely of good feelings, possibly sprinkled with a few less enjoyable ones, such as disappointment or guilt. If he has been less fortunate, he will be much more likely to hurt. He will be more familiar with feelings of loneliness and despair. The person who typically grows into a successful executive, in fact, may have no experience whatsoever with the deep, abiding despair, the feeling of utter hopelessness, which the chronic loser discovers early in his childhood. (This lack of firsthand experience with such things on a *feeling* level can cause many an executive never to understand what really goes on inside the heads of his more pessimistic or depressed subordinates, particularly those who always seem to be putting themselves down and forever setting themselves up to fail.)

But no matter what feelings a young person actually experiences as he starts growing up, once these feelings recur often enough and become familiar enough to be adopted as part of his script, he becomes almost fanatically possessive of them. As he grows older, and they suddenly come upon him from time to time, he consistently does his best to hold on to them. And whenever he feels them starting to slip away, he goes to almost any extreme to recapture them.

In fact, *feelings*, these feelings which we all have but which we all so often ignore or deny, are among the most significant elements of our life script. Rather than merely wait for them to come upon us randomly, most of us actually go to great lengths to *recreate* them—frequently through the use of games. Virtually every game has some feeling associated with it—either as its payoff or as part of the buildup towards its payoff. Thus, the Child in us, through its vested interest in perpetuating the familiar feelings it once felt (and reconfirming its script), typically selects *games which assure the return of those old feelings.*

NIGYSOB (Now I've Got You, You Son of a Bitch)

One of the most common games played in an office setting is NIGYSOB. This game starts when one person sets another up so that he can *zap* him, entrap him, stomp on him, figuratively exclaim, "Now I've got you, you SOB!" and as a result make himself feel better. (He also makes the other person feel worse in the process.) It is frequently played by bosses at the expense of subordinates.

Bill, sales manager of a small electronics company, never goes through a day without getting angry about something or at somebody. Anger—loud, malicious, cutting anger—is an important emotion in his life, and he has a knack for setting up other people as objects of his wrath. The following transactions are typical of the way Bill handles things.

BILL: I thought you were going to have that report finished today.

FRED: I was, but I got tied up all day with customers.

BILL: That's no excuse! *(Zap)* One more fool move like that and you'll be finished around here! (*Zap, zap.*)

The key to identifying this as a game is the first sentence. It has the appearance, on the surface, of being a statement of fact—what Bill happened to think about the situation. Its secret purpose, however, becomes evident once the game unfolds. It is clearly to zap Fred. (Remember, not only must a game always have a payoff, but its transactions are always on *two* levels, with a surface meaning as well as a secret meaning.) Bill gets his payoff from the satisfaction of having told Fred off, and having thus relieved his own anger. Fred gets zapped? Bill justifies his anger. End of game.

NIGYSOB is a particularly fascinating game in that it provides not only a payoff feeling in the relief of anger—achieved by zapping the other guy, but it also provides the opportunity of building up lots of anger and tension in the first place, making the payoff that much more significant. Although the spoken transactions between Bill and Fred actually involved only three or four sentences, Bill could easily have started feeling bad about Fred literally hours earlier, wondering if Fred would have the report in on time and planning his moves in case Fred did not produce. In practice, Bill frequently takes several days working himself up to a really good zap, often building up pressure inside himself for hours on end.

Good NIGYSOB players have clear-cut programs for reproducing their feelings of anger. These programs are often quite detailed, including such things as whom to associate with, how to set them up, what to say, what to expect—as well as, of course, what to feel. Bill's program for anger goes like this:

PROGRAM 1—ANGER

A. WHOM TO ASSOCIATE WITH—People who like (are used to) being picked on.

B. HOW TO SET THEM UP—Find something they don't want to do. Tell them to do it. (Or, find something you're sure they *want to* do, and tell them *not* to do it.)

C. WHAT TO SAY—"Don't make me angry!"

D. PAYOFF—Feel angry.

E. BASIC DEMAND AND TYPICAL ORIGIN—"Do what I want you to do because I never got my way when I was little." (I can't cope, otherwise.)

F. WHAT TO EXPECT OF YOURSELF—The power to always control people.

G. HOW TO DESCRIBE YOURSELF—"Hot-headed."

The victim of a NIGYSOB game, often unable to get back at his persecutor, will typically learn the moves of the game so well that he can then go out, find his own victim, and successfully vent the anger he feels within himself at not being able to handle his own difficulties.

In this case, Fred immediately returned to his office and proceeded to question Barbara, his secretary, about a message he was to have received earlier which she had neglected to pass on to him. Their conversation, a bit longer than Fred's conversation with Bill, went like this:

FRED: A very interesting thing happened. Someone said he left a message for me earlier this morning. Isn't that strange? No one told me about the message!

BARBARA: Was it Mr. Smith who left the message?

FRED: Yes, it was. How did *you* know?

BARBARA: *(Beginning to feel trapped)*: Because I talked to him.

FRED: Ah ha! *(Pausing triumphantly.)* Can't you even take a message without bungling it? *(Zap.)* Can't you even do *that* right! *(Zap, zap.)*

Barbara, having already had a bad day, went home that evening in a vile mood, ready, in turn, to NIGYSOB her husband and perpetuate the injustice. The irony of the NIGYSOB game is that the victims always seem to know how to victimize others.

Kick Me

Another game frequently seen in office situations is Kick Me. Kick Me occurs when the central player sets himself up for a good, old-fashioned negative stroke (or *kick*), sets someone else up to give it to him, and then, lo and behold, actually *gets* it. Kick Me is used to induce any one of a number of negative feelings, from mild depression to deep-rooted, hard-core despair; but perhaps the most common feeling associated with it is simply that of *rejection*.

Marvin, assistant auditor in a city controller's office, is a past master at the art of getting himself kicked and then feeling rejected. Rejection is actually something of a way of life for Marvin. He looks like a loser, acts like a loser, and more often than not manages to do enough things to *prove* to himself that he is a loser. One morning, after having made a fool of himself at a staff meeting for the umpteenth time, Marvin stopped by Ted's office to bemoan his ineptness. Ted was already wrapped up in a project, but Marvin didn't notice.

MARVIN: I wonder why I always foul things up like that.

TED: *(His mind on other matters)*: You ought to know. You do it often enough! (Not a bad kick, but not quite what Marvin was looking for.)

MARVIN *(Plaintively)*: But I try so hard *not* to. . . .

TED *(In utter exasperation)*: Marvin, can't you see I'm busy! Won't you just get out of here and leave me alone!

MARVIN *leaves silently, having finally confirmed that he was completely unwanted, and feeling utterly rejected*

Marvin's skill at getting kicks is so well developed that he often doesn't even need to say anything! Since the first move in a game need not necessarily be spoken (it can be either verbal or nonverbal), Marvin frequently just has to *glance* at someone in his typical pathetic, woebegone manner for the negative strokes to start raining in.

"Uh oh! Here comes Marvin again. . . ."

"For God's sake, Marvin! Stop acting so foolish!"

"Marvin, it's about time you did something about your personality."

"Hi, Marvin. Sorry, but I've got to go now."

"Marvin, why can't you just shape up!"

He has heard them all his life, ever since he was a little boy, and his favorite game, Kick Me, is structured to make sure he continues hearing them.

Marvin's program for reproducing his old feelings of rejection is every bit as detailed as Bill's program for reproducing anger. It goes like this:

PROGRAM 2—REJECTION

A. WHOM TO ASSOCIATE WITH—People with a stern, critical Parent who easily find fault or become exasperated.

B. How to set them up—Act dumb, stupid. Fumble a lot and do foolish things. In particular, demand positive strokes from people when you're least likely to get them.

C. What to say—Anything stupid and irritating.

D. Payoff—Feel rejected.

E. Basic demand and typical origin—"Don't reject me, because Mommy always did."

F. What to expect of yourself—Loneliness.

G. How to describe yourself—"I never have much luck with people. People like to take advantage of me."

All good Kick Me players do not necessarily act like born losers. Marvin is something of an extreme example. The mark of a good Kick Me player is merely that he frequently sets himself up to be kicked. He is typically someone who received enough negative strokes in childhood to decide to incorporate his recurring negative feelings into his script, but he may not have received enough negative strokes to decide to feel (and act) like a loser all the time. The trick in identifying a Kick Me player, therefore, is not to look for a certain type of person, but merely to be alert to the kinds of payoffs people get from their transactions. If someone seems to be setting himself up to feel bad and appears to be trying to get others to help him, then he is quite likely a Kick Me player. His appearance may occasionally provide supporting evidence, but it may also sometimes be misleading—some Kick Me players simply do not look the part. *What he is doing* is the key.

Becky, a pert young research assistant of twenty-two, is absolutely the last person one would ever suspect of playing Kick Me. An attractive, bright girl, she not only acts pleasant and engaging, but she *looks* like a winner. Becky, however, was raised in a family where little girls never did things for themselves. They just sat around looking like ornaments. As a consequence, Becky grew up feeling totally helpless, unequal to many everyday tasks, and not really capable of holding her own in the world.

Unable to do many things for herself, Becky learned to survive early in life by getting others to do things for her. An attractive girl, she found that by assuming a façade of utter helplesseness she could often manipulate people into helping her. (Who could resist a pretty, helpless girl?) This approach was very useful to Becky when she was little—girls in her family were not permitted to do things for themselves, and it *did* get things done, but in the long run it served merely to perpetuate her own helplessness (she never, ever, learned how to do things for herself), and for all her efforts, Becky never really quite got rid of the bad, helpless feeling inside herself.

When she finally left home to go out into the world (college, and then a job), Becky's helpless feelings began to recur more and more frequently. Not only was she increasingly required to do things on her own, but she found that people in the real world did not respond to her overtures for help nearly as readily, or as consistently, as the folks at home once had. Even those who did respond soon tired of it. Her most familiar transactions at work (those geared to avoid having to do things), more and more often brought the responses: "Oh Becky, who don't you do something on your own for a change!" or "Becky, it's time you stopped depending on people!" or "Becky, if you don't start doing *something* by yourself, your chances of making it around here are pretty slim."

As one might suspect, these statements served merely to intensify Becky's longstanding feelings of helplessness—feelings which by now frequently reduced her to a state of hopeless internal panic. When uttered with a tone of finality or one of severe disgust (embellishments which Becky herself induced with her helpless looks and gestures), such statements ranked among the most effective kicks Becky's friends could give her.

Becky, attractive as she was, had a sophisticated, detailed program for getting her kicks and recreating her old feelings of helplessness. It went like this:

PROGRAM 3—HELPLESSNESS

A. WHOM TO ASSOCIATE WITH—People who easily tire of helping others.

B. HOW TO SET THEM UP—Act inept, passive. Stand around a lot. Look like you expect *them* to handle things.

C. WHAT TO SAY—"Please help me."

D. PAYOFF—Feel helpless.

E. BASIC DEMAND AND TYPICAL ORIGIN—"Please help me, because everyone did when I was little."

F. WHAT TO EXPECT OF YOURSELF—Not much.

G. HOW TO DESCRIBE YOURSELF—"Not very good at things."

One of the tragedies of recurring script feelings is that when they do not recur often enough, we typically devise new ways—new games or different twists on an old game—to recreate them. On occasion, Becky would go about this by *reversing* her requests for help. Whenever several days had passed and she had not needed help, or had not asked people for assistance (had not felt helpless), Becky would actively go out *and try to help others!* In spite of her own ineptness, she would actually take the initiative and ask others if she could help *them!* Naturally, those people who knew her would immediately point out the ridiculousness of such a request, and Becky's secret reason for asking it would suddenly become clear. Once again she had induced them to kick her!

Many people use this approach to seduce others into their game, particularly if they are badly in need of a payoff. The rule is: ask or demand the reverse of what you really want ("Don't make me angry," when you really want to feel angry; "Let me help you," when you really do not want to help); and be sure to do it in an irritating enough fashion so that they comply not with your spoken wish, but with the secret one.

Uproar

Uproar is sometimes confused with both NIGYSOB and Kick Me. It is characterized by lots of hostility and loud fighting, and either player may occasionally appear to be zapping the other, or setting himself up to be kicked. The difference between Uproar and these other games, however, is in the payoff. Uproar players generate lots of intense feelings in the midst of their game, but they never seem to be able to release those feelings. There is no payoff feeling as there is for the Kick Me player, nor any relief from pent-up feelings, as with the NIGYSOB player. The feelings in Uproar just continue to build up, and build up, until one of the players simply cannot stand it any longer and abruptly leaves the scene (stalking out of the room, throwing up his hands in disgust, and slamming the door behind him).

Uproar frequently begins when Player A assails Player B with a statement similar to the final zap in a game of NIGYSOB or to the final kick in a game of Kick Me:

"What's the matter with you?"
"Can't you do *anything* right!"

"Here we go again. . . ."
"If I've told you once, I've told you a million times. . . ."

Player B then has several alternatives. If he isn't affected by these comments—if they just roll off him with no measureable impact—he has effectively declined the game. If he responds by feeling depressed or rejected, he is probably hearing such remarks as a response to some of his own earlier nonverbal overtures in a game of Kick Me (if he had in fact made such overtures) and has prepared himself to take his kicks like a good little Kick Me player. If he chooses not to accept the kick, however, and instead reacts *defensively*, his next move will be to accept the invitation to a game of Uproar. This move will typically be some defensive remark like:

"What do you mean by *that?*"
"Why don't you mind your own business!"
"You've got some nerve!"
"What's wrong *now?*"

The argument will then get hotter and hotter, as feelings intensify, but the cross borne by all Uproar players is that the other guy will never back down, and the only way out of the game is some sort of hostile withdrawal.

Like many games, Uproar often takes just a few minutes to play from start to finish. As with other games, however, it can also take much longer, with many smaller episodes over many days and months leading up to one final confrontation—when one or the other of the players decides to leave permanently (quit the company in a huff) or get the other guy to leave permanently (fire him, get him fired, force him to resign). The final move is often preceded by a sentence like, "If you do that just one more time, so help me, I'll. . . ." At this point, the other player, now knowing exactly what to do, will normally take very little time in escalating the game to its explosive ending.

Uproar is frequently played between boss and subordinate when both players have real difficulty in dealing with each other and in their mutual frustration are easily seduced into old unproductive ways of handling things. As Uproar is principally a means of intensifying bad feelings to the point where "getting rid of people" becomes the only alternative, both players have virtually guaranteed an economic loss to the company immediately upon undertaking the first few moves in the game. (A loss, caused not only by time wasted playing the game, but by the ultimate withdrawal of one of the players.) Uproar is a characteristic game of organizations with lots of employee turnover.

How Games Reflect Our Life Position

People often display a need to be comfortable through experiencing familiar feelings, however negative such feelings may be. They feel a sense of security with the familiar, even if it is unpleasant. This leads them to repeat their most familiar feelings by selecting games which help recreate those feelings. In doing so, they establish a pattern of behavior in which certain games and feelings tend to recur over and over again. This pattern maintains the forward impetus of their script, and reinforces their basic life position.

While a person may have some familiarity with all four basic life positions, most of his games tend to reinforce one dominant position. For most people in business and in other organizations, this position will usually be either I'm OK—You're not OK, or I'm not OK—You're OK. The position I'm OK—You're OK (we're both OK) is generally game-free. It is characterized by an attitude of openness and trust; by a willingness to share, to give, and to unconditionally accept other people as they are. There is basically no need to manipulate others for one's own personal emotional gain, or payoff. The fourth position, I'm not OK—You're not OK, is reinforced by games, but it is literally self-destructive, and characteristic of people who ultimately cannot cope with the real world.

I'm OK—You're not OK

Games which reinforce the position I'm OK—You're not OK typically center around such feelings as anger, scorn, superiority, or disgust—where someone else (other than the person experiencing the feeling) is identified as the object of the anger, scorn, superiority, or disgust. These games are usually played from a strong Parental stance, or from the stance of an angry, sulking Child. They involve such common, everyday practices as blaming, criticizing, and putting people down.

Great resentment can be expressed in such games. Some people spend most of their early lives constantly subjected to unrelenting, irrational, external demands—demands placed on them by their circumstances, environment, and occasionally by particularly domineering, distressed parents. (Do this; do that; *don't* do this; *don't* do that; be what I want you to be, not what *you* want to be; feel what I say you feel, not what you really feel; be inferior, because I say you are; be inept, foolish, and clumsy, because I don't want you to be better than me.) People resent the imposition of these demands (a normal reaction of the natural Child). Unable to relieve the pressure or to lash out at the source of the demands, they often build up great resentment inside themselves. They learn to play their games with particularly fierce intensity. Later, whenever they feel bad, they unleash this pent-up resentment at whoever seems to be the current "cause" of their bad feeling. Such resentment, directed at someone in the present (wife, husband, boss, subordinate), typically has nothing at all to do with the person or persons currently seen as the target of the resentment. It is merely the expression of all the pent-up anger produced by years of unrealistic pressures and demands placed upon the person demonstrating it as a youngster. Finally, it is "safe" for him to lash out and put people down. (Mommy and Daddy are no longer around.)

Many games which reinforce the position I'm OK—You're not OK descend from the early childhood game Mine Is Better Than Yours (a subtle way of saying "I am better than you!" or "I'm OK—You're not"). NIGYSOB, the "big people's" format for zapping others, is perhaps the most widely encountered descendant of this universal childhood put-down. There is virtually no other formula for feeling so much better, so quickly, at someone else's expense.

Many other games which reinforce the position I'm OK—You're not OK are variations on the NIGYSOB theme; games like Blemish (played by people who can't relax until they find the other person's "blemish," or by groups who single out one particular person for his "blemish" in order to make themselves feel collectively more secure); or games like Critique, where the person reviewing someone else's progress, behavior, or attitude uses the process as an excuse to make himself feel better. (His "critiques" are often spontaneous—occurring whenever he unconsciously feels the need to pick on someone to relieve some pressure or bad feeling of his own.)

Frequently a good Critique player will move from Critique directly into a game of You're Not Good Enough (so I'll do it for you). If the player is a boss, and if he has a subordinate to play with, the preordained goal of his critique will often be to show that his subordinate is incompetent. He can then justify taking over, and relieve the anxiety he felt at watching someone else try something he could do better. This situation is typical of the performance-oriented boss who sees delegation as losing control and who fears the mistakes his subordinates may make in learning to come to grips with a problem. Knowing that he can handle it and that they probably cannot (yet), such a boss, operating from an I'm OK—You're not OK position, will take over, perform the task he has always been able to perform, and create a situation in which no one ever learns anything.

When his subordinates complain, this boss may then switch to a game of I'm Only Trying to Help You in a futile attempt to maintain their loyalty. Then, if by some chance things continue to go wrong, he will immediately deny responsibility, frequently switching into some form of the game You Got Me into This. All his games focus on other people as the source of his problems. With this rationale, he need never examine his own contribution to his difficulties, need never move in a direction of positive growth or change.

Sometimes games which reinforce the position I'm OK—You're not OK may be three-handed games, as with Let's You and Him Fight. Many a person has been seduced into fighting with others for some reward (job, promotion), only to discover, even if he wins, that his victory is hollow. (The job is not what it was cracked up to be, the promotion does not bring a raise in salary, and all the glory he thought he would find is not there.) In fact, he may soon be fighting for his life all over again. Some brief undercover work will usually reveal that this game has been set up by some third party so that the players can eliminate each other, much as a fickle woman might eliminate her unwanted suitors by getting them to fight among themselves.

Hardly a day goes by when we cannot find someone playing a game reinforcing the position I'm OK—You're not OK. But observing someone playing one game one time in no way guarantees that we have uncovered that person's basic life position. People operating from any of the other three positions may be familiar with any particular game, and may play it frequently. Some, for instance, may operate generally from the stance I'm OK—You're OK, but still have occasional difficulty relating to those who represent values, ideals, or life styles in conflict with their own. It is as if all their early experience focused on how OK they were, or on how right they were, or on how superior they were, but left them with little information on how to deal with those who did not meet their own (Parental) standards in life. Such people will occasionally be very comfortable playing NIGYSOB, Critique, or Blemish.

Other people operate basically from an I'm not OK stance, but may be backed into a corner, or reach their boiling point, and flip into I'm OK—You're not, more or less as a last resort. These transitions between positions, these flippings in and out, can take place instantaneously. One minute a person will be in the doldrums, beating on himself, or accepting kicks from others, in an I'm not OK—You're OK position. An instant later, almost in the twinkling of an eye, he will be lashing out at others, having flipped into I'm OK—You're not OK. Then, just as quickly, he may flip back, having expended his energy, and quite possibly having scared himself.

A person's dominant life position therefore cannot be determined by examining one or two of his games. His basic position will involve many, many games. It will be determined by his over-all game pattern, as well as by the intensity and frequency with which he plays his games. It is something which may only be verified by constant observation, and which isolated instances may only hint at.

I'm Not OK—You're OK

Games which involve depressive feelings, feelings of being put down, blamed, attacked, abused, or hurt, tend to reinforce the *I'm not OK* aspect of the position I'm not OK—You're OK. They structure time in ways which produce unconscious negative strokes (secret payoffs). They are usually played from the stance of a compliant (not defiant, or sulking) not OK Child. They help the player remind himself that he is not OK and recreate all the negative feelings associated with his depressive stance.

Of all the games reinforcing the position I'm not OK—You're OK, Kick Me is perhaps the most prevalent. It also has many other games related to it. Give a new project to a good Kick Me player, and he will immediately start thinking of all the reasons he cannot do it. ("Never could do it," "Never did it before," "Not good at that sort of thing," "Can't work alone," "Can't work with people.") He will get wrapped up in all the negatives of his past, until he nearly paralyzes himself. Then, with all the old feelings of ineptness rising around him, he will move smoothly into a game of I'm Not Good Enough (so you do it for me).

If no one is willing to play this with him, he may then start work on the project. He may, in fact, appear to make a valiant effort to come to grips with it. If so, it is less likely with an eye towards succeeding, and more likely with an eye towards phasing into a game of Look How Hard I've Tried, which will justify his unconsciously planned failure. If he does fail, he may bring his cycle of bad feelings to a close by trying to find comfort in a quiet game of See What You Made Me Do. On the other hand, if he still hasn't satisfied his need for negative feelings, he may look for a nurturing Parent with which to play Ain't It Awful, or perhaps Why Does This Always Happen to Me (WAHM).

These games do not necessarily occur in sequence, nor do they necessarily take just a short time to play. They do, however (with others like them), represent a class of games which emphasize and reinforce the not OK aspect of their player's life position. Very often, they represent a stubborn, almost life or death effort to maintain the not OK status quo. Such games as If It Weren't For . . . (You, Me, Them, Life, Circumstances) and Wooden Leg (what can you expect of a man with a wooden leg, poor personality, no education) are particularly effective at this. At times, their surface appeal to logic can be very seductive.

To much of the world, people who play games based on an I'm not OK—You're OK life position often seem modest, quiet, unassuming, and the embodiment of many worthwhile, noble traits. In truth, however, they often see themselves quite differently. They typically see themselves as victims; victims of life, victims of the system, and victims of all the pressures and influences ebbing and flowing in the world around them. They go through life feeling buffeted by fate, victimized by the people they live with. More often than not, they see themselves as powerless to do anything about it. They believe themselves to be powerless. To gain control over their lives, to put their own show on the road, would destroy the elaborately conceived scheme their Child has devised to retain its own control over their script (and destiny). While they may well see themselves as victims of their surroundings, the ultimate irony for such people is to learn that, in the long run, they have only victimized themselves.

Games That Are Played in Pairs

An almost foolproof way to spot a NIGYSOB player is to look for the Kick Me players on the other end of his transactions. Conversely, the best way to spot a Kick Me player is to look for the NIGYSOBers he gets to kick him. NIGYSOBers and Kick Me players are virtually always on opposite ends of each other's transactions.

When a good NIGYSOB player and a good Kick Me player get together, they can be so accomplished, and their moves so subtle, that it becomes almost impossible to tell who actually makes the first move. Alfred, senior attorney for a large metropolitan law firm, particularly delights in zapping Ed, one of his junior attorneys. One day, when he had a hunch that Ed had not done much work on a particularly difficult case, Alfred approached him. Their conversation went:

ALFRED: Ed, what's happened with the Johnson case?
ED: Nothing so far. I haven't had a chance to get to it.
ALFRED: You haven't! What kind of a firm do you think this is! *(Zap.)* If we all put off our hard cases, we'd be out of business! *(Zap, zap.)* You better stop loafing or you'll be looking for another job real soon! *(Zap, zap, zap.)*

While on the surface it looks as if Alfred set out to zap Ed, by posing his initial, innocent-sounding question, "What's happened with the Johnson case?", the truth is that Ed knows Alfred likes to be kept up-to-date on his projects. Ed is an accomplished Kick Me player. In pursuing his quest for negative strokes, Ed will frequently neglect to inform Alfred about his more troublesome cases, putting them off on purpose. He will thus assure himself of his negative strokes, even if Alfred is not in the mood to voluntarily zap someone that particular day. When Ed does put a case off, he starts the game. When he doesn't, Alfred starts it. Both are so skilled, however, that neither usually knows who really makes the first move.

Many games are played in pairs. Particularly widespread in organizations are those games, like NIGYSOB and Kick Me, which pair off a stern, controlling Parent with a compliant, not OK Child. Don and Jess, the director and assistant director of a large government agency, provide an excellent example of how this works. Don is the Parent in most of their transactions, operating from the position I'm OK—You're not OK. Jess, his subordinate, is the Child, operating from the stance I'm not OK—*You* are. They each have at least half a dozen games which fit smoothly into this framework. Following, in eight steps, is a condensed version of what frequently happens between them.

Step 1. Don assigns Jess a project.

Step 2. Jess works diligently, but is programmed by his script to fail.

Step 3. Don notices the projected failure. He stands by, pointing out possible pitfalls, then makes an effort to help.

Step 4. Jess resists. Plea: "Look How Hard I've Tried" (when the trying, all along, was never related to succeeding with the projcct).

Step 5. Don reluctantly assumes control of the project, justifys his actions with "I'm Only Trying to Help You" (when he doesn't help in any way that's meaningful to Jcss, or from which Jess might learn. His help is no help at all).

Step 6. Jess plays "Look How Hard I've Tried" to Don's "I'm Only Trying to Help You." Both are comfortable.

Step 7. Complications develop. Don denies responsibility for possible failure through the use of "You Got Me into This" (when he really got himself into it by making his own decision to take over). Don drops the project like a hot potato.

Step 8. Jess is left holding the bag and immediately takes the remaining steps needed to complete the failure, pleading "See What You Made Me Do" (which was exactly the sort of failure he had programmed for the project from the very beginning).

In Step Four, it may be noted that Jess's resistance to Don's taking over is really a surface resistance. His secret message to Don is "Take over, I'm a failure." In Step Five, Don's apparent reluctance to take over is also merely surface reluctance, as is his stated interest in "helping" Jess. Don takes over because he has to take over in order to confirm that he is OK at someone else's expense.

Don and Jess need each other badly. Jess can only avoid dealing with his failure script (and continue never to succeed) by having a secret contract with Don wherein Don always rescues him. Don can only avoid dealing with his own unconscious need to prove he is OK at someone else's expense by having a secret contract to always rescue Jess.

Thus Don and Jess use the nonreality of their complementary games to maintain the integrity of their respective life positions. Each accepts the other's fictional view of the world so that he himself may not be unmasked. With diligent effort they may go through their entire lives that way.

Many other games are played in pairs (when Don plays Blemish, for instance, Jess can slip comfortably into Ain't It Awful). Identifying them isn't always easy. Knowing the name of a game, however, is far less important then being able to recognize that a game is, in fact, in progress. Naming games can often become an end in itself—an intellectualized process which rarely produces change. Far more important than being able to find a label, is the ability to understand what is happening.

Regardless of what game someone might be playing, he usually has at least one other person who is responding to him—someone who is in some way supporting his dysfunctional behavior. Without such a person, he couldn't play his game. (When he cannot get someone to accept his game, he will either stop playing, or leave to find someone else who will.) Thus, when it isn't clear what the central player is doing—what game he is playing—it is often helpful to observe the supporting player, or players. This practice can frequently provide useful information for the central player himself. Any person who isn't certain what he is doing, but who has, for instance, lots of Kick Me players around him, can be pretty sure he is playing NIGYSOB. Similarly, any person who isn't sure of the exact name of his game, but who has people around him playing *something like* Kick Me, may rest assured his is playing *something close to* NIGYSOB (a near-relative game, perhaps). He can then take steps to stop his game without ever knowing, or ever really needing to know, its name.

How to Avoid Losing Games

We often get caught up unconsciously in our own and other people's games. We get hooked into either initiating or responding to transactions on a Parent or Child level. Once we are into a game, we rarely come out ahead. There is no victory in keeping oneself depressed or in getting kicked. There is no glory in getting the upper hand and feeling good about it or in making the other fellow feel worse and gloating over victory. Any transaction designed to make someone feel good *at the expense of someone else* is guaranteed to keep the perpetrator victimized by his own archaic behavior patterns.

Since we cannot win, once we are in a game, our only hope is to avoid losing. This is best done by understanding the emotional underpinnings of the game and by being able to get ourselves, and others, out of the game to a more productive place.

Identify What You Feel

In order to get out of a game, you must first know that you are in it. Games are most clearly identified at the feeling level. They are evidenced, as they reach their conclusion, by looks and sounds of such feelings as anger, depression, and self-satisfaction. Thus you will often find it helpful to ignore the surface appearance of events and to look instead for what occurs at the feeling level. Where is the frustration, the hopelessness, the anger, the rejection? Who creates pressure in order to relieve it later? Where is the conflict? Where is the resistance? How do they build up? Who feels what, and how is it important to him? Most of all, where does it all seem to be leading?

Get in touch with what you feel as you go through your day—particularly when you are transacting with others. Learn to recognize when people seem to be frustrating you or getting on your nerves. They may be setting you up to zap them. Get a feel for when *you* seem to be frustrating others. You may be setting them up to kick you. Notice when you are starting to get angry; when you are beginning to feel depressed, put down, or inadequate. Look at how things are going and determine if you will soon be feeling better, or worse. If your feelings are intensifying, the game itself may be escalating.

Make the Implicit Explicit

One of the most effective ways to rescue yourself from a game is to recognize what is happening, describe it to your fellow players, and express your own wish to withdraw. Sometimes, if you have a good Child-Child relationship with the other players, you can do this quickly, and suggest a switch to some more enjoyable transaction.

Mike, regional sales manager for a manufacturer of ladies sportswear, had gotten into a heated telephone argument with one of his district managers over how many salesmen to send to a forthcoming trade convention. As their words became more and more pointed, Mike could feel himself becoming more and more agitated. He could feel his position hardening. Not wanting to escalate into Uproar, and unwilling to zap his district manager, Mike thought of another approach. "Look," he said matter-of-factly, "We're not getting anywhere this way. Let's start over again, okay?"

His district manager, equally anxious to avoid a confrontation, readily agreed. Mike's Child, directed by his Adult, had found an easy way out for both of them.

Sometimes things are not that simple. One of the players may be too deep in his game to withdraw so quickly. Chris, a young aeronautical engineer, had been quietly trying to comfort a friend of his who had just been passed over for promotion. It was an unfortunate setback for his friend, but it was not the end of the world. Nevertheless, whenever Chris tried to change the subject, his friend returned to it, each time with greater intensity. He kept saying, "What's wrong with me?", "How can they do this?", "I suppose I'll have to resign now," and "Couldn't they leave me with *some* self-respect?" He seemed to know all the phrases for an almost endless game of Ain't It Awful, or Poor Little Me.

While Chris had joined the conversation out of genuine concern for his friend, he was beginning to feel frustrated in his attempts to provide consolation. He suddenly realized that his efforts were proving fruitless and that he himself was tiring. He decided to withdraw. He said to his friend, "I know you're sad, and I realize this is a big blow, but there's nothing either of us can do about it now, and we're certainly not getting anywhere sitting around like this. I'm ready to do something else. You can join me if you wish."

His friend, still deep in his game, could tell that Chris would no longer play. Faced with the choice of keeping his game, but losing Chris's companionship, he decided to give up the game and go along with Chris. By being explicit about his plans to withdraw, Chris had managed to clarify his friend's immediate choices. By stroking him, with a show of understanding and with an invitation to join in some other activity, Chris had also succeeded in helping his friend trade in some useless (game) strokes for some potentially better, more meaningful reality-based ones.

Sometimes, when you are caught up in a game just as strongly as the next player, getting out can be much more difficult. Here it is helpful to openly explore all the Adult implications surrounding the game—the opening moves, the escalation (if any), and the predictable payoff. In addition to stating your own wish to withdraw, it is helpful to ask the question, "*After the payoff, what next?*"

Glenn, one of eight staff attorneys in a local public defender's office, found himself in a pointless, nine-handed game with his fellow attorneys and their boss, the community's public defender. The public defender, a good lawyer, was something less than a capable administrator. Their office was chaotic. One secretary (the boss's) opened everyone else's mail (it was done, allegedly, to control the work flow), treating other secretaries as her inferior. Lawyers were required to sign in and out each day on time sheets, as if they were punching a time clock. The case load had increased dramatically, beyond the point where any lawyer could treat his clients fairly. More than this, the atmosphere in the office was extremely tense. It was hard to work there.

The lawyers, confronting their difficulty, had finally convinced their boss to hold a staff meeting at which they could offer suggestions and participate in management decisions. It was here, in the meeting, that Glenn found himself in the game. As each lawyer spoke, giving his view on what troubled him, their boss responded, "That's how it was before I took this job," "I'm aware of this, but it's the best we can do," and "That's how other offices do it." Regardless of the issue, his answers were always the same—he knew about it, but there was nothing he could do. He heard all their comments only as strong personal criticisms—attacks on his own ability as a manager. He responded with defensive statements—the reasons things were as they were, the "Yes, but's," implying that he was not to "blame" for the difficulties. Never once did he actually hear his lawyers in terms of how *they* were being adversely affected by the stress in the system.

As his frustration mounted, Glenn suddenly realized the futility of what they were doing. He and his fellow lawyers were merely escalating a stalemate. Their boss was not hearing them, and they were not hearing their boss. Glenn didn't know exactly what to do, but he did know he didn't want to continue participating in the game. He said, "I feel frustrated by what we are doing. When each of us says what's bothering him, hoping the boss will do something about it, the boss answers in a way which means he won't do anything about it. We seem to have discovered all the things he won't do, and these are the things that trouble us most. As we bring up each new item, our frustration only deepens. The boss's frustration seems to deepen, too. We can probably bring up new items for the rest of the meeting, and feel that much worse when we're finished. But what *then?* We'll feel worse, and nothing will have changed. Frankly, I feel bad enough already. Isn't there something more productive we could do?"*

The public defender, hearing Glenn's words, and for the first time seeing clearly how he himself participated in the stalemate, offered to help restructure the meeting in a more positive fashion. He also agreed to do his share in relieving the tense atmosphere which hung over the office.

This particular approach to getting out of a game is especially valuable when both sides have (or are aware of) a vested interest in no longer playing. It exposes the secret motives each Child had in originally participating, and it gives the Adult of each player a chance to assess what is happening. Without an explicit statement of what was happening in the meeting on the *feeling* level—a statement of how the feeling itself was being maintained and escalated—all the players in the game might well have continued playing indefinitely.

This approach can be used not only for getting out of T.A.

*Most people, at least in their first efforts, will not be as clear or as articulate as Glenn in exploring the Adult implications of a game. Any effort, however, will be better than no effort, as it will automatically stop the game by breaking the string of transactionally expected responses.

games, but for dealing with any number of other gamelike circumstances in life. Many life situations are characterized by transactions with secret payoffs and certain stylized rules, and regulations. Many business and political negotiations, as well as wars between nations, are entered into and kept alive through the use of transactionally expected responses. Often, they are escalated at the feeling level. ("He called me a liar, I'll have to shoot him." "He bombed my village, I'll have to blockade his port.") Responses are typically tied to feelings and are programmed in such a way as to keep the other players always in the game. Many of these moves, and their programmed responses, have been passed down from generation to generation, usually in the form of Parent data about what to do in the face of a threat or an attack.

Most traditional responses in such situations involve efforts to beat the other fellow *within the context of the game,* frequently in ways which produce great personal harm to both sides. While it may often be important to react spontaneously to a real attack with a satisfactory defense or counterattack (it may well be a matter of life or death), if no threat exists or if it has successfully been warded off, such games can benefit from having their moves exposed and their players confronted with the realistic consequences of where those moves are leading. Most people never see beyond the (harmful) payoff. Many never see even that far. Few ever ask themselves, "After the payoff, what then?"

6. Living in the Past, Future, and Present

The Concept of Time Competency

Many people go through life unaware of their surroundings, unresponsive to the world around them. They spend their time in their heads—evoking memories of their past, anticipating the future, dwelling on what has gone before, and worrying about what is yet to come. They think unproductively. They become so wrapped up in what they are doing, they completely block out the present. In doing so, they prevent themselves from responding spontaneously to their environment and often learn to mistrust whatever natural responses to life they might once have had.

Such people are typically victims of early lessons which taught (erroneously) that their natural feelings and responses were not accurate, and were to be ignored. They were taught not to feel what they felt, but rather to feel what they were told to feel or what they were permitted to feel. They were taught not to stay in the present and experience life, but rather to fit life into some predetermined framework provided by their parents. What they were experiencing at the moment was only relevant if it fit into what they had been told about it before.

Such people grow up handling things in stereotyped ways. They always look to how things *should* be, to the way they *ought* to respond or feel. They try to force simple solutions upon complex situations. When their old (Parent) ways do not fit, their solutions, applied to present problems, only compound their difficulties. Failing to solve their problems, they reach dead ends, frustrating themselves and feeling bad rather than seeking new solutions. ("This *has to* work. It *must* work. If it doesn't, I'm hopelessly lost. I'm a failure.") For such people, the past either dulls or completely obliterates their perception of the present, leaving them unable to deal effectively with reality.

Other people have just as much trouble with the future. The future is so important to them it intercedes in the present, keeping them unaware of what is going on around them. When they were young, if they ignored the future (if they forgot to consider how Mommy would react to what they were doing, for instance), the consequences were often traumatic. (Some kids can barely breathe without incurring the ill will of their parents.) The only way they can survive is to always attend to the probable (catastrophic) consequences of their actions. They learn to consider the future out of fear. It can become an obsession with them. It keeps them from seeing, hearing, and feeling in the present.

For still other people, the future holds little promise; the past, little relevance. When they were young, there was often no connection between what was happening and what had gone before. People were inconsistent and events occurred randomly, without rhyme or reason. Trying to make sense of it was most often an exercise in futility. Later in life, efforts to understand their past and to anticipate their future serve little more than to escalate their confusion.

These people fail to grasp the true relationship between the past, the present, and the future. For them, the past and future are either too relevant or not relevant enough. Their memories and expectations are either too alive, too meaningful for them, or they are not alive and meaningful enough. Such people are not *time competent*. They use time unproductively. Unlike the time competent person, they permit the past and the future only to confuse them. They fail to put the present in its true perspective, to see things in terms of what has gone before and what may yet occur.

The person who is time competent lives in the present, using information from his past and expectations of the future to enhance his perception of the present, not to limit it. The past and the future extend his perspective; they don't interfere with it. They help him plan, to assess probabilities, and to alter his present actions and his commitments to the future in terms of how he sees those probabilities. They broaden his understanding of the relationship between events—his sense of continuity between what has been, what is, and what is yet to be. Above all, the past and the future help the time competent person, rather than hinder him.

Seeing and Hearing with Eyes and Ears of the Past

Many of us live much more in the past than we realize. Certain incidents make a very strong impression on us when we are young. Whenever similar events occur later in our lives, our old tapes replay so automatically, and so strongly, that we can become totally blinded to what is actually going on around us. In a very real sense we exist and are living in the present, but we are seeing and hearing with eyes and ears of the past.

Stage Fright

David, a rising young oil company executive, was attending an oil marketer's conference. He was seated at a large table with a dozen other company representatives, his mind wandering briefly over the events of the day. Suddenly the conference moderator, who had been reviewing the week's agenda, turned to him, saying, "So, Dave, what do you think about it?"

David sat up abruptly, his train of thought shattered, panic coursing through his every nerve. All eyes turned to him expectantly. "What do I think about *what?*" he thought, terrified. "The agenda? I don't care about the agenda. Why ask me?" But was it the agenda? How could he be sure, before answering? "What am I supposed to *say?*" he asked himself, panic-striken.

All eyes still bore in on him. David searched desperately for a response, but nothing came. He tried to calm himself, but his panic only worsened. As the seconds dragged on, he knew he would have to force himself to answer. Pulling himself together, he replied lamely that he really didn't have anything to say at that time. It was anticlimatic. The eyes turned away, but David knew they weren't satisfied. He knew he would have to make up for the fumbling sometime during the conference.

Fortunately, David's awkward moments are rare. He is really going places in his company. Yet he is still plagued by a very uncomfortable problem. Whenever he is startled or is asked something unexpectedly—particularly when others are watching—David becomes paralyzed with *stage fright*. His early life was governed by parental demands to perform well; and he did perform well, particularly when he knew he was being watched. His best strokes still come when others watch him perform. But the converse is also true. When all eyes are on him and he has nothing to say, he continues to feel the obsolete demand to perform and panics at the thought of not being able to.

Sitting at the conference table, he does not hear the moderator's genuine interest in what he might have to say. He does not see the attentive looks on the faces of those around him. He sees and hears only the *demand*. It is a demand which is not really there in the present—at least not there with anywhere near the intensity with which he feels it. The demand is a nonexistent demand, one that lives only in David's past.

When people respond to situations in ways inconsistent with the reality at hand or inconsistent with how others see that reality, they are very likely living in their past. They do not see or hear what is available to be seen and heard, and they prevent themselves from finding current solutions to current situations. David, had he not been in his past, might easily have explained to the moderator that his mind had wandered and that he simply had not heard the question. The moderator might then have repeated what he had said, and David might have replied in a manner more appropriate to the situation at hand. But at that moment at the conference table, with his Adult turned off, David was totally unable to process reality data. Seeing and hearing with eyes and ears of the past, he responded only with the old panic he used to feel at his inability to perform on command. He ended up mumbling and fumbling, unable to express himself, and having to make sure to recoup his losses later in the conference.

One way to identify when we are living in our past is to recognize those moments when we respond with great fear, terror, or anger to situations which do not really call for such responses. Actually, few day-to-day situations require extreme emotional responses of any sort. Our daily existence is rarely a life or death proposition (where such reactions might be warranted). The world goes on, and we usually go on with it. Few situations are hopelessly unsalvageable. Given freedom to operate, the Adult can almost always find acceptable solutions to current problems.

Parent-Child Transactions

Stanley, age thirty-five, had always floated through life. He took things as they came. As a youngster, he had been quiet and unassuming, never pushing very hard. In college he took courses everyone else seemed to be taking, and when he graduated, he went with one of the companies which happened to be recruiting people on campus one day. Life, in a sense, came to Stanley. He never had to chase it. Sometimes it was good to him, sometimes it wasn't. But he was always content to take it as it came.

Stanley was much like his father in that way, and that was something his mother had never quite forgiven him. He could still hear her nagging, "Stanley, if you don't get off that rear end of yours and make something of yourself, you'll end up just like your father!" But his father had enjoyed life. Although he had never advanced very far, he had enjoyed where he had been—something Stanley had always secretly admired.

One morning Stanley was called into his boss's office. It was time for another performance review. Stanley never much liked performance reviews, but he dragged himself in, looking appropriately concerned. Within minutes his boss launched into an extended discussion of Stanley's "deficiencies" frequently referring to a Performance Review Sheet on his desk. He ticked off various boxes on the sheet, mumbling phrases like "lacks initiative," "poor self-starter," and "needs direction."

As soon as his boss started speaking, Stanley's eyes glazed over. To Stanley this scene was fraught with memories—memories so strong they simply overpowered him, imposing themselves on the present. He could no longer see or hear what was actually happening. His boss droned on, dwelling on Stanley's "problems," but Stanley was once again back in his past, hearing his mother nagging at him. His boss's voice became his mother's, his boss's frown, his mother's. Stanley's past simply enveloped him, and he no longer saw or heard in the present. He heard his boss's comments only as old Parental criticisms, and as he did so, all the old, defensive, placating responses about "being sorry" and "trying harder" came trippingly to his tongue.

It does not take much to get us in our past. Often, all we

need is the inducement of a very familiar Parent-Child transaction. With a really qualified partner, one who fits an old, familiar role in our script, we can succeed in tuning out the present for hours at a time.

Very often, in playing old games and pastimes, we fail to see the person we are playing with as himself. We see him, rather, as someone from our past—typically as the person who first created the role he happens now to be playing. When we do this, we automatically repeat our former unproductive solutions to past problems. There is nothing new in an old, preprogrammed series of transactions. There is nothing different. All the moves are known, and the outcome is predetermined. What did not turn out well before will not turn out well now. By bringing the past into the present, we assure an ever-consistent (unproductive) outcome of events.

Each of us has a past different from that of the person next to us. We all have different key experiences in our lives which, when they recur, throw us back into our past. These experiences vary widely between individuals. What is important for one person may not be important for the next. The impact of a nagging mother, for instance, may not be the same even for two people with the same nagging mother. (One may have disregarded the nagging in his youth; the other may have been traumatized by it.) By living in the past, however, no matter what our reasons, we merely repeat in current situations the endless frustrations of our early life. We never change them.

Fear of Failure, and Guilt

John, a twenty-seven-year-old engineer, had been assigned a fairly difficult, somewhat complex, new project. He had no sooner received it than he felt himself vacillating, wondering whether or not he could handle it. Instead of starting on it, he was building up anxiety by starting to *worry* about it. As self-doubts from his past loomed up before him, John found himself responding in the present to old Parental expectations of his past—expectations that his every decision be the right one, expectations that he always be perfect. (His folks had never tolerated mistakes.) John had always been careful never to tackle a project he was not sure he could handle. Faced with one he had doubts about, fears from his past coursed through his body, wave after wave.

John's boss, on the other hand, had a different problem. He was a considerate, well-intentioned person. He had not wanted to make John uncomfortable. Having given John a project he might not be able to handle, and noticing John's discomfort, he immediately started feeling guilty. He knew, somehow, that he was responsible. Worst of all, he could not rid himself of the guilt feeling. It was making it impossible for him to concentrate on his own work. There he was also, living in his past by feeling bad in the present for something that had taken place hours earlier.

Both John and his boss, each in his own way, were now uncomfortable. They were both in their past, unable to process reality data, unable to recognize that as soon as John started work on his project, he could ask for more data to clear up anything he did not understand. If he needed more direct help, he could ask for that, too. There was nothing in the *present* to feel bad about. Both keeping themselves in their past, John and his boss managed to keep from handling their work effectively for hours on end.

Some of the most clear-cut examples of how we get into our past stem from our transactions with other people. Someone says something that hooks us, and we instantly replay an earlier, similar transaction from our past. We become startled and flip into our past so suddenly that almost anyone can tell that something is wrong. But people *can* get into their past without a crossed transaction, without a bit of help from anyone else. They do it all by themselves, frequently at times when no one else is even around. They do it through the use of *rackets*.

Rackets

Rackets are designed to keep us perpetually in our past. When someone is in his racket, he is engaged in recreating an old, familiar feeling, all by himself. He is not playing a game with anyone, and he does not need a partner. If it looks like he is playing a game (but there is no one around), he is, at best, playing it all by himself, recreating his old feelings and finding his old payoff, all in his own head.*

*Many T.A. experts speak of the racket as the *feeling* itself which a person recreates, whether he does so by himself, through fantasies, or with others, through games. Thus, by this definition, a racket can also be the payoff of a game. I find this sometimes confusing, and prefer to speak of the racket as the process through which a person recreates

Racket feelings, like game feelings, are generally artificial. They are not spontaneous, natural Child responses to real-life situations. They are manufactured feelings, feelings a person brings upon himself to maintain the sameness of his past, feelings which, when he experiences them, have little or nothing to do with the reality of life around him. Anger, in a racket, will persist long after the event which produced it. It will not be the sudden, natural reaction which someone feels when an unwanted external demand is placed upon him, an anger which later subsides. It will be a long, drawn-out expression of resentment that endures long after the occasion which produced it. It will sometimes appear to be spontaneous, but in such instances it is most likely to be merely *apparent* anger, usually related to an event which has itself been manufactured (as when someone picks a fight with someone else and becomes "incensed" when the other fellow fights back). Sorrow and despair, in a racket, will not be genuine responses to a real personal loss (such as the loss of a loved one), but will be similarly manufactured depressions, serving merely to maintain the integrity of an already depressive life script.

For Warren, still a junior accountant at thirty-eight, life is full of disappointments. These disappointments, however, are not a series of isolated external events, as one might think. They are rather a series of self-created internal feelings—feelings of disappointment, *racket* feelings, feelings so important to Warren that he rarely misses a day without recreating them. How he does this is extremely clever! Warren has a Parent which is so demanding, so unyielding in its requirements, that its expectations for Warren always exceed Warren's capacity to produce. No matter where he is, at the office or at home, Warren always bites off more than he can chew, fails (by design) to accomplish his objective, and ultimately manages to disappoint himself. (Warren learned this from his father, who had always expected more of him than was physically possible. When Warren could barely walk, his father had him on a bicycle. When Warren could barely throw, his father had already given him a regulation football. Warren could never live up to these expectations, and was always "causing" his father extreme disappointment.) Now

---

feelings by himself, as distinguished from the process through which he recreates them with others—games. In this context, a racket can be seen as a game someone plays by himself, using only the Parent and Child in his own head.

Warren never starts anything without expecting too much of himself, and naturally, he ends up disappointed. Even when he looks in the mirror each morning, he sees only an image of how he would *like* to look, and he manages to disappoint himself by not living up to that image. Warren perpetuates his disappointment racket by attaching unrealistic expectations to everything he does, indeed, to virtually everything about himself. By expecting the impossible, Warren always guarantees the inevitable—disappointment.

Warren does not always stop here. He frequently gets others to help him create his disappointments. He asks more of them than they are willing to give and makes demands on them which they are not willing to accept. When they do not come through, he typically overreacts by appearing totally crushed, as if to say, "How could you do this terrible thing to me?"

Warren uses this disappointment racket to manipulate people. Many of us have Parent tapes which, like Warren's, forbid us from disappointing those who are close to us. When Warren wants to demonstrate how terribly disappointed he would be if someone were to let him down, he gets such a sorrowful look on his face, and acts so utterly chagrined, that the other person is very hard pressed not to accommodate him. If that person's tapes on not disappointing people are strong enough, he will submit to Warren's manipulations time and time again. In fact, Warren has used this technique to twice avoid being transferred and to get at least three minimum raises he did not deserve. Eventually, of course, people *do* disappoint Warren, making his ultimate disappointment that much more intense. In the long run, Warren's Child always wins.

Like most rackets, Warren's manufactured feelings of disappointment mask other, more basic, natural Child feelings. With Warren, this more basic feeling often surfaces when he is disappointed by someone who really does not threaten him. His disappointment then becomes a prelude to NIGYSOB. Warren sets the other person up with phrases like "Don't disappoint me!", gives him appropriate looks and gestures, and when the person finally comes through with the disappointment, Warren zaps the hell out of him. Disappointment turns to anger, and as the anger surfaces, people get an accurate picture of the real, hidden feeling behind the disappointment. Warren is clearly angry, not disappointed. Although openly he only beats on others, he secretly beats on himself by keeping himself perpetually disappointed. People close to him can almost taste Warren's pent-up frustration; they can almost feel the latent anger he harbors toward his own disappointment script.

Racket feelings almost always act as substitutes for spontaneous, natural Child feelings. This substitution first occurs in a person's youth, in situations where the natural feeling he experiences is never identified, acknowledged, or permitted by his parents. Only a substitute feeling is permitted, and the substitute feeling soon becomes the person's racket. In Warren's case, Warren was never allowed to feel angry, nor was he permitted to express the very real resentment he felt toward a father who always placed strong, unrealistic expectations on him. He was only permitted disappointment.

A young person can develop real confusion about what he feels, confusion about what is real and what is not. The youngster who suddenly has a new baby sister, who is getting all the attention and most of the strokes he himself used to get, can feel extremely hostile towards her. When he expresses his resentment and is told, "You don't *hate* your sister, you *love* her," he is not being permitted to even *identify* what he feels. When a youngster whose mother beats on him is constantly told, "You must never be *angry* at mother, you must *respect* her," that youngster may have real trouble in later life differentiating between anger and respect. The young person who hates his little sister may develop an artificial "sweetness" racket to disguise his hidden resentment, a racket which may ultimately give him great difficulty in expressing real affection. The youngster who must respect an overbearing mother may develop an artificial "respect" racket, one in which he always seems to respect people he really dislikes.

Identifying a racket can sometimes be quite difficult. It is often hard to suspect someone of not really feeling what he seems to feel. The greater danger, however, is that once we accept a person's racket, we open ourselves to his manipulations. We let him blackmail us. We avoid doing things so as not to disappoint him, we let his depression ruin our own happiness, and we believe he respects us, when what he really feels towards us may run much closer to a carefully concealed resentment—one he himself may not be aware of.

Living in the Future

Gus, operations manager for a small automotive parts plant, started for work one sunny spring morning, hardly noticing what a lovely day it was. The air was fresh, the grass had just turned green, but Gus paid absolutely no attention to his surroundings. His mind was on other things. The rains of the previous week had caused a large leak in his cellar. Gus knew that if it got much worse he would have to call someone in to fix it. "I wonder how much that would cost?" he asked himself as he turned out of his driveway. "Probably a lot. Maybe even a few hundred dollars." Gus felt bad about that. He would have to hold off buying the new set of golf clubs he wanted.

As he drove down the parkway, Gus noticed an empty car parked by the roadside, its left rear tire flat. "That reminds me," he thought, "I need a new set of tires. The last ones only held out for 15,000 miles. I've almost gone that far on this set!" Gus drove the thought from his mind. "I'll just not look at them for a while, and pray for the best. With luck, they'll last through the summer."

The summer! It would be a rough one, with the kids home from camp. His wife would probably start using her charge cards again. Gus scolded himself. "This is just useless daydreaming," he muttered under his breath. "I better think about something more constructive. I've got an important meeting today. I'm nowhere near prepared. Gosh! he thought suddenly. "I bet I'll have to give a report! Nobody's said anything, but that's just like them—waiting till the last minute. But what will I talk about?" Gus shuddered at the thought. Meetings were not his cup of tea.

The subject was too intense to dwell on. Gus's mind continued to wander. He thought of his secretary. He wondered if she had finished typing that long memo he had given her several days earlier. "I told her it's important," he mused, "but I'll bet she still hasn't finished it." His secretary caused Gus a problem. Somehow, he always had trouble getting through to her. Also, he did not want to push her too hard, for fear she would quit her job. But he needed the memo! "If I don't have that memo ready," Gus mumbled to himself, "the boss will probably have my head. He's been acting strange lately, anyway. That's all I need, to get fired now!" The anxiety created by this prospect caused Gus to swerve from the road. He quickly turned his attention back to his driving.

As one can easily see, Gus is a worrier. When his mind is free to wander, he gets into the future, fantasizing about all the catastrophic things which might happen to him. He does not see how lovely a day it is, nor does he feel the fresh, spring air around him. He lives only in a time which is yet to come. He lives there in a catastrophic way, feeling bad about everything which he thinks might happen and bringing that bad feeling with him into the present.*

Gus does not live in the future only when he is daydreaming. Even when he talks to his secretary, he is dominated by the fear that if he pushes her too far, she will quit. He does not know how to stroke her. He does not realize how important a few good, honest strokes can be. The thought that his secretary might work harder, just for strokes, does not enter his mind. Gus believes the only way to increase her output is to push her, a tactic which he carefully avoids for fear she will leave him. Living in fear in the future, he prevents himself from seeing simple solutions to his problems in the present.

Since Gus deals with his secretary only on a you-take-the-orders-and-I'll-give-them basis, operating solely from his Parent, his catastrophic fantasy about what might happen is not far wrong. His secretary actually has little regard for their relationship, and even less interest in the only part of his personality she ever sees—his Parent. Thus, by keeping their relationship on a Parent-Child basis, Gus manages to maintain some validity to his catastrophic expectation. By remaining in his Parent, he reinforces his need to live in the future.

Gus's dealings with his boss operate the same way. He gets into the future, worrying about "What will happen if. . . ." His fantasy here is that he will be fired (and the world will collapse), if he does not do everything his boss says to do. Whenever he talks with his boss, his fears force him to re-

*Everyone who lives in the future does not necessarily worry and feel bad. "Rainbow chasers," people who dream of good things to come, may live in the future every bit as much as worriers. Their future fantasies may be every bit as unproductive. (They may just be more pleasant.)

main in his compliant Child, accommodating his boss's every wish. When he is not talking with his boss, his own Parent takes over. It is so demanding, it generates enough pressure for five bosses. His Child is still fearful! Actually, Gus's real pressure comes from the Parent in his own head, not from his boss. By operating from his Parent, he continues to reinforce his need to live in the future, this time by worrying about what might happen if he fails to live up to his own expectations of himself. (This situation is far from unusual. When Gus was young, he used to fear his mother and father. Now that he has grown up, his own Parent is much the same as he once experienced his mother and father to be. Only now he fears himself.)

Living in the future rarely causes problems when it is just idle daydreaming. At such times it can be a harmless form of withdrawal. It does cause difficulties, however, when it interferes with our ability to plug in our Adult and process data in the present. Sometimes people carry around so many catastrophic expectations of what *may* happen that they live in a state of almost constant fear. Never able to get into the present and do something about their problems, they stay in the future, feeling the terror associated with the worst possible outcome of events, feeling it so strongly that it totally immobilizes them, keeping them from any productive problem-solving activity in the present. (Consider the student who is so scared of flunking his next exam that he cannot concentrate on studying; or the salesman who is so excited at the thought of his first big sale that he cannot prepare himself properly—so that he muffs it.)

Many people never let their understanding of what *might* happen contribute positively to what they do about it in the present. Instead, they worry. They keep themselves uptight. When they do try to prepare for the future, they do not succeed. They do not know how to go about it. They try to control the outcome of events. Rather than assimilate the data they need, planning to respond spontaneously to the future when it arrives, they rehearse, hoping the future will fit some predetermined plan they devise for it, and that when it becomes the present, it will suddenly become predictable.

Ruled by their fears and expectations, such people are not tuned in to where other people are. They do not know what to respond to, let alone how to respond. They do not trust themselves. Unaccustomed to living in the present, they try to program their lives. They turn automatically to their Parent to determine what *should* occur. Then they plan around it. They plan their words, their moves, their every gesture. Sometimes they perform well, if nothing interferes with their program; but they usually fumble miserably when required to respond spontaneously to the unexpected. The unexpected throws them. The spontaneity of life throws them. They memorize and they play-act well, but life in the present is usually a replay of what they have previously prepared, and they are somewhat less alive for it.

Living in the Present

When a person can say, "Here I am in the present, playing old tapes from my past," he is no longer in his past, but in the present, aware that he has just come from his past. When he can say, "Here I am in the present, projecting myself into the future," he is no longer in the future, but in the present, aware that he has just come from the future. The very process of identification is one which is carried out in the present by the Adult.

The person who lives in the present is time competent. His Adult is always plugged in. His Child may still react spontaneously to events, but he is always aware of what is happening, and he is always able to alter his responses instantaneously, if need be. The person who lives in the present is relaxed, yet alert. He is aware of his surroundings and comfortable within them. If he is *not* comfortable, if his surroundings are producing stress, he is aware of his discomfort. He does not need to deny it, nor does he need to distort himself by making believe he is comfortable. It is a *real* discomfort, not something from his past which he carries around in his head.

The person who lives in the present is aware of what he feels from moment to moment. His computer is plugged in to his senses. He uses his senses (as we all must do to live), but he uses them with awareness. He does not eat without tasting, or play without enjoying; nor does he exist in the same room with other people without sensing where they are. When he sees, it is with true perspective. When he listens to someone, he gives that person his full attention, intuitively providing him with one of the best of all possible strokes. He strokes people automatically. Every look, every gesture, every expression on his face, tells people that he is aware of their existence and that he accepts them. He validates people. He does not ignore them. He does not tune them out. If he happens to be in his head, it is because his computer is on and he is processing data, solving problems, or dealing with abstractions. He is not stuck in his past or in his future; nor is he playing archaic Parent or Child tapes. If he is in his head, he can return to the present, relaxed and alert, instantaneously.

The Value of Identifying Where You Are

The person who really knows where he is has the jump on almost everyone else around him. When he is clear, most of those around him will still be uncertain, confused, flipping in and out of the past and future, and vacillating back and forth between their Parent and Child. They will often be unclear, even if they appear not to be; confused, even when they seem to have strong, forceful opinions on matters. No one is more uncertain than a Child who is not sure what he feels; no one more misguided than a confident, know-it-all Parent who has managed to miss most of the facts.

The person who is clear on where he is can often use this insight to make others more clear on where *they* are. People intuitively lean toward the person who can help them through their confusions (even if they are not consciously aware that they are confused).

Dick, vice president of a large electronics company, and a member of his city's Chamber of Commerce, was attending an evening meeting called by the Chamber of Commerce to complete plans for redeveloping the city's central business district. As the meeting wore on, it became more and more clear that little was going to be accomplished. Rival factions were engaging in petty arguing. Tempers were flaring. Absolutely no progress was being made, and everyone was becoming extremely restless. Finally, Dick could contain himself no longer. He rose to speak. "Gentlemen," he said. "I arrived here this evening expecting to accomplish certain things, but I have only become more and more disappointed."

He paused a moment. Then he continued, "So far, we have done nothing but bicker and fight, and I have somehow found myself caught up in it all, hesitating to commit myself and avoiding the real issue that brought me here." (A statement, in effect, that he knew he'd been hooked by whatever game they'd been playing.) "Now, it is getting very late, and although we can continue the way we've been going, I, for one, would prefer to stop arguing and get down to business."

Immediately, four other members who had been silent spoke out. "Yes," they exclaimed. "Let's stop the foolishness!" "Let's get down to brass tacks." "Let's get to work!" "We're with Dick!" Others soon joined in, and in less than a minute Dick had galvanized the entire committee into action.

Later, when several other members thought back about how Dick had stopped the chaos and drawn everyone together, they were unable to pinpoint any specific strategy he had used. He had not expressed his convictions on any of the issues or called upon others to follow his lead. He had not offered any new compromises or proposed any new initiatives. He had focused only on how he himself felt. He had dealt only with his own expectations and reactions, while acknowledging the very real probability that the meeting might well continue on its existing aimless course. That could hardly be called a sophisticated strategy, yet, almost as if by magic, it had somehow been able to mobilize the committee in a way no one else had dreamed possible.

People can often be brought together by someone able to clarify their own unexpressed feelings for them. But even if their feelings as a whole are so mixed, or so varied, that they simply cannot be united, the person who has identified where he himself is will still be way ahead. He will be able to extricate himself smoothly from the game without having to play Uproar and without having to bend to any other irrational whims of his Parent or Child. He will always be in charge of himself—a position of clarity intuitively sensed by those around him, most of whom deny it to themselves by remaining uncertain as to where they are in the first place.

Staying in the Present

Although you can bring yourself into the present by identifying where you are (once you are aware you are in your past, you are no longer in your past but in the present, aware you have just come from your past), this will often not be enough to *keep* you in the present. It is too easy to slip back. Sometimes it is almost impossible not to. In order to stay in the present, therefore, you must get in touch with your surroundings; you must plug your Adult into your senses and experience life in the present, from moment to moment. Use your senses with awareness. Your senses, ultimately, are your only anchor to reality. Get in touch with what you feel. *Know* what you feel. *Feel* what you feel.

Projecting Onto Others—A Way to Avoid What We Feel

Identifying what we feel is not always as easy as it sounds. We have many habits and many ways of expressing ourselves which often defeat our efforts. Tom and Frank, two middle-aged executives who frequently played golf together, were chatting about Curt, another crony, who often livened up their weekly outings on the golf links.

TOM: I feel sorry for Curt. He's been working so hard lately, and his wife's been after him so much, it looks like he won't be around much this summer.

FRANK: Yeah. I really feel sad. I miss having Curt around. Things sure are quiet without him.

Both Tom and Frank liked to have Curt with them. Whenever he was with them, Curt brightened things up. There was never a dull moment. When he wasn't with them, both Tom and Frank felt a sense of loss. But while Frank could identify what he felt (sad) and recognize that he missed having Curt around, Tom had real trouble getting in touch with his feelings. He could only say that he felt "sorry for Curt." But "sorry for someone" is not a feeling. Sadness, anger, frustration, and the like are feelings. Being "sorry for someone" is a nothing—a projection onto someone else; a projection onto someone outside ourselves; a projection which hints at what we might feel, but which skirts the issue and often adds to our confusion.

"I feel sorry for *you*," "I feel glad for *him*," and, "I am worried for *her*," are all confused ways of saying, "I am sad," "I am happy," and "I am worried." They are substitutes for clear, positive identification. They are left-over Parent phrases, passed down from earlier generations when our forefathers still burned witches, when they needed to deny responsibility for those endless, irrational waves of anger, insecurity, and guilt which always came over them. Such projections are merely old ways of sidestepping the unknown, gimmicks to avoid acknowledging what we feel. Given enough gimmicks, a person could avoid getting in touch with himself forever.

How Our Parent Can Keep Us from Feeling

Terry, a rookie business machine salesman, had been told to spend several days in the field with his supervisor, so that he might learn his new job a little faster. While sitting in a customer's office, his supervisor remarked to Terry that he looked depressed.

"I feel stupid," Terry replied. "Whenever I open my mouth I say the wrong thing. I don't have anything worthwhile to contribute, and I just feel foolish tagging along like this."

Lydia, a middle-aged librarian, came to work one day wearing a new dress a friend had given her. The dress was stylish, attractive. It made Lydia look nice, but it was definitely not the kind of dress she had been used to wearing. When a fellow worker announced how much he liked it, Lydia remarked, "Oh, but I feel so *silly* in this. It makes me look so funny!"

Terry says that he feels "stupid" and "foolish." Lydia says she feels "silly." Yet stupid, foolish, and silly are not *feelings!* They are judgmental words which come from a person's Parent. They are not expressions of what a person feels; they are expressions of what he *thinks*, or more accurately, of what his parents used to think of him in such situations. Such words suggest that the person using them, at least in certain situations, may simply not permit himself to feel (and may not have been permitted to feel as a youngster). Instead of feeling, he operates from his Parent and continues to remain out of touch with himself.

This happens more often than we ever realize. Pretty girls will look at themselves and say they feel "ugly." Competent businessmen will fumble briefly and say they feel "dumb." While even a casual observer could recognize that at such times these people are evidencing feelings of disappointment, frustration, or possibly depression, the people themselves are often simply not aware of it! They are totally turned off, tuned out, completely unaware of what they feel.

Checklist for Staying in the Present

Living in the present for any extended period of time—for any person—can be an enormously difficult task. Although we all live in the present part of the time each day as part of our normal living pattern, the *extent* to which we do so varies greatly from person to person and from day to day. Many forces tend to pull us from the present. The number of minutes and hours we actually stay in the present each day and the degree of alertness and responsiveness we bring to these minutes and hours are so varied, and so easily disguised, it is something each of us can ultimately know only for himself.

Someone interested in increasing the real time he spends in the present may do so by stopping himself periodically during the day and following these three simple steps.

1. *Get in touch with what you feel.* Turn your attention to what is going on inside yourself. Identify what you feel, both emotionally and physically. When we keep ourselves out of the present, we don't know what we feel. You can reverse this process by focusing on what is going on inside yourself. Which muscles are tense? Is your stomach tight? Are your eyes strained? How about your neck and shoulders? Are you tired? Alert? Are you angry, depressed, or sad?

2. *Get in touch with your surroundings.* Become aware of what is happening around you. What is your environment like? What is the temperature? The humidity? The lighting? Is your environment comfortable? Is it pleasant to be in? If it is, are you responding to it naturally, by being relaxed, or are you doing something in your head to stay out of touch with your surroundings, and are you keeping yourself out of the present?

3. *Check to see that you are not substituting projections and descriptions of feelings for real feelings.* Don't talk yourself out of getting in touch with yourself. Permit yourself to identify what you feel. Only when you first know what you feel can you then take over for yourself and feel something different.

7. Contracting for Change

Learning to See Yourself

Darrell, a middle-aged utility executive, had been exposed to Transactional Analysis but was having trouble relating it to his own life. One morning, while chatting with his friend John, Darrell expressed a very common frustration. "John," he said, "I'd *like* to use T.A. to gain some autonomy over my life, and maybe change part of my script, but I just don't know *what* to change!"

John hesitated a moment, then asked quietly, "How do you spend most of your day, Darrell?"

Darrell stopped, and knit his brow. He hadn't thought about how he spent his day. But the more he considered the question, the more he knew the answer. After a moment of silence, he responded, slowly. "Well, to be frank, I mainly spend my day shuffling papers."

John looked at him thoughtfully. "Is that satisfactory to you?" he asked.

Darrell seemed to have reached a decision. "Not really," he replied. "I seem to spend more time looking busy than *being* busy."

"Sounds like that's something you'd like to work on," John remarked, ending the conversation.

In less than thirty seconds, Darrell had found something about himself worth looking into, without any effort whatsoever. He had merely focused, with John's help, on how he spent his day.

Often, unless we have some special relationship that is not going well, or some specific, bad transaction that causes trouble, finding something about ourselves which we want to look into can be fairly difficult. The awkward, troublesome moments usually provide our best clues to things worth changing. Without them, we frequently don't even know where to start. Yet many people who don't have moments of extreme anger, or severe depression, or who don't get into really destructive games, still lead lives programmed to turn out in ways that they don't intend. It can be helpful for them to learn to examine their behavior in ways which provide insight into what they do and clarify where they are going.

What Do You Get Out of What You Are Doing?

Perhaps the most useful way to examine what you do is simply observe *how you spend your day*. Look at yourself as if you were a disinterested observer. Notice how you use your time, and how you expend your energy—your two most valuable personal resources. From moment to moment, ask yourself how you gain from your decisions to use these resources. *What do you get out of what you are doing?* We typically structure much of our day in ways learned in childhood. This behavior was once geared to gain strokes and to make us comfortable. It may still have the same purpose, or it may now be geared merely to structure time in ways which gained us strokes and made us comfortable *in the past*. If at any time there is no immediate, or future gain from what you are doing—especially if it is something you do more or less repetitively, the odds are you once did get something out of it, but the reasons for doing it no longer exist. It has become an unproductive habit.

In using this technique—in looking at yourself this way, be sure to put away your critical, judgmental Parent and your fearful, guilty Child. They will serve only to confuse you, and will short-circuit your Adult quest for data. The person who finds himself shuffling papers, for instance, unless he temporarily deactivates his Parent and Child, might well become wrapped up in the guilt or the fear involved in not doing his job "right." He might punish himself for being lazy, and never get to deal with the fact that as a child he was stroked for being active, for *looking* busy, and was never stroked for actually accomplishing things.

The number and variety of habits from childhood which can interfere with a productive later life are almost endless. People receive strokes in their youth for *appearing* busy, rather than for *being* busy (that way they stay out of mother's hair and she doesn't have to keep after them); for *working* on projects, rather than *finishing* them (they still stay out of mother's hair, but are stroked for being "hard workers"); for *creating* inefficiencies, rather than *eliminating* them (this way there's always something for everyone in the family to be busy at—especially important in a family where the real strokes are for staying busy); for creating ideas, rather than implementing them (that is, for *dreaming*, rather than *doing*; a pattern prevalent in families where there's a high premium on ingenuity and brilliance); or, for *implementing* ideas, rather than *creating* them (found in families where the premium is on practicality).

Sometimes our current behavior patterns are leftover reactions to our earlier environment—reactions we carry with us to an environment which no longer exists. Alvin, an aspiring young real estate broker, found that he spent most of his day *avoiding* work, rather than seeking it. He also remembered quite vividly that as a youngster back on the farm, he had always been given more work than he felt he could handle, and had spent most of his early life trying to get out from under it. He had unfortunately carried this avoidance pattern with him into the real estate business where it was doing him considerable harm.

Many of our unproductive habits—what we do as well as what we say—involve behavior we were once stroked for but which we have no longer reason to continue. Such habits are comfortable only in the sense that they are familiar. Anyone willing to examine what he does, and willing to both do and feel something different, will find many new options available to him. In order to do so, however, he must free himself from his need to maintain the status quo—to always repeat the same feeling in the same situation, to keep the present consistent with his past. He must be willing to accept the temporary uncomfortableness of feeling something different in familiar situations, and his desire to rule his own life must be greater, and of more consistent strength, than the combined force of all his fears.

"I Hear Myself Saying . . . ."

One of the most important moments in a person's life can come when his Adult *sees what he is doing when he is doing it*, and is able to say, in effect, "This is my Child." This is the very first step to continuous personal autonomy.

Bill, regional manager for a national business machine

company, was speaking to a group of his district managers about their poor showing of the previous few months. As he warmed to his subject, his voice grew louder, and his face redder. He was visibly distressed. "And furthermore," he said, "I'm getting damned *tired* of all this nonsense. . . ."

Then he hesitated, as if he were suddenly aware he was in his Parent. He hesitated only for an instant, picking up where he'd left off, almost in midsentence. "And I feel myself getting angry, and *I hear myself saying* that this is 'nonsense,' and that I'm tired of it. . . ." He paused again, grasping the full import of where he was, and taking a deep breath. "But I'm sure we're *all* tired of it, and it's really more important for us to sit down and see what we can do about it, than for me to yell and scream about how tired I am."

At that, his district managers, each of whom, to the very last man, had previously been buried in his Child, perked up their ears, sat forward in their chairs, and prepared to process data on an Adult level.

The key to altering unproductive Child and Parent behavior is, essentially, to recognize it when it is happening, not after. One of the best methods of acknowledging that you know what your Child or Parent is doing, even in the midst of a conversation with someone else, is simply to say "I hear myself saying. . . ." (whatever is being said). Statements like these will often completely alter the direction of a conversation, reorienting it to a clearly Adult level. They are clear-cut evidence to those around you that your Adult has begun to speak.

To do this effectively you must learn to listen to yourself. It is important to hear what you are saying *when you say it.* It is also important to become aware of your internal (feeling) responses to situations as you respond; to know what you are feeling *when you feel it.* (Your feelings typically trigger your words.) While it is not always necessary to say what you feel, it does let people know you are unhooking yourself from your automatic Parent and Child responses, and provides them with incentive to do the same. The person who lashes out at people or who begs for sympathy operates from his Parent or Child. The person who identifies where he is and says, "I feel angry" or "I feel depressed" or "I hear myself saying things that are unproductive," operates from his Adult.*

*Be sure not to say such things, looking for a transactional response. Example: You say, "I feel angry," expecting the other person to say,

How to Obtain Feedback

Rarely do we see ourselves as others see us. Even when we learn to listen to ourselves carefully, and when we learn to examine what we do with real perspective, we can still benefit from checking out where we are with others around us. There are several ways to do this. The easiest way, is merely to watch how those around you react to what you do. Spontaneous reactions provide the most reliable data, but are sometimes hard to interpret unless the other person's attitudes and prejudices, if any, are known. Frequently what he sees will be filtered through the eyes of his Parent or Child before being returned to you, and it may be difficult to interpret the distortion. ("That was dumb!" or "That was funny!") Spontaneous reactions, when they do occur, provide relatively unguarded, honest feedback, and are usually worth noting for that reason alone. Many people disguise their reactions either for their own protection or to avoid "hurting" you, and will simply not be able to provide you with any useful data at all.

An even more accurate way to obtain feedback, and one infinitely more satisfying, if it can be done, is through an Adult "feedback" contract with the Adult of another person (spouse, friend, associate); a contract under which that person provides nonjudgmental, uncritical, and undistorted information about how he sees you—what he sees, and what he hears, without placing any special demands on you in return. When asked for data, he will respond only in terms of what he perceives. He will look for the secret purposes, if any, of your transactions—some purpose which your Child may know about but which may be beyond your Adult awareness. He will look for your hidden payoffs, for what you seem to gain from what you are doing. He will notice what you feel, and how you seem to sustain the feeling. He will look for how you get strokes. He will observe if you are in your Parent—blaming, judging, and controlling; or if you are in your Child—placating, making excuses, or being controlled. He will note anything relevant about what you are doing which you seem unaware of; and he will let you know what he sees.

"I'm sorry," or "Okay, I'll stay out of your way." The purpose of this is only to get your Adult to speak; not to rehook your Parent if others do not live up to your expectations.

Such a contract can only be undertaken with someone willing to participate on a "no strings attached" basis. He must be willing to let you do whatever you want with the information. He must also be willing to let you do nothing at all with it. He must recognize that your life is your life, not his; and that his contract is to help you see you, not to lay any special demands of his own on you. He must have no vested interest in manipulating you to meet his own personal needs, and no secret need to dilute or distort the content of the information he provides.

Implicit in such a contract is the understanding that at no time need you necessarily accept the information he provides you. Indeed, it may not always be accurate. He may be missing something; he may not be able to stay in his Adult long enough to express what he sees; or his words, being his words and not yours, may be misleading. If he raises his voice, starts telling you what you "should" do, or acts resentful, you will know he has left his Adult. If you start feeling any sort of pressure from him, it will signal that he has at least temporarily violated the contract.

The most realistic part of your contract will be the recognition that his data, when it is available, is really only for you to check out and verify for yourself. Although it may often be more accurate than data you could obtain by yourself, it is not the last word. Final authority on what to accept, as well as on what to do with the information you do accept, rests with you.

Seeing Yourself in the System You're In

Every group of two or more people—a family, a social club, a department in a company or other organization, or a board of directors, can be seen as a system of people. No matter what its size, each system has its own unique character—a special quality all its own which distinguishes it from every other system. Within each system, people have their own special ways of interacting, ways in which they either contribute or detract from what goes on within the system. Take away just one person, and the system itself changes.

Of all the factors influencing what happens in a given system of people, the most significant will be *the undercurrent of feelings which exists within the system at any given time.*

Systems of Feelings

Whenever two or more people get together, each brings with him a dominant life position as well as a more temporary set of feelings associated with the immediate circumstances at hand—his state of alertness, his tiredness, the stress he is under, and his attitude toward the other person, or persons. Under these circumstances, a *system of feeling* is created—a system generated by the combination and interaction of the feelings of the people involved. (The people will either be comfortable with each other, or they will not.)

This system of feelings sets the tone for all the transactions which occur. It often determines the *outcome* of the transactions. (Whether things go well or don't go well will often be determined at the feeling level.) It is a tangible, *feel*able reality. Walk into a room full of depressed people, and *you* feel depressed. Walk into a room where everyone is exuberant, and *you* feel exuberant. Similar feelings tend to reinforce each other. (Two happy people often create more joy than either could by himself.) Opposing feelings tend to detract from each other. (You feel good, I feel bad, and the system ends up somewhere in between.)

It is useful to recognize how each person within a system contributes to the total feeling of the system—who gives off the OK vibrations, and who gives off the not OK vibrations. Who produces stress; who relieves it. OK feelings and not OK feelings are incompatible. When both are found in the same system, each will be vying for supremacy. Both types of feelings are extremely responsive to pressure, and while the not OK person may find solace and end up feeling better as a result of their interaction, the OK person, to his dismay, may end up feeling worse.

We often find ourselves being hooked into not OK systems without knowing what is happening. Feelings are, in a sense, contagious. When we enter a system where the balance of feelings is not OK, where the people engage in unproductive pastimes such as Ain't It Awful and Poor Little Me or play destructive games like NIGYSOB and Let's You and Him Fight, we will usually be under enormous pressure to join in the games and feel bad with everyone else. Unless we carry a good deal of perspective with us, we can easily be forced into a not OKness of our own. If we protect ourselves and maintain our own OKness by not joining in the games, we run the risk of being kicked out of the system. Most not OK systems simply will not tolerate a healthy person for very long.

Systems Under Stress

Some systems are more stressful than others. Some families are less fun to be in, some companies less comfortable to work for. Stress within a system may have any number of causes, but it can usually be traced to someone within the system who feels bad about himself, bad about others in the system (often from his Parent), or who feels just plain bad, in general (depressed, unhappy, unwanted, from his Child). Stress is placed on the system if that person insists that others acknowledge and respond to his own bad feeling. If he is in his Parent, dissatisfied with something (life, events, the work output, the smile on a subordinate's face), he will want others to accede to his demands, live up to his expectations, and feel the internal pressures that he feels (put the same pressures on themselves). His dissatisfaction, coming from his Parent, is often a reflection of how his own parents were dissatisfied with him. If he is in his Child, fearful or hurting, he will be insisting that others absorb his bad feelings, nuture his hurt (which may often be a racket), or in some way help relieve the burden he carries around with him. He essentially wants others to feel bad with him.

The stress in a system does not occur when the person attempting to create it cannot elicit a response from others. It occurs when others in the system cannot respond comfortably.

The president of a large manufacturing company, a true financial genius, had been appointed when his company was in deep financial trouble. He had rescued the company from disaster, but when he stayed on as president, he created more stress in the system than the system could comfortably tolerate. He could handle money well, but he couldn't handle people. Although he knew this, he was unwilling to give up his high salary and important title once the crisis was over. He decided to hang on, regardless. He soon felt threatened by everyone close to him. He fired people for irrational reasons: they weren't "right" for the job; they were "weaklings"; they needed to be taught a lesson; they needed to be used as examples; they were disloyal (which meant they talked back to him). He treated his executives like children, often calling them into his office without warning, firing questions at them without explanation, then dismissing them without comment. He overruled them without telling them. (They would find out later, often when their own subordinates would disregard regular instructions and be seen reporting directly to the president.)

He made assignments according to people's weaknesses, not their strengths. His sales vice president, whose strength was in recruiting and training people in the field, was told to stay in the office and be more "available" to the president. His administrative vice president, whose strength was in home office administration and who didn't handle sales people too well, was told to spend more time in the field "helping" with field office administration.

He played his executives against one another. He would invite three or four of them in his office at the same time, chew out one of them unmercifully, and force those remaining to join in the game of NIGYSOB or be labeled disloyal. His behavior engendered an ever deepening, irreconcilable mistrust among his subordinates.

The difficulty in keeping the system intact—in keeping the people working together as a team—was that there was virtually no way in which those in the system could respond comfortably to the president's demands. If they disagreed with him, they risked being fired. If they agreed, they risked being sucked into his web of mistrust and intrigue, often sacrificing their own sense of human worth and dignity. The choice between personal survival and the loss of personal integrity was not a comfortable one. Those who chose to remain in the system and survive, economically, found themselves stuck in a situation in which they could no longer survive emotionally.

Since we all operate within systems of people, both at home and at work, it can be helpful to recognize how we affect the systems we're in, as well as how we're affected by them. Very often, people will distort themselves, absorbing great pressure or abandoning life-long moral principles just to accommodate a system, just to remain in it or keep it intact. This holds true for family systems, as well as business systems. Time and again, men and women with children of their own unwillingly submit to the irrational demands of their parents, all for "the good of the family." Against their better judgment, they put up with all sorts of emotional blackmail just to avoid hurting someone in the family system, just to keep the system intact.

Time and again, mature businessmen force themselves to stay in systems detrimental to their personal health—organizations dominated by the irrational Parent or fearful Child that exists in the head of one or two bosses who keep the system in chaos. Often, people trap themselves into staying in unhealthy systems out of fear (afraid to leave a job for fear they won't find another), inadequate planning (by keeping up with the Jones's, they can't afford to quit, or spend time looking for another job), or useless Parent data (quitting is for cowards, job "loyalty" supersedes personal goals, no one likes a failure). Whatever their reason, when the personal distortion required of such people is too great, the system itself may remain intact (the people may remain in it), but it will become an uncomfortable system. Unless they can somehow manage to change the system or unless they're protected from it, such people will usually have to choose between leaving the system or feeling bad within it.

How to Make the System OK

We can either add or detract from a system by increasing or relieving the pressure we place on others within it. While we may not always contribute positively, we can almost always avoid a negative contribution to a system by learning how we put pressure on others, and by making a positive effort not to do it.

Identify the Demands You Place on Others

Don, a tax attorney in his late forties, had unusually high standards of achievement. He prided himself on giving his clients work of the highest quality. One morning, after a client had just informed him that he, Don, had somehow neglected to sign the last letter mailed to that client's office, Don turned to his secretary and asked, his face turning purple and his eyes bulging, "Why in the world did you let that letter go out unsigned!"

Like many other of Don's seemingly innocent sounding

questions, this one masked a very strong, implicit demand. It was an irrational demand, one that denied the fact that his secretary, like everyone else, was a mere human being. It was a demand which carried the implied message, "BE PERFECT!"

Doris, a capable young secretary of twenty-seven, had a boss who frequently left the office without saying where he was going. This caused Doris no end of frustration as she never knew what to say when people called and asked where he was. (She felt that a competent secretary should always be able to say where her boss had gone and when he'd be back.) One day, after her boss left for a minute to go to the men's room, Doris had felt particularly inept at explaining his absence to a caller. Later, when he returned to his office, she blurted out in exasperation, "Why don't you ever tell me where you are going!"

Humorous as this might seem, her boss was actually dumbfounded at the demand he heard behind the question. Not recognizing where Doris was, he could hear only the very strong, compelling demand behind her question; a demand which translated, "LET ME KNOW WHERE YOU ARE *EVERY MINUTE!*"

Often, when we are in our stern, critical Parent or our fearful, not OK Child, we will inadvertently place unwanted, irrational demands on others around us. These demands may be expressed in many ways. Some may seem trivial, or insignificant. Some may seem very subtle. But no matter how trivial, how subtle their expression, they almost always cause tension within the system. They affect the other person (or persons), causing him either to absorb the demand (and possibly feel worse) or to reflect it back upon its source (creating even more dissension). Rarely can a person remain within a system without eventually responding in some way to the demands generated by others in the system.

Behind each demand can usually be found some basic, unexamined not OKness—some need to control, some catastrophic expectation. This not OKness will typically reinforce the position *I'm* OK—You're not OK (so I can make demands on you), or I'm *not* OK—You're OK (so I need to make demands on you to validate my own not OKness). It will exert great pressure on the OKness of the remaining participants in the system.

A system operates best when each member feels good about himself and feels good about others in the system, when each member deals with others from the position I'm OK—You're OK, and places no special demands of his own on his fellow members. The system will work most smoothly when each member is available to actively stroke the others, or if he is not available to stroke them, when he is at least willing to permit them to be themselves and "do their own thing" without incurring any ill will or suffering recriminations.*

Rescind Your Demands

Stan, an office supervisor with trouble at home, was bringing tension with him into the office. He had become very short tempered, and was leaning hard on his subordinates. His subordinates had responded, in turn, by becoming increasingly more resentful, creating more problems for Stan than he had counted on. One day, he decided to remedy things by openly acknowledging how he contributed to the tenseness. When his secretary walked into his office, he remarked in a subdued voice, "I've been very frustrated lately, and I know that I've been hard to get along with."

His secretary, a woman who spoke her mind quite frequently, replied heatedly, "Well, I'm glad you realize it. But that still doesn't do me much good!"

And it didn't. They soon ended up arguing louder than they ever had in the past. Stan's Adult awareness of where he was had brought the subject out into the open, but it had not taken any pressure off his secretary, and it had not cleared anything up.

Acknowledging the demands we place on a system will not normally be enough to make the system itself OK. When I say "I am angry," or "I am frustrated," or "I am hard to get along with," I speak only about one person—*me!* Yet a system involves more than one person. It involves *me* and *you.* A statement about *me* is an incomplete statement of my understanding of the system as a whole. It deals with only one part of the system. Indeed, in saying "I know I'm hard to get along with," I can easily transmit the Parent assumption that

*In an organization, "doing one's own thing" does not mean doing whatever you want, without regard to the good of the organization. It means doing your own job, at your own pace, and in a manner which is most comfortable for *you;* but it does mean doing your job. (See Chapter Ten for more on the three-part position, I'm OK—You're OK—and the context is OK.)

I believe *you* must still get along with me, and accommodate yourself to me, or else! (In effect, I'm OK, but *you're* not!)

In order to make the system OK, any statement I make regarding the demands I place on a system must be followed by an additional statement containing the implications of my Adult awareness. Namely, "I am hard to get along with, *but that's my problem, and whatever you do is OK with me!*" or "I may be having trouble with my own OKness at the moment, *but I don't mean it to affect you, and you are still OK in my eyes.*" This approach rescinds any implied demands which my actions or words might have previously carried, and explicitly relieves others in the system from having to respond in any way to my own not OKness.

Sometimes the situation is reversed. The other person may be responsible for the bad vibrations, and may be placing his demands on me. If so, there is much less I can do to make the system OK. I can't, for instance, stop the other person from continuing to make his demands, if he doesn't want to stop. I can, however, clarify how his demands affect me, and I can make explicit the basis on which I will, or will not, remain in the system. (I can also express my willingness, if any, to remain in the system with an Adult contract to work out the difficulties, and I can express the terms of the contract.)

This approach often entails a certain degree of risk—one must, in fact, be prepared to leave the system. The other person may not change, he may hear your explicitness as a threat, or he may escalate his demands in a one-handed game of Uproar. If he does, it will merely confirm that the system would, in any event, never have been OK. Your explicitness will have saved you many months, or possibly years, of waiting around and hoping for something that would never occur. In reality, however, it will often be to the other person's advantage to keep the system intact, and to learn how his not OKness influences the system as a whole. (If he doesn't, he will probably continue undermining systems the same way for the rest of his life.) If you can achieve an Adult contract with him, a contract in which you may call attention to his not OKness in a way which is helpful to him, so that he can recognize it, deal with it, and rescind any implied demand attached to it, you may succeed in both keeping the system together and making it a truly OK system. The risk is not insignificant, but the alternative is to perpetuate a not OK system with no real hope for change.

How to Go About Changing Yourself (for Those Who Are Interested)

Not everyone wants to make himself over. But most of us, at one time or another, do try to make certain adjustments in our lives—perhaps to make our lives more productive, more enjoyable, or in certain ways less self-defeating. Unfortunately, many of these efforts fail to succeed. More often than not, we're just not certain what we really want. We may decide, for instance, that we want to get ahead in life; but once we see what it entails, we have second thoughts. We may want to become more patient, and more understanding of others; but when we find how much effort it takes, and how much concentration, we soon give up. Sometimes our Parent says one thing (like "Work hard and earn lots of money"), and our Child says another (like, "Be happy and enjoy life"), and without a plan to integrate the two messages (some means of working hard and enjoying life at the same time), we vacillate, never really working hard enough, nor enjoying life enough, to satisfy us.

It isn't unusual for a person to receive some sort of mixed message in his childhood. John, a thirty-six-year-old marketing executive, had been given both the "be happy" and "work hard" messages from his mother ("be happy," secretly, from her Child to his Child; "work hard," explicitly and verbally, from her Parent to his Parent). John has gone through life acting out a drama in which he periodically tries to resolve the dilemma posed by the conflicting messages. Since his script doesn't call for a solution, he goes through life frustrated and confused. (His mother never had a solution and neither did his father, who always agreed with his mother and who actually provided a model after which John could pattern his own confusion.) John continues to work moderately hard at a job he only halfway likes, sensing something is wrong and waiting for something magic to rectify it. Although nothing ever does, he still doesn't really want to make the hard decision to do something positive about it.

When we find ourselves not changing—even if it's something we thought we wanted to change, the truth is, on balance, *we really don't want to change!* People change only what they want, and they change only when they want to. We often think we want to change, and make stabs at it, but if this process goes on very often it is most likely just part of our script. We play at changing, but we're never really serious. In order to really change, we have to really *want* to!

Decide What You Want

The first rule about changing, then, is: *Decide what you WANT to change!* Not what you *think* you want, or what you *might* want, or what someone else (or your own Parent) thinks you should want, but what you really WANT! This want must come from deep within your natural Child. Give yourself time to think about it. Mull it over. If you should find that you don't really want what you first thought you wanted, don't beat on yourself. Don't feel guilty. Recognize that at the moment you simply don't want it. Be content with that decision, for it's your real decision. Later, you may change your mind. but for the time being it will be more productive to work on something else. Nothing further can be accomplished until you have firmly decided on something you want to change and are willing to stick to that decision.*

Make a Contract

Once you have decided what you want, the next step is to make a contract. Your contract is with yourself. It will help assure that you get what you want. It must be an honest contract, and it must be reasonable. With a dishonest contract, you will defeat only yourself.

PART ONE

Part One of your contract must be a clearly defined, operational statement of what you want. To be operational, this statement must be worded in such a way as to make certain that the contract itself will be sure to work. Your *want* must be stated in precise, practical terms. It must not be stated in vague terms, such as "I want to be successful" or "I want to be happy." It must be stated in terms that will enable you to periodically measure your progress. "Happiness" and

*See Chapter Ten for more insight into the process of deciding on a contract; particularly, for more information on what you may need to give up in order to keep your contract.

"success," as generalized goals, cannot be measured. For contracts of the "happiness" and "success" variety to be operational, they must be worded to specifically answer the questions, "I want to be happy—*when?*" (When I get up in the morning. When I meet my customers. When I come home at night and see my wife in the doorway.) Or "I want to succeed—*at what?*" (Getting a raise next fall. Balancing the budget. Getting to the office on time.)

The more operational a contract is, the better. Among the most operational contracts of all are those in which you can identify *something you no longer want to do.* (I no longer want to feel bad when I come home at night. I don't want to wait until the money's half gone to start balancing the budget. I don't want to feel tongue-tied in the boss's office.) To be this precise, you must first spend some time examining what, in fact, you actually do! The value of such an approach is that it is much easier to *stop* doing something you already do than to start doing something you know nothing about. It is also much easier to measure your progress. When we stop living in our Parent or Child, we automatically come into our Adult; and when we stop living in the past or in the future, we automatically come into the present. By *not* doing something we ordinarily do, we indirectly achieve the somewhat more illusive, but often more important goals of turning on our Adult and living in the present.

Part Two

Once you have firmly decided what you want, you must then decide what you are willing to do to *get* what you want. Part Two is the "will do" section of your contract. There is an important distinction between what you *want* to do and what you *will* do. What you want to do, no matter how operationally stated, may still be no more than idle speculation, little more than wishful thinking. What you *will* do is the practical data which turns wishful thinking into explicit contracts.

In order to determine what to state under the "will do" section of your contract, you may want to ask yourself one of the following questions.

1. When your decision involves something you don't do (but want to), ask *How do I prevent myself from doing*

what I want to do? (How do I arrange not to do it? What do I do to avoid it?)

Examples:

How do I prevent myself from enjoying my work?
How do I keep myself from relaxing?
How do I stop myself from being spontaneous?
How do I keep myself from getting promoted?

2. When your decision involves something you do (but no longer want to), ask *How do I do what I no longer want to do?* (How do I keep myself doing it? What do I do to keep doing it?)

Examples:

How do I make myself unhappy?
How do I frighten myself?
How do I set myself up to be zapped?
How do I keep myself from turning in projects on time?

Don't accept an "I don't know" answer from yourself. "I don't know" answers will come from your Child, which may occasionally try to undercut your efforts. Whenever this happens, simply disregard your Child and continue searching for your answer until you find it. An accurate answer will always, eventually, be available from your Adult.

Your answers to your "How do I prevent myself . . ." questions will be as varied as your wants. We typically prevent ourselves from doing what we want in an infinite variety of ways. Here are just a few of the many possibilities:

> I prevent myself from doing what I want by convincing myself I shouldn't do it. (I get in my Parent and stop myself from enjoying life.)
>
> I keep myself from wanting too much by reminding myself I'm not worthy of it all (just like my parents taught me).
>
> I keep myself tense by clenching my jaw.
>
> I keep myself overworked by never finishing anything.
>
> I keep myself overworked by not wanting to say no to anyone—especially my boss. I keep myself from saying no by staying afraid, and by not learning to explain from my Adult what I can and cannot accomplish comfortably.
>
> I keep myself from liking my job by not knowing what I like.
>
> I keep myself from getting a good job by believing the

world owes me a living. (I never learned to provide things for myself when I was young.)

I tire myself by restricting my breathing.

I keep myself a victim of the system by always keeping up with the Joneses.

I frighten myself by not concentrating on what I'm doing and by letting my mind wander all over the place.

I prevent myself from meeting new people by panicking at the thought of not having anything to say. (I've never learned pastimes.)

I prevent myself from changing by not asking myself what's wrong. I don't ask what's wrong because I don't realize things are so bad.

Sometimes your answers may seem silly. They may sound trivial and foolish. But whatever answer you come up with—remember, it is *your* answer. What is real for you at the moment *is real!* Stick with it! It will be an important insight.

Your "How do I prevent myself . . ." questions, answered honestly, will provide you with a list of things to stop doing. Your next step is merely to decide whether or not you will stop doing them. Those that you will stop, make explicit. Those that you won't, also make explicit. You may always refuse your own contract, but always be sure to make your refusal explicit.

If your initial answers to these questions prove unsatisfactory, if they fail to give you enough data to make an intelligent contract, simply continue applying the same questions to the unsatisfactory answers you have already obtained. For example:

BASIC WANT: I want to be more aware of what's going on around me, particularly when I'm engaged in a conversation.

QUESTION: How do I prevent myself from being aware?

ANSWER: I keep on talking, even when others have stopped listening.

(But a contract to stop talking probably won't, by itself, make you more aware of what's going on around you, so keep questioning.)

QUESTION: What do I do to keep myself talking, even when no one's listening?

ANSWER: I want to make a point and I get so wrapped up

in my explanation it becomes more important to me than whether or not anyone hears it.

QUESTION: Why do I get all wrapped up in my explanations?

ANSWER: I convince myself that people will think I'm dumb if I don't explain everything right. But that's stupid! They've already stopped listening! I guess I'm just stroking myself for having the right answer!

This process will almost always produce a statement of what you will need to do to fulfill your contract. In the above example, the last answer led to a "will do" contract that read, "I will stop trying to always have the right answer. Instead of talking endlessly, I will become aware of how others react and of what *they* are thinking."

Both the Child and the Adult work together to reach the "will do" portion of the contract. While the stimulus and the final decision come from the Child, the questions come from the Adult. The Adult also does the reality testing needed to determine whether or not the "will do" items are actually appropriate to undertake, particularly at the time you will need to undertake them. The "will do" statement is ultimately decided by the Child and the Adult together.

PART THREE

One last step in writing a contract, to assure that your not OK Child doesn't undercut your efforts at the last minute, is to ask yourself, "*How will other people know I have completed my contract?*" That is, what external evidence will there be of your success? If your answer is "There's no way they can tell. Only *I* will know," then you must not accept it! You will be giving yourself an easy way out. (If no one will know you've completed your contract, then no one will know if you've cheated, and it will be much too easy to cheat.) Don't stop writing your contract until you have a clear statement of how others will know when you've completed it. A clear, operational, explicit contract might read like this:

PART ONE

My contract is that I will not be hooked by my boss's Parent.

PART TWO

I will accomplish this by becoming aware of when he is speaking from his Parent, and will recognize that what he says really has nothing to do with me.

PART THREE

People will be able to tell that I have kept this contract because they will feel the OKness of my responses.

Or this:

PART ONE

My contract is that I will not avoid the part of my job I dislike most.

PART TWO

I will accomplish this by estimating the time it will take to do it, set that time aside, and do it.

PART THREE

People will be able to tell that I have kept my contract because I will never be behind in my work.

Or this:

PART ONE

My contract is that I will not be an accommodating Child.

PART TWO

I will accomplish this by:

1. Making a decision on the basis of what I want to do (no matter what others think I should do, and disregarding what my Parent tells me).
2. Stating my decision to myself and to whoever is concerned.
3. Believing my decision is sound and from my Adult.
4. Standing by that decision and being proud of it and carrying it out without hesitation.

PART THREE

People will be able to tell that I have kept this contract because:

1. I won't be a bundle of nerves.
2. I will be more confident and sure of myself.
3. I will also keep my word and not alter it.

The exact words of a contract are important only insofar as they are real to the person making the contract and are believable to anyone listening. In the above examples, Part One, the "want" portion of the contract, had already been transformed to a "will" at the outset. The contracts thus became even more firm and more believable.

How Do I Prevent Myself from Keeping My Contract?

Once you've got a contract with an explicit statement of what you will do to achieve what you want as well as a statement of how others will know when you've achieved it, *there is still no guarantee you will complete your contract.* To assure the completion of your contract, you must check it out from time to time. You must measure your progress. If you find that you are not, in fact, making much progress, you may ask yourself, *How am I preventing myself from completing my contract?* More often than not, you will know the answer, and you will be able to quickly make the appropriate adjustments to get back on course.

As you practice making contracts with yourself, and as you check out how you prevent yourself from completing them, you will gradually learn to make sound contracts. The first few may not work. You may find, looking back, that you settled on contracts you didn't really want, or that you forced yourself to agree to do things you didn't really want to do. You may find that some contracts were not, in fact, reasonable contracts and that you prevented yourself from keeping them by making them unreasonable in the first place. If you keep working at it, you will soon become more skilled. Each new discovery will bring you that much closer to success and will help you achieve a truly high degree of personal autonomy in your life.

8. Making Decisions That Pay Off

More people have agonized more often, more intensely, and in more diverse situations, over the question, "What should I do?" than perhaps over any other question ever posed by members of the human race. Their answers have determined how they run their lives, how they run their families, how they run their businesses, and, inevitably, how they run the nations they live in. How they arrive at their decisions is a process few appreciate and fewer still understand.

The question itself, "What should I do?" (used by most of us at one time or another), implies a childlike need for a Parent solution to problems. ("What *should* I do?") In childhood, the most efficient and often the safest way to decide what to do is to get the answer from Mommy and Daddy. In the absence of direct Parent input, most children will either examine data for themselves (from their Adult) or respond directly to stimuli out of fear, instinct, or whim (from their Child). As they grow older they continue to do things the same way. In situations where their Child once dominated, it continues to dominate. In situations where their Parent once ruled, it continues to rule. While Parent and Child decisions may themselves be unpredictable, the situations in which they occur are often very predictable indeed.

We all have our unique patterns of decision-making. We reserve our Parent, Adult, and Child for certain specific situations, and when our Parent or our Child is in charge, our Adult may be excluded. Each of us is different from the person next to us. Although most of us like to think that our really important decisions come from our Adult—or from our Parent or Child with the agreement of our Adult—this is typically not the case. The reality in most situations is: once a Parent, always a Parent; once a Child, always a Child. And unless the script is changed: once dysfunctional, always dysfunctional.

Decisions Made by the Child

More often than not, we fail to realize when our Parent and Child have the upper hand. This happens to people from all walks of life and at every level of personal achievement. Some of the most tragic instances occur when people in high places make disastrous Child decisions not easily recognized by their peers.

In the board room of a large industrial corporation, fourteen directors of the corporation sat comfortably around a large circular table and listened to the president—a strong, forceful man in his late fifties. The company had been operating in the red for the past six months. The president was explaining how this had come to pass—how the company had misjudged demand for its product, miscalculated in its labor negotiations, and had been unable to anticipate a downturn in the economy. He stood erect, his shoulders back. In a booming voice he went on to say, "Gentlemen, although we have had recent setbacks, we are now preparing to take full advantage of the anticipated upturn in the economy. Rather than lay off workers and cut back production because sales are down, we plan to recoup our losses by borrowing more funds and gearing the company up to maximum strength. When the upturn comes, we will be ready."

Two directors squirmed noticeably in their seats. This was risky business, gearing up while the economy was still soft. There were mixed opinions in the economic community about when the upturn might come. If it did not come soon, their company would plunge even deeper into the red. Somehow, the president was disregarding some of the most important facts in the case. The economy had not turned up *yet*, and the company was already losing money by not selling all that it was producing. While there were times in running a business when it was appropriate to take calculated risks, these times were not when the company was already flirting with disaster. The president seemed more involved in his own "do or die" effort to save face and to recover from his earlier poor showing than he was in deciding matters in the best interest of the company.

Although the plan looked risky, the board as a whole was

inclined to let the president have his way. Theirs was a clubby atmosphere. Discord and embarrassment had always been unwelcome. A strange kind of etiquette prevailed—an etiquette whose rules forbade one member from seriously questioning the actions of another, including the president. To question him was to challenge him, and to challenge him was to imply a lack of confidence in him (which would presumably impair his ability to function capably forever after).

So the two directors said nothing. When the time came to support the president's plan, the motion passed without serious discussion. Six months later, when the economic upturn had not come and the company was in receivership, each board member, to the very last man, emphatically denied that any reasonable person could ever have foreseen the disastrous consequences of the continued economic downturn.

This story, not uncommon in the annals of corporate tragedies, illustrates two different kinds of dangerous Child decisions. The first, made by the president, had to do with his inclination not to bide his time but rather to make something of a last-ditch effort to vindicate his past performance while he still had the power to do so. It was a decision to sink or swim. The president was apparently under tremendous pressure, from his own Parent or possibly from the cumulative Parent (real or imagined) in the heads of his peers, to do something spectacular or bow out. To his Child, it made little difference whether he sank by himself (was fired or forced to resign) or took the whole ship with him (forced the company into bankruptcy). The risk to himself was the same in either case, but by risking the fortunes of the company in this supreme effort to work things out, his Child knew that he might still be able to salvage his own reputation, turn the company around, and carry on in glory.

The second Child decision, unfortunately, was made jointly by the members of the board of directors. It was the decision to retain the structure of the system they were in, the decision to keep their "club" intact (ultimately, the undoing of the system). It was the decision to ignore any reality data which might threaten the fabric of their system as a whole, and to do so by honoring all the secret contracts about what subjects to avoid, about etiquette, and about having "confidence" in one another. It was the decision, made by the Child of each board member, to uphold their secret contracts above all else. With each member's Child having joined in the signing, little wonder that the Child of the President felt it had carte blanche to do with the company as it wished!

Many systems of people sustain themselves and keep themselves intact through the use of secret contracts. These contracts restrict the ways in which members of the system deal with each other, limiting them to certain prearranged, "safe" transactions. In particular, they limit the amount of reality data that can be introduced into the system. (How many families stay together but keep themselves miserable in this very same way?) If the secret contracts restrict the introduction of reality data to the point where the system itself becomes vulnerable (because realistic external forces are actively at work ready to bring it down), the contracts will eventually have to be exposed or the system will in fact collapse. If, however, there are no external forces involved (as in many families and bureaucratic organizations), the secret contracts may indeed keep the system intact, but they will ultimately serve merely to maintain and reinforce the rackets and fantasies of the members.

Many Child decisions in business are difficult to pinpoint. Many on the surface seem productive. Some involve doing things (or *not* doing things) to avoid being blamed or to avoid being found at fault—by one's own Parent or by the Parent in others. ("Don't look at *me! I* didn't do it!") Others involve lifesaving devices geared to maintain one's own survival (such as setting subordinates up to play Let's You and Him Fight). In the long run, however, virtually all such decisions are more productive if first checked out by the Adult. There are usually better ways to survive than by simply avoiding things or by systematically eliminating competition. Strengthening one's Adult is almost always more useful than making one's Child more manipulative.

Decisions Made by the Parent

The Danger of Parent Slogans

One day, many years ago, a famous general was agonizing over whether or not to attack a warring nation that had just invaded a small country friendly to his own. As he grappled with his decision, he gathered his advisors around him, assessed the relative strength of his army, estimated the ability of the smaller country to withstand the invasion, and calculated the effect of prolonged aggression on all three countries. He carefully reviewed all the data that could possibly shed light on his problem. Still, he could not make up his mind. Finally, an advisor spoke. "General," he said, "I am astounded that it is taking us so long to go to the rescue of a nation so friendly as this nation has been to us. What are friends *for* if they cannot be counted on?"

"Ah, yes," said the general. "What are friends for if they cannot be counted on. We shall go to war!" And with that the general committed his nation to a war that lasted twelve long, hard years, twelve years that drained his country of virtually all its productive resources and cost the lives of tens of thousands of its young men.

The general, like many people in moments of stress, found an easy solution to his problem by abandoning his Adult approach (processing data) and embracing an old, sloganlike Parent message ("Stand by your friends"). Typically, when our Adult efforts at processing data produce no clear-cut solution to our problems—when the balance of available information is neither for nor against a particular decision, we end up disregarding the data we have so carefully processed and turn, instead, to some more simplified Parent solution. Appropriate or not, the advantage of a Parent solution is that it requires no thought, and it relieves the frustration of being unable to reach an Adult solution. Moreover, if the Parent data we draw upon is universal enough, our solution, relevant or not to the real problem, will meet with widespread acceptance.

One of the most seductive aspects of Parent data is that it is often couched in catchy phrases—slogans that are easily understood and easily transmitted from generation to genertaion. ("Spare the rod; spoil the child." "Never forget a friend; never forgive an enemy.") Slogans express ideas in simplified (and sometimes oversimplified) terms. Although the ideas themselves may well be Adult before being reduced to slogan form, they often lose something in the translation. People who take such information into their Parent with no insight into how it was originally intended may forever use it indiscriminately in situations where it was never meant to apply.

Parent slogans are particularly useful to politicians, generals, and other leaders of large, organized groups of people.

They provide such leaders with simple concepts for their followers to identify with and to rally around. Common Parent data give people a unity of purpose. It enables them to more readily support their leaders. (Who can deny the universal appeal, the "rightness," of "Stand by your friends"?) For the leaders themselves, it is often more important to resolve their problems with Parent solutions that everyone can accept than it is to find Adult solutions that no one understands. Whether or not a Parent solution works in fact is often much less important than that everyone agrees it should be tried.

Parent Slogans for Every Occasion

Leo, a middle-aged bank trust officer, handled all his bank's security transactions. Leo dealt directly with the brokerage houses, buying and selling stockes for the bank's trust portfolios. One day, when he wanted to sell a thousand shares of a stock that had been sinking steadily, he phoned one of his brokers. A new voice answered the phone.

LEO: I want to sell one thousand shares of Magnum Industries at 21½.

VOICE: Okay.

LEO (*concerned that the voice may not be familiar with the regular procedure for handling telephone orders*): Got that? A thousand shares at 21½.

VOICE: Right. A thousand shares of Magnum at 21½!

LEO: Okay. Thanks a lot.

Leo had misgivings about not having talked to his regular broker—maybe he should have asked for him—but he was very busy, and in Leo's mind, it was up to the brokerage house, not the bank, to see that things were handled properly.

Later that day Leo learned that the brokerage house had not *sold* a thousand shares, but had, instead, *purchased* a thousand shares! The voice on the phone had been that of a new clerk, and the clerk, in his excitement, had mixed up the buy and sell orders. Leo was beside himself. Instead of having sold his shares, he was now saddled with twice as many shares as he had originally owned. Without hesitation, he picked up the phone, called the brokerage house, and announced to the manager that his bank would no longer do business with the firm. The next day, in explaining his actions to an associate, Leo said, "There's absolutely no margin for error in this business. A mistake like that is inexcusable!"

An interesting decision. Hardly a well-reasoned one, however. Certainly not one that took into consideration the long-term performance of the brokerage house, the ill-feeling that might develop between the brokerage house and the bank, the needlessness of all the pain. Certainly not a decision that concerned itself, from an Adult standpoint, with the quality of the communication of data that had taken place during the phone conversation of the previous day.

Leo's associate, hearing in Leo's statement certain Parent data about inexcusable mistakes, and hearing it as irrational and inappropriate to the situation at hand, still did not know what to do. Like many of us, he was stymied when confronted with an irrational Parent. Rather than do nothing, however, he decided to swap Parent data with Leo. Perhaps, if he were adroit enough, if he could hit on something that might trigger a responsive chord in Leo, he might get Leo to change his mind.

ASSOCIATE: Isn't this treatment a little harsher than these people really deserve, Leo? *(Parent data: "Don't treat people harshly unless they 'deserve' it.")*

LEO: Not one bit! They know what kind of business they're in! *(No real Parent data here. Just an irrational justification of an irrational stand.)*

ASSOCIATE: But Leo! Everyone's allowed at least *one* mistake! *(A direct confrontation of conflicting Parent data: "Everyone's allowed at least one mistake" versus "No one's allowed any.")*

LEO: Well, you've got a point. But if I give in once, I'll have to give in all the time. *(A concession made by one Parent to the next: "You've got a point," followed by a corruption of the Parent slogan "Do it for one; do it for all.")*

ASSOCIATE: Okay, but can't you make an exception, just this once? *(A plea for mercy, implying that Leo's judgmental Parent can also show compassion.)*

LEO: I don't know. I'll think about it, but I'll have to have a darn good reason to change my mind! *(The only reason good enough for Leo will be if he is threatened enough, or harassed enough, or possibly rewarded enough to make it worth his while. It is doubtful that any direct confrontation with differing Parent data will, by itself, cause him to change his mind on this one.)*

Changing a Parent decision by confronting the Parent with other, conflicting Parent data is at best a chancy operation. The Parent's time-honored position is that it is always right—regardless of the data. The Parent is not interested in reality, nor is it interested in the consequences of its actions. Only by randomly hitting upon something that works, or by wearing down the Parent in the process, can anything worthwhile ever really be accomplished by this method.

This dialogue is typical of many centered on decisions made by the Parent. Many conversations with people in positions of authority—with bosses and executives (and many conversations in court between attorneys and judges and juries)—involve the exchange of relevant (or irrelevant) Parent messages. Both sides display the slogans most likely to influence the Parent of the person making the decision. Little or no exchange of reality data actually takes place. The purpose of the conversation is only to uncover sufficient Parent data to either neutralize or undermine the opposing position. Reality is not relevant. Usually, the person with the largest store of offsetting Parent slogans, and the one most accomplished in presenting them, wins.

Much time and energy are spent by people in organizations as they ponder the applicability of Parent slogans to current situations. For some it is the safest way to decide things (widely accepted Parent data are rarely subject to question); for others it is the only way (they don't know any better). Some widely utilized Parent slogans are particularly seductive. They include the following:

Stick to the company policy. ("It's safer this way, Elmer. . . .")

Don't change horses in midstream. ("We can't back down now, Charlie.")

The organization (family, company, church, or state) comes first. ("I don't care *what* your wife says, Harry, you go to the Congo or you go on unemployment.")

Don't mix business and pleasure. ("I'm not taking you to Miami, Myrtle, because all our seminars at the Lido are going to be high-intensity, business-oriented workshops.")

Never abandon (compromise) your principles. ("We're gonna *win* this price war, Bert, even if we go broke in the process!")

Never let people take advantage of you. ("We better not let them help us much more, Fred. It may be a trick.")

While blind reliance on such Parent slogans can be the source of much humor, it can also be the source of much confusion, and, sometimes, much tragedy. People who truly believe it is wrong to abandon their principles need only latch on to some inappropriate, obsolete principle to cause all manner of problems for themselves and others around them. People who use Parent slogans in *any* situation to avoid further thought, discussion, or the processing of data on an Adult basis severely limit their effectiveness in dealing with real-life situations, in an everchanging, real world. Their decisions may come easy, but their dilemmas will persist.

The problem with Parent slogans is that they offer no valid substitute for Adult thought. They provide simple guidelines for simple lives, but for thinking people, they often bring more confusion than clarity. The tendency to use them, however, can frequently be very strong. The inclination to force reality to fit the slogans of the past, rather than to incur the frustration produced by accepting the unresolved aspects of reality in the present, is very powerful. It is often far easier to locate an acceptable slogan than it is to sift through all the available reality data related to a particular subject and still not find an answer!

Fortunately, not all people who use Parent slogans to express their decisions employ Parent methods in reaching them. Many Parent slogans are really short-hand expressions of truly Adult decisions—the end result of Adult processing reduced to slogan form for ease in communication. ("Stick to company policy," for instance, may be the expression of an Adult decision if the reasons for diverging from the policy are not significant enough or easily enough expressed to risk the hassle.) Often, the only way to determine if a decision is truly Adult is to talk to the person making it, to get a feel for the process he has gone through in reaching his decision. If this cannot be done, the final test is simply to wait and see how the decision itself fits with the reality of life as events unfold in the future.

Sometimes, the Parent inadvertently reveals itself through the use of double-talk in justifying or rationalizing its position. By sticking to traditional Parent phrases, a skillful Parent can assume a meaningful façade, yet say nothing, for literally hours on end. Take, for instance, "We fired him because he wouldn't work hard enough. He wouldn't work hard enough because he was just plain lazy. He was lazy because he was spoiled. He was spoiled because his upbringing was bad. His upbringing was bad because he wasn't given proper standards. He wasn't given proper standards because . . . (further Parent rationale)."

Or "You won't ever amount to anything because you don't care (or don't try). You don't care (or try) because you're lazy. You're lazy because . . . (etc.)."

Around and around the Parent goes, using its own special brand of mumbo-jumbo, trying to get a handle on life (and sometimes getting close), yet never quite succeeding.

How Parent Polarities Box Us In

Gary, staff director of a large juvenile court system, had a difficult decision to make. Two of his probation counselors (all of whom spent their day driving from one school to another checking on delinquent children) had asked to be excused from having to sign in each morning at eight o'clock. The two counselors lived at a considerable distance from the courthouse, and their school districts were situated near their homes. Driving to court each morning to sign in and then back to their school districts to work took up more than an hour of valuable time. The counselors already worked long hours, and the extra travel seemed a needless imposition. Gary had a difficult choice. His Parent said that everyone should sign in at eight, yet he knew his counselors' case was unusual. "On the other hand," he said to himself as he pondered the question, "their job is already pretty attractive. Why should I make it even more so?" The solution, for Gary, centered around whether or not the request itself was a fair one. If it was fair, he knew he should grant it. If it was unfair, he shouldn't.

How could he be sure it was fair? Certainly, the administrative staff would resent such a request. *They* would still have to sign in. Yet the counselors worked late, and occasionally would even have to see a youngster at his home in the evening, sometimes as often as twice a week. Also, they were usually shorthanded, frequently carrying a larger caseload than might normally be expected. "Still," Gary thought, "changing the rules for some but not for others, might look like favoritism. It might cause more trouble than it's worth."

Fairness, it seemed to Gary, was an illusive quantity. He knew his counselors were already underpaid compared to those with similar jobs in other cities. Why shouldn't he try to help them when he had the opportunity? They only stayed with him out of loyalty anyway. They could always leave and get better jobs elsewhere—probably at much higher salaries! "Damn it," mused Gary, "This decision is harder than I thought!"

The more Gary thought about it, the more uncertain he became. His frustration grew. As he kept swaying back and forth, vacillating from one side to the other in his "fairness" box, he kept getting further away from settling the issue to his satisfaction. The longer he stayed in his box, the more his frustration mounted. The more his frustration mounted, the greater were his chances of just stopping at one side of the box in exasperation and declaring the request either "fair" or "unfair" solely on the basis of which side he happened to be on when his frustration peaked.

This process of trying to fit circumstances into a black and white framework—of trying to force reality to conform with either one or the other of two extreme views on an issue (fair or unfair, good or bad, right or wrong)—is a common approach to decision making. It is seductive in its simplicity. Once we are convinced a position is fair, right, or good, we can unhesitatingly support it! This approach works well (is efficient) whenever we have enough Parent data to provide the label we need for a situation—when our Parent says something is clearly fair, right, or good. (But the decision itself will only be appropriate if the relevant Parent data happens to be appropriate.) This approach barely works, however, in the absence of Parent data, or in situations where existing Parent data is inadequate. The more we try to force *reality* into this predetermined, restrictive parental framework, the more frustrated we become, and the less appropriate become our decisions. Reality, as it turns out, has nothing to do with fairness (or rightness or goodness, for that matter).

These opposing "extremes" we so often use in making decisions, these opposite ends, or poles, on any existing scale of values, are called *polarities*. Like Parent slogans, Parent polarities represent simple methods, passed from the Parent of one generation to that of the next, for trying to resolve complex situations. In the past, when life was, in many ways, much simpler than it is today, both people and situations could be more readily understood in terms of such polarities—in terms of fair and unfair, right and wrong, weak and strong, superior and inferior, or smart and dumb (the list is virtually endless). When a person was your friend, you could trust him, care for him, help him, support him, and depend on him. When he was your enemy, you could disdain him, ignore him, beware of him, fight him, and destroy him. But you also had much more Parent data to help determine if he were friend or foe! He was your friend if he talked the same language (or dialect), went to the same church, had the same skin color, or belonged to the same political party. If he was not your friend, then, by definition, he was your enemy!

Today, when people are frequently neither friend nor foe, when friends are often of a different race (let alone religion), when enemies frequently look and act exactly as friends once did, life is not so simple as it once was. By trying to fit life in the present into the polarities of the past, we often succeed only in boxing ourselves in—forcing ourselves to deal with problems in an obsolete, inappropriate frame of reference.

How much easier Gary's decision might have been had he avoided his fairness box, stayed away from Parent polarities, and dealt solely with the problem of optimizing the job effectiveness of his subordinates (which, presumably, was what he was hired for). Since he was dealing with people, he need only have concerned himself with the content of his transactions, in the present, and the quality of his relationship with his counselors. Were his counselors really dealing with him from their Adult? Were they genuinely concerned to maximize the time they could spend productively on the job? Were they actually interested in conserving the time and energy used in their morning ride to court? If they didn't have to make the trip, would they reallocate the time more productively?

If the answers to these questions were yes, then it was really not important whether or not the counselors signed in at eight. Only switchboard operators, certain administrative personnel, and a few secretaries *had* to be in at that time (to make the office run). On the other hand, if the counselors' request had really come from their trouble-making Child—if they were the kind to try to get away with as much as possible, to minimize their own work load at the expense of others, and to lord it over the rest of the staff when receiving special favors, then there was no reason to consider the request in the first place.

If Gary had granted the request, his only problem would have been in explaining it to the rest of the staff. Yet a truly Adult contract between two or more Adults can always be explained to the Adult of a third party (in this case, the rest of the staff). If some of the staff refused to hear (from their Adult), choosing instead to react miffed, spoiled, or hurt (from their Child), they would have then isolated themselves as the source of stress in the system, exposing their subtle use of negative control to try to influence the outcome of events. (Negative control is that exercised by the Parent or Child when it uses threats, manipulations, and the fear of implied action to keep others from doing things.) Gary would have then known which employees he could more easily afford to risk losing. With few exceptions, an available, sincere Adult is much more valuable than an obstinate, manipulative Child.

For Gary, the best solution could only be achieved by avoiding the rules, guidelines, and polarities of the past and attending to what was actually happening in the present. If people operated from their Adult, he could acknowledge such transactions and build on them. He could use such transactions to strengthen other relationships in the organization. If people operated from their Parent or Child, he could identify such transactions, but recognize their limitations. People operating from their Parent or Child, would need rules to follow and would react unfavorably in situations where they had more freedom than their Child could comfortably tolerate.

How Scripts Can Keep Us from Making Decisions

Typically, when we want to improve our decision-making skills, we look for new ideas, new techniques, and new rules that might help us accomplish our objectives. We focus on new behavior and new ways of doing things, totally ignoring our old behavior, our old ways, and all the things we have done before (and continue to do) to prevent ourselves from making decisions in the manner we would like. This can be a tragic mistake. Before learning new ways, it is often more important to *unlearn* our old ways. Many of us are burdened with scripts that prevent our Adult from making decisions. Our scripts cause difficulty not only by suggesting inappropriate Parent and Child solutions to problems, but by frequently keeping us so tied up, and so confused, that we simply avoid making any decisions at all! Indecisiveness, frustrating as it may be, is not necessarily an abstract character "flaw" that fate randomly bestows on unsuspecting individuals. It is very often an easily identifiable script element, the outgrowth of an early life experience in which there was never a payoff for any decision of any sort.

One of the most common situations involves the person who was zapped hard enough and often enough as a youngster to forever after adhere to the admonition, "Do what you're told, and don't get into trouble." Rather than risk a mistake and face the possibility of punishment, such a person learns early in life that the only safe way to decide something is to ask someone else. As he grows up, he makes decisions based only on what other people tell him. If there is no one to tell him what to do, or if he does not think to ask, he simply does nothing. This pattern permeates his entire decision-making process. It is not a question of "When in doubt, ask." It is a question of "*Always* ask," and if no one says anything, do nothing. Such a person may sometimes get so tied up in the process of asking that, even after he's told, he still doesn't do anything. He frequently goes around asking people what to do, often answering himself (usually from his Parent), but still not doing anything because his payoff is only in the asking and the answering—not in the doing! (It's still too risky.) He remains stuck in the negative inertia of a script that says, essentially, "Never, never risk a decision."

The Parent-Child Box

Wilfred, age forty-two, a middle management transportation executive, manages to keep himself stuck in a related, but somewhat different way. One day, while trying to decide what to do with a subordinate whom he had inherited, but really did not like, Wilfred noticed that he had avoided doing anything with this subordinate for months on end. Wilfred wanted to fire him; but he didn't fire him because he couldn't find a really good reason, and he knew that in the long run he would only feel guilty about it. The subordinate was having some problems on his job, and as a good boss, Wilfred knew that if he wasn't going to fire him, he should at least offer to help him overcome these difficulties. But Wilfred didn't do this, either. To help him, when he really wanted to fire him, would have simply been asking too much. So Wilfred remained stuck, doing nothing.

As Wilfred later expressed it, "My Parent says one thing (what I *should* do), my Child another (what I *want* to do), and I manufacture a box for myself in which I end up feeling bad *whatever* I do (guilty if I do what my Child wants, but what my Parent says I shouldn't; resentful and put upon if I do what my Parent says, but not what I really want). The way not to feel bad, therefore (I convince myself), is to do nothing. But somehow, by staying stuck and not resolving the issue, I continue to remain anxious and unsettled over the whole thing."

Wilfred is not unusual. Many people have tapes that tie their feelings to their behavior, tapes that say, "When you do such-and-such, you will automatically feel such-and-such, and the only way to avoid the feeling is to avoid the behavior." These messages create no-decision boxes in which the Parent says, "Don't do what the Child wants," and backs up its position with the threat of a strong feeling (guilt); and the Child says, "Don't do what the Parent says you should," backing up its position with an equally strong feeling (deep resentment, deep feelings of being put upon). When you believe that what you feel is tied to what you do, your decision to avoid bad feelings from both sides can often result in total inaction. The resulting unresolved situation may then produce an anxiety far worse, and of far greater duration, than either of the feelings you started out by trying to avoid. (This anxiety may then become a racket.)

The Child-Child Box

Another way many people keep themselves from making decisions is by never learning to resolve the dilemma posed by two conflicting "wants." This dilemma is typified by the familiar picture of the spoiled child sitting in the middle of the floor, crying because he cannot have his cake and eat it, too. (His fantasy is that he can have both. Reality, unfortunately, is not on his side.) In his frustration, he neither keeps his cake nor enjoys eating it. Although many people who evidence this pattern in later life may never have been spoiled in their childhood, they still have never learned how to decide comfortably between two conflicting wants. (I want *this,* and I want *that,* but I cannot have both, and if I don't determine which "want" has the greatest yield, I don't get either.)

Closely related to this dilemma is that of the person who has ambivalent feelings towards someone, or something, and never acts decisively because he fails to resolve the conflict between these ambivalent feelings. Barry, a metallurgical engineer of thirty-five, had been thinking of leaving his job for some time. He had been hired six years earlier by Pete, an old fraternity brother. Barry and Pete had enjoyed some fine times together in college, but as soon as they started working together (and Pete had become Barry's boss), their once comfortable Child-Child relationship had disappeared into thin air. It had been replaced by a very uncomfortable Parent-Child relationship. Pete, finding hinself in the role of "boss," had started operating entirely out of his Parent, placing many unrealistic, irrational demands upon Barry. ("Do this." "Do that." "Do this *better!*" "What's *wrong* with you?" "Can't you do any better than *that?*")

At first, Barry had tried to retain their good relationship by accommodating himself to Pete's wishes. He had played "good little boy," acceding to Pete's demands and trying to live up to Pete's expectations as best he could. But it was an impossible task. Pete's Parent was totally irrational. His demands of Barry at any one time were a reflection of the pressures and frustrations which he himself at that moment was unable to cope with. As the moments changed, so did the demands. All Pete's screaming and yelling had little, if anything, to do with Barry. (It was merely *Pete* feeling bad.) But Barry didn't know this, and their relationship deteriorated accordingly. Bewildered, hurt, and discouraged, Barry still refused to seek a new job because, as he put it, "Basically, Pete was still a friend."

From time to time, when tension between the two became unbearable, Barry and Pete would try to salvage their friendship by getting together after work for a few drinks. They would relax and reminisce a bit, and for a while things would be better. But the new luster rarely lasted. Before long, Pete's Parent would reemerge, and things for Barry would be worse than ever.

This then, for almost six years, had been the substance of their relationship. Escalate tension, increase stress, have a few drinks, patch things up; escalate tension, increase stress, a few more drinks, and so on. For the last two or three years, on and off, Barry had been thinking of quitting. As he expressed it: "The problem is, I simply can't make up my mind! Things get really bad around here, and I just about decide to quit, when Pete and I go out one night and have a hell of a good time. Then, for some reason, I usually decide to hang around a while longer. But it's a vicious cycle. Before long, Pete becomes impossible to deal with all over again. I really like Pete, and he's a capable guy. I don't understand why he always does this."

Barry likes Pete, but then again he doesn't. He wants to quit, but then again he wants to stay. He keeps waiting for his feelings to shift permanently in one direction, but they never do. Like many of us, Barry denies himself the reality of his mixed emotions. He wants things in black and white so he can make *firm* decisions, yet his feelings rarely fit this mold. Like most of us, at one time or another, he feels both good and bad about the same person at the same time. (He likes Pete's Child, but not his Parent.) His fantasy is that someday Pete's Parent will disappear and his conflict will miraculously be resolved.

But Pete hasn't given any signs of changing in over six years. Sometimes he hints at it, but only to manipulate Barry into staying on the job. Pete needs Barry's expertise and doesn't want him to leave (hence, the after-work drinking sessions). Yet he does not want Pete to stay badly enough to bother to change himself. By maintaining this uncomfortable equilibrium, however, and by making conciliatory gestures whenever necessary, Pete manages to keep Barry's services. Barry, on the other hand, by basing his decisions on his need for clear, unambiguous feelings, perpetuates his indecision racket and keeps himself stuck.

For Barry, the only clear way out is to acknowledge his ambivalent feelings, to identify that *this is where he is,* feeling ambivalent, and to recognize that what he hopes for just may never come true (it hasn't come true in six years and *won't* come true unless Pete has some reason to change). By doing this, Barry can free himself to make decisions based on reality and not based on his own self-satisfying fantasy to how he would *like* life to be. Life, as it turns out, is full of ambiguities.

The Santa Claus Fantasy, and Other Ways to Avoid Decisions

This inclination to live in a dream world year after year, constantly waiting, hoping, and wishing, is a severe deterent to effective decision-making. Often referred to as the Santa Claus fantasy ("Don't worry [and, mainly, don't do anything] because Santa Claus will eventually come and all will be right"), it represents a philosophy widely encountered in our society. It reflects the naively optimistic (and to some, religious) view that all we need to do is be good and tend to our own business, and everything will eventually turn out as we would like. Once this wait-and-hope philosophy is taken into our script, many of us end up waiting and hoping forever. Unfortunately, most of the rewards this approach suggests are not readily available upon this earth.

Other effective script methods to avoid decisions include those of the carefree person who prevents himself from making decisions by "believing" that decisions "aren't fun." His position is that making decisions involves "being serious" and doing things that are essentially anti-Child. Early in life he observed that all the spontaneity and joy went out of people once they grew up and assumed responsibilities. (For all the grown-ups in his life, there was never any way to mix seriousness and pleasure.) Consequently, he decided that the only way to save himself was to keep himself a child, avoiding decisions, steering clear of responsibilities, and staying away from anything remotely connected with growing up and being serious. As he continues to go through life this way, he succeeds in preserving his spontaneity at the expense of gaining his autonomy.

Other people may avoid decisions by deciding something one day (smokers, for example), but deciding something different the next. (The decision is to *change decisions.*) Some make decisions with no understanding of how to carry them out. (No plan for getting from Point A to Point B.) Such people are really making incomplete decisions. In theory, their decisions are related to their actions, but in practice, their actions do not correspond to what they say they have decided. They are much like arm-chair diplomats, sitting at home deciding when and how to handle international trade with Russia or Red China, with no practical mechanism available to connect what they decide with what happens in reality.

Someone really interested in improving his decision-making ability can do well by first examining how he prevents himself, and how he has prevented himself in the past, from making decisions the way he would like to. Many of our difficulties with decisions are based on earlier, unconscious decisions that conflict with what we want to do now. We keep ourselves from making decisions in the present because we have already made earlier decisions to do something different. By understanding our earlier decisions ("Asking others is safer than deciding for yourself," "When your Parent and Child disagree, avoid the bad feeling by doing nothing." "If you can't have your cake and eat it too, forget the whole thing," "If things aren't going right, just wait for Santa Claus," "If you make decisions, you'll stop enjoying life"), we can free ourselves to make *new* decisions based on our current lives, and not based on what might once have provided an important payoff for us in the past.

Adult Decisions Based on Reality

Realistically, many situations are handled more appropriately by the Parent or the Child than by the Adult. Parent decisions are often the most efficient (particularly in terms of "how" things are done) and the most immediate (and the most effective, when immediacy provides needed impact). Parent guidelines and instructions frequently provide the only way to move people who will simply not be moved by other, less forceful methods. Child decisions are often the most fun, the most enjoyable; in situations involving creativity and intuition, the Child will frequently find ways to do things—new, imaginative approaches to help solve old, perplexing problems—that the Adult could not even guess at.

Left to their own devices, however, the Parent and Child may cause great tragedy, bringing disaster and ruin to events where even a moment's clarity might save the day. Only consistently under the watchful eye of the Adult can the Parent and Child bring highly effective solutions to situations where the Adult itself might not function effectively. A really effective Adult knows when to turn to the Parent and Child. It will be guided by reality. It will have the freedom and flexibility to select the most appropriate approach from among all the available alternatives.

Interestingly, it is often difficult to tell if someone is operating from his Parent or Child *at the direction of his Adult,* or if he is simply hooked, with no control over the situation! The best clue is the speed with which he can get *out* of his Parent and Child, once he is in them. We can all get *into* our Parent and Child quickly (we can be hooked instantaneously), but we can only get *out* quickly when we are really there only at the direction of the Adult.

To use his Parent and Child effectively, a person must learn to understand them implicitly. He must know how his Child creates, how it plays, what it fears, and he must understand its vulnerabilities. He must recognize his Parent, and be familiar with its fixed positions, its expectations, and how and when it expresses itself. He must be able to recognize when fatigue, stress, frustration, and impatience interfere with his thought processes, and when exasperation or annoyance cause him to listen selectively, hearing only what he wants to hear, disregarding things he feels irrelevant, and rationalizing away all pretense to objectivity. With understanding, he will come to develop a sense for when his Parent and Child can help him, and he will also know when he can, and when he *must,* disregard them.

Even if his Adult is always in charge, a person cannot always be assured optimum results. He must learn to see that his Adult receives data of adequate quality and quantity to make decisions both responsive and suitable to each new situation. Even a well-oiled, high-speed Adult is useless without adequate information. While objectivity is obtained by staying in the Adult, perspective can be obtained only from exposure to the widest possible range of circumstances and information bearing upon any particular decision. In addition, the Adult cannot be effective if it waits forever to make a decision. It must know when it has collected enough data to assure a reasonable probability of success, and it must be willing, when necessary, to act on the basis of such probabilities. Decisions that really pay off may sometimes be made by the Parent and Child, but for consistency, the Adult must always be in charge, and must have both the perspective and insight necessary to handle its job successfully.

Decisions about People

Some of the most frustrating decisions we make about people deal with how and when to alter or terminate relationships. In organizations, the biggest questions usually are: when to hire, when to fire, when to stick with people in the hope that they will change, and what to do about them in the meantime. Many people faced with such decisions typically make them from their Parent or Child, based on what they think *should* happen, or on what they hope might happen, without regard for the realistic probabilities of what is in fact likely to occur based on people's scripts.

Two professional managers were attending a management seminar. As they sipped coffee during a break in the program, one said to the other, "My biggest problem is motivating my people."

His companion sighed, nodding his head in agreement. "Mine, too. I just wish I could come up with something which would really work. We have high salaries and good working conditions, and still I have some people who just don't seem to care. I've tried everything I can to motivate them, but nothing seems to help."

In their never-ending search for reality data, businessmen are constantly discussing motivation. Unfortunately, they often look on it as some supreme manipulative technique, some universal carrot to thrust before the rest of the world, some technique which, once understood, will enable them to get others to do their bidding willingly. By taking this approach—by searching for a device with universal applicability—they often overlook what has been before their noses all along.

People motivate themselves! They do so by seeking the same sort of payoffs that have been important to them ever since childhood, and they usually give off all sorts of clues, in their everyday behavior, as to what these payoffs are. Sometimes a person's personal payoffs clearly coincide with the broader goals of his organization—as when a performance-oriented person works hard to please his own Parent, but at the same time produces results which benefit his company. Sometimes his payoffs *conflict* with the goals of the organization—as when a Kick Me player compulsively continues to fail, time after time, without ever showing any signs of changing. The confusions for the professional manager occurs when he fails to realize that motivation, in its manipulative sense, is merely the process of finding out what payoffs are important to a person, and then setting him up to achieve them. When a manager says that he cannot motivate a Kick Me player, he is wrong. *He can!* In reality, a Kick Me player can be manipulated just as easily to kick himself and get his negative stroke as a performance-oriented person can be set up to work hard and get his performance stroke. The process is identical. The difference is that motivating a Kick Me player to kick himself usually has no broader value to the organization.

Unwilling or unable to see this reality, managers continue to frustrate themselves by trying to find new rewards for performance (money, power, recognition, fame, raises, promotions, plush surroundings) to fit scripts where such rewards are irrelevant. They continue trying to force the stroke to fit the script (which never works, and merely sustains the frustration) rather than change the script to fit the stroke (which frequently has the possibility of working.)

Many organizations devote considerable effort to the process of fitting their top men to their top jobs. They screen their executives carefully, they define their job requirements, and they see that the men selected fill the jobs in terms of their personal skills and talent and their actual interest in handling their jobs successfully. It is a process of finding a fit—a congruency—between the man, his skills and interests, and the job. It is an enormously difficult task. Few scripts readily fit a set of independently conceived job specifications. Yet if there is no fit between a person's script and the context in which he works (the goals of the company, the specs of his job), the person will either accommodate the goals of the company without following his script (which causes anxiety and stress, and doesn't last very long), or he will follow his script without regard to the goals of the company (which produces anxiety and stress for his superiors, and also doesn't last).

Unfortunately, in their intuitive efforts to find a fit between job specifications and the people they hire, most executives restrict themselves to the rigid framework of predefining their job specifications and assuming that a person's script is unchangeable. This greatly complicates the task. Once having hired a person whose script does not fit the context, they typically either live with the stress or fire the person. Rarely is consideration given to the simpler and much more practical solution of changing the context to fit the script, changing the script to fit the context, or both.

Job specifications are often much more flexible than they appear. (People typically mold their jobs to fit their scripts, within certain limits, anyway.) By acknowledging this reality, and by making a conscious effort to define the reasonable limits within which a person might continue to operate with impunity (and still be paid), a manager can go far towards easing the fit between script and context. He can often *optimize* this fit by learning to determine which subordinates are in fact changeable and by learning to help them through this occasionally tedious, yet always rewarding process.

In broad outline, this can be done by establishing a system in which unconditional, positive strokes are given frequently (just because people are people) and jobs are structured in such a way as to provide people with the opportunity for receiving conditional strokes for good performances. (Jobs that are trivially easy provide little opportunity for such strokes. Telling someone he did a good job, when even a moron could have done it, is rarely effective. In addition, fragmenting someone's job so that it is impossible for him to feel any sense of personal accomplishment also undermines this process.) Local profit centers, where each person in the organization can identify his own contribution to the company's profit (or other goals), are extremely helpful. In such a context, those people who seem not to be responding to positive strokes may then be invited to examine their scripts with an eye towards determining what creates the difficulty and what, if anything, they might be interested in doing about it.

Decisions about Systems

Susan, an enthusiastic young school teacher fresh out of college, was having trouble fitting herself into a school system where all her lessons about teaching seemed inappropriate. Susan wanted to be a good teacher, but wherever she turned, her actions seemed to backfire. Less interested in adopting the style and posture of the traditional teacher than in exposing children to the exciting possibilities of learning, Susan concentrated on developing good relationships with her students. She stroked them, she tried to challenge them, and she did whatever she possibly could to pique their interest in learning.

Everything Susan did met with resistance. She wanted to upgrade her curriculum, but was told she couldn't, because if she did, the teacher in the next grade would not have anything to teach. She wanted to take her students on field trips, but was told that the legal risk of dealing with children after hours and off school grounds was too great. She became friendly with several delinquent students in the faint hope of possibly salvaging their lives, but was told to back off, as she was infringing on the responsibilities of the children's parents and counselors. When she signed a student petition about safety measures, hall duty, rest rooms, and fire drills, she was reprimanded for "siding with the students." She was even attacked for wearing the youthful clothes generally associated with young people of her age because she appeared to be "too closely identifying with the students."

As all her efforts to fit into the system and become a good teacher met with resistance, Susan became increasingly distraught. In explaining her dilemma to a friend, Susan said, "I really don't know what to think about this school system. Sometimes it just doesn't seem to make any sense!"

To that, her friend responded with remarkable insight, "Where did you learn that systems always have to make sense?"

And there it was! The crux of Susan's frustration! She was trying to make sense out of a system that did not make sense! She was using all her lessons and all her instincts about how to treat people and build relationships to try to fit into a system that did not value such things. She was trying to become a good teacher in a system that rewarded only ineptness. In the final analysis she could fit into the system only by distorting her own sense of reality, by adopting as her own the special craziness of the system.

Whether we are aware of it or not, whenever we enter, or become part of a system, we make a decision regarding that system. Most often, we assume that the system itself makes sense. Nothing could be further from reality. Whether or not a system makes sense depends entirely upon the circumstances surrounding its creation, and the attitude of the person or persons exercising greatest control over it. Many systems of people are organized not to make sense. They reflect the particular confusions and distortions in the circumstances which bred them. School systems organized by law, supervised by uninformed school boards, and run by teachers who cannot teach and students who will not learn are just one of many examples. *Any* system in which the context is not OK, any system where people are brought together and kept together for poorly defined and unrealistic purposes; any system that nurtures itself by denying the integrity of the human being, simply will never make sense. Trying to make sense out of it will always be a useless pursuit.

This holds true particularly of bureaucratic organizations—many of which are preorganized by law to carry out specific functions and populated after the fact by people both unfamiliar with the system's goals and unable to establish the meaningful relationships necessary to achieve them. It also holds true for nonbureaucratic organizations when the person (or persons) in charge of the system is plagued by certain critical confusions or distortions in his own head—distortions which he insists on nurturing and passing on to others. These distortions often result from inconsistencies between what his Parent and Child may think about something or, sometimes, between what his Parent thinks and what really is.

The person in charge of a system sets the tone of the system. He either gives permission to members of the system to think for themselves while they remain in the system, or he forces them to distort themselves and alter their behavior to conform with his own Parental (and often irrational) views of what life is like. The head of a system who has a confused system in his own head will often rule only over confusion.

In making decisions related to people, both as individuals and as a part of systems, it is important for the person in charge to understand, in his Adult, the reality context in which he is operating. He must know "where" people are, and he must be familiar with what is happening within the system. Aware of the real possibilities for change, he must have a fair idea of the reasonable time frame in which change is likely to occur, and he must also know the circumstances under which positive change, as a realistic probability, is in fact not probable at all.

9. Refining the Art of Management

The insights of transactional analysis are enormously valuable in managing and supervising others. Merely by getting in touch with oneself, a person can vastly improve his dealings with other people. When a manager or a supervisor gets a feel for whether or not he is in his Parent or Child, replaying old tapes or seeing and hearing with eyes and ears of the past, he can vastly increase his chances of altering future transactions in a more useful or productive direction. When he gets a feel for where other people are, he can use this knowledge to alter his automatic reactions and responses to accommodate more productive or more realistic mutual goals. Beyond this, as a manager or a supervisor develops a sense for the potential of giving unconditional strokes and of establishing I'm OK—You're OK game-free relationships, a sense of how such relationships promote creativity and encourage people to develop themselves to the fullest, he can dramatically affect the climate of interaction in any group of people he may be held accountable for.

The greatest benefit, however, comes when a manager develops skill in actively helping a person (subordinate) identify where he is and becomes capable of helping that person get from there to another, more productive, place (where he would like to be). Large numbers of people in business have scripts calling for working without succeeding, trying without achieving, and structuring time in ways that only confirm their not OK life positions. With practice, a manager may help his people rewrite these scripts. He can help them become more aware of themselves and gain greater autonomy over their own lives. In doing so, he can effect change which will systematically increase a subordinate's personal productivity and significantly enhance his economic value to the company. The secret is in understanding that no one can *make* someone else change, but that, with help, many people are quite willing to change by themselves.

Basically, a manager has only two problems to overcome. The first is that he must often remain Adult in the face of many familiar, time-honored overtures on the part of others to hook his Parent and Child. The second is that he must establish an atmosphere of OKness in which it is safe for a subordinate to undertake the difficult and sometimes fearful task of reprogramming himself. The first problem—that of remaining Adult—is almost always with us. The second problem—that of establishing an atmosphere of Okness, a climate for change—can be solved by consciously learning to sense "where" people are, neutralizing one's own expectations of other people, and actively working to achieve their personal trust.

Learning to Sense "Where" People Are

Dealing with the Not OK Child

Sally, a young clerk new to the bookkeeping department, was sitting at her desk one morning. As her supervisor walked by, she put her pencil down, glanced up with a discouraged look, and said, "I'm no good at making these calculations."

Her supervisor, a woman in her mid-forties who had heard such complaints from Sally before, replied, "You say that about everything, Sally."

This pretty much set the tone for the rest of the conversation.

"I *know* it. I'm miserable at a lot of things."

"No, you're not. You just need to try harder."

"But I *do* try. It just never works out."

"Don't be silly. You'll never get anywhere acting that way." *(Walking off.)*

Sally returned to her work more depressed than ever. Her suspicions about herself had been confirmed once again. She *was* incompetent, and no one could understand her.

This scene could have had a more constructive ending, had the supervisor been able to identify where Sally was, and had she also managed to get out of her Parent and into her Adult. She might have said to herself, "When Sally says she's 'no good' at something, what she's really saying is that she feels unhappy or depressed. This makes me feel disgusted with her, because she's always saying that, and never buckling down to work. My Parent easily gets hooked by her not OK Child. And that's the *last* thing I want."

In searching for an Adult statement which Sally might accept, the supervisor might have focused on the way Sally seemed to *feel*. When Sally said, "I'm no good at making these calculations," the supervisor could have said, "You look depressed, Sally," or "You seem dejected." (Or "Sounds like you're having a rough time," or "Looks like you're having some trouble.")

Sally, thankful to have someone understand her, might well have answered, "I sure am. Things just aren't going well today." The supervisor could have nodded, patted Sally encouragingly on the back (stroking her), and walked off leaving Sally in much better shape to get back to her calculating.

By doing this, in one step the supervisor could have made an Adult statement of fact (how Sally appeared, to her), and avoided judgmental statements which only served to confirm Sally's not OKness to herself. (She doesn't try hard enough. She's silly. And she won't get anywhere.) Both the supervisor and Sally would have felt better. A simple nod and a pat on the back would have cemented things. At least for the time being.

In learning to sense where people are, it is often helpful to avoid responding directly to what they say. It is much more important to understand the secret messages from their not OK Child. These secret messages are transmitted in code. They are secret in the sense that they are never stated explicitly; but they are not *really* secret, because they can be clearly understood by anyone who knows what to listen for. The Child level of a transaction is the feeling level, and the Child's secrets are about its feelings. Its messages, therefore, can always be recognized by listening not to what someone says, but to what his words (and actions) say about what he feels. By responding not to the words, but to the feeling, the secret code can always be cracked.

Responding at the feeling level can sometimes be difficult, particularly when we are accustomed to responding only to words. Someone interested in gaining skill at this can benefit greatly in face-to-face situations by asking himself four key questions:

1. "What is this person really saying (nonverbally, and in verbal code) about the way he feels?"

2. "How does it make *me* feel?" (What do I feel at this exact moment?)

3. "How am I responding?"

4. "Is this what I want?"

Not OK Interpretations of Everyday Conversations

John, a thirty-four-year-old insurance salesman, sat in his office one morning making telephone calls to people for appointments. As time went by, it seemed as if no one at all was interested in talking about insurance. He couldn't get any appointments! Shortly before noon his manager passed by his office and invited him to lunch. As John put on his jacket, he turned to his manager and said, "I'm terrible at making telephone calls."

His manager, knowing it to be true, replied, "You can't be good at everything."

Things seemed to get worse from that point on.

"But I don't think I'll ever improve."

"It takes time. Keep at it, though. Otherwise you soon won't have anyone to sell to."

"I just don't have the knack, I guess."

"You'll probably get better with more practice."

"I don't know. I've already done quite a bit."

Feeling they were starting to go around in circles, the manager decided to wind up discussion of this particular subject by saying, "Tell you what. If you'd really like, *I'll* make some phone calls for you this afternoon."

John replied, "Okay," still preoccupied with his own bad feelings as they walked out the door together.

This conversation is deceptive. It seems to end on a constructive note. The manager is offering John some comfort, encouragement, and, apparently, some direct help. But is he really being helpful? Compare this, for instance, with what might have happened if the manager, feeling John's depression, had said to himself, "When John says he is 'terrible' at making phone calls, what he is really saying is that he feels discouraged and not OK. I know telephoning for appointments is not his strong point. When he gets this way, my impulse is to cheer him up and be encouraging to help get rid of the bad feeling. I guess it makes me uncomfortable. But there is really no good reason to play 'comforting Parent' to his not OK child. Also, I don't want my Parent to take on his responsibility for making his calls. Rather than get hooked, my best bet is to answer from my Adult and make statements which reflect my observation of the way he feels."

Had the manager looked at things this way, the conversation might have gone, "I'm terrible at making telephone calls."

"You look discouraged."

"I don't think I'll ever improve."

"It really seems to upset you, John."

"Yes. I just don't have the knack, I guess."

"I know how that feeling is. If you'd like, perhaps we could work together on improving your telephone skills sometime soon."

"Thanks very much. I'd appreciate that."

In taking this approach, the manager could have avoided the pitfall he fell into during the first conversation. In both cases John was using the subject of the telephone as a substitute to express what was really bothering him—that he was feeling bad. In the first conversation, the manager did not understand what the real subject was. Not in tune with John's feelings, he was unaware of how his own responses reinforced John's not OKness. His impulsive answers devastated John, who, without the manager's knowing, chose to interpret them as confirmation that he really was, in fact, not OK. Someone deep in his not OK Child can easily interpret such statements in the worst possible way. For instance,

"You can't be good at everything" might mean "It's true, you really *are* not OK. OK people *can* be good at everything."

"Keep at it, or you soon won't have anyone to sell to" may be heard as "It won't be long before you're out of a job."

"You'll probably get better with practice" might translate "Since you've already had plenty of practice and still can't do it, it looks like you're all washed up."

"I'll make some calls for you myself" might well be heard as the clincher, "This is it! It's the last straw. You're so helpless someone else has to make your own calls for you."

In the second conversation, the manager's statements did not lend themselves to misinterpretation. "You look discouraged," "It really seems to upset you," and "I know how that feeling is" translate "I understand, and it's OK."*

It takes two people to make a conversation, each person having his individual set of feelings and reactions to what is going on. The secret to developing a feel for dealing with people is to be able to identify what is happening on both sides of the transaction. Where are *both* people? What is *he* feeling? What am *I* feeling? Are we hooking each other? Is that what I want? Once this identification has been made, a person has the option of switching to his Adult and redirecting the transaction.

Neutralizing Your Own Expectations

How Expectations Cause Trouble

It was Amy's first day at her new job. Amy was fresh out of secretarial school and eager to make a good impression. Because she felt a little nervous, she arrived at work early to be sure to get off to a good start. Her new boss, known to be a perfectionist, had called her into his office to take some dictation at about 10:00 A.M. An hour later, after working very hard on it, Amy handed him her first piece of typing, waiting expectantly for her first words of praise. Her boss took the typing and looked it over quickly. Then he glanced up and in a matter-of-fact tone of voice said, "You'll have to do better than this or you won't last very long around here."

Stunned, Amy stood speechless in front of his desk. Sensing that she was not going to say anything, her boss continued, "They sure don't teach you girls much in school these days, do they?"

Amy broke into tears and ran from the room.

Exaggerated? Unusual? It happens somewhere in this country every day. Only two ingredients are needed. One person needs to decide in advance of an event how he *expects* some-

*Incidentally, if you do this and the other person does not acknowledge the reality of such statements, or does not accept them as strokes, check your demeanor and tone of voice. You must always be honest, sincere, and stroking.

one else to act. Then the other person needs to go and do it differently. The first person, particularly if he is the boss, will then feel he has every right to come on Parent, hooking the second person's Child. If the Child does not submit, it will revolt. Time and time again, our expectations completely undermine our ability to deal with people on an Adult level.

Frank, regional sales manager for a medical supply firm, had just been given a new territory to open up. Instead of going out and immediately hiring some new salesmen, as his boss might have done, he spent his first week quietly visiting competing companies in the new territory. Most of Frank's new competitors had not met him yet, and he felt that this would be a fine opportunity to obtain valuable information about how they were operating. It might enable him to avoid making costly mistakes of his own later on.

Frank's plan worked to perfection. At the end of the week he returned to his office with much useful information. Immediately upon returning, he headed straight for his boss's office to tell him about his good fortune. As he walked in the door, however, Frank could tell something was wrong. Before he was fully inside, he was cut short by, "What's wrong with you, Frank? Can't I trust you to do a job right?"

Taken by surprise, Frank could barely answer, "What do you mean?"

The conversation continued on its destructive path. "I heard what you were up to last week. I'll bet you haven't hired even *one* salesman, have you?"

"No, but I picked up some valuable information."

"I don't care what you picked up. When you open a new territory, your job is to hire new salesmen, not fool around."

"I'm sorry."

"You better be. There's only one way to do this job, and you're starting out on the wrong foot. I want to see you back here a week from now with something accomplished!"

Frank hurriedly backed out the door, completely deflated. Fortunately, he would be able to accomplish something next week, but his relationship with his boss would be strained for weeks to come. Indeed, it might never again be quite the same.

This situation could have had a much happier ending. Each man could have given some thought to what he expected of the other. Frank might have been able to avoid the confrontation entirely had he "checked" with his boss in advance of his trip. Even if he had not checked, his boss still might have said to himself, "Frank has been given a new territory to develop. By not checking with me, Frank is saying that he assumes I have confidence in his ability to do the job well. I feel myself getting annoyed with Frank because I expect him to do things the way *I* would. I know my way works because it works for me. Other approaches are hard for me to understand. But Frank's got a good head on his shoulders. Maybe he'll find a better way for himself. What's really important is that he knows the responsibility is his. I certainly don't want my Parent to get hooked and relieve him of that responsibility. Least of all do I want him to feel forced to play humiliated Child."

As Frank opened the door, his boss, not expecting anything in particular, might have said, "Hi Frank, how did things go this week?" If he had, Frank quite likely might have started in on an enthusiastic description of events of the past few days, explaining how much valuable time he had saved. Having neutralized his expectations, his boss would have been able to fully appreciate Frank's success. He might have said to himself, "Frank doesn't always do things the same way I would, but they still seem to turn out pretty well. He's really a pretty clever guy." To Frank he might have said, "That's great!" All would have ended well.

We often cause ourselves difficulty by our expectations of other people, especially when those expectations have not been spelled out in an Adult contract between ourselves and others. People can be unpredictable. When they do not do things the way we expect, it may cause bad feelings. If we are in a position to come on Parent, we may do just that, undermining any Adult relationship we might have. Small, inconsequential matters often cause the greatest problems, as they are rarely spelled out in a contract. If a person agrees to "A" (an important point), we will often expect him to hold to "B," "C," and "D" (unimportant points), *even if these points were never discussed!* The surer we are of our position, the more likely we are to come on Parent. But, often, people need to come around to their own way of doing things. What is best for us is often not best for the other person. Carrying around preconceived notions of how other people should do things can sometimes be a very real hindrance.

How Expectations Lead Us into Games

Ted, a struggling young insurance salesman, was seen by his sales manager walking into a movie theater one afternoon when he was supposed to be working. This created something of a dilemma for the manager. While he did not want to confront Ted in front of the theater, he knew he would have to speak to him the next day. He spent the rest of the afternoon puzzling over what to say. He felt sure that punishment was not the answer, but he also knew that Ted could not go on taking off afternoons to go to the movies. Finally, he decided on a course of action. He would get Ted to admit he had been to the movies. Once Ted had admitted it, the manager planned to excuse him this once but warn him firmly not to do it again.

The next morning the manager called Ted into his office. He decided to ease into the subject slowly.

MANAGER: Hi, Ted. How are things going?

TED: Okay, thanks. What's up?

MANAGER: Nothing much. I was just looking for you yesterday and wondered where you were.

TED: Oh. I was out seeing some customers.

MANAGER: Someone said they thought you took the afternoon off.

TED: Not yesterday.

MANAGER: You worked all day?

TED: Sure. Just because you couldn't find me doesn't mean I wasn't working!

At this point the manager's good intentions vanished. Ted had been trapped in an even bigger sin: *lying*. And lying demanded punishment. The manager found himself acting out a script that he had been over many times in his childhood.

Nothing was working out as he had expected. The conversation went on like this:

MANAGER: Don't pull that sort of stuff with me! I *personally* saw you walking into the movies! How dumb can you get?

TED: Me? At the movies?

MANAGER: Yes, you! Now are you going to own up like a man and admit it?

TED: It must have been someone else you saw. What time were you at the movies?

MANAGER: It doesn't make any difference what time I was there! I'm going to dock you a half day's pay, and if I catch you doing it once again, you're fired. Now get out of here and get back to work.

There it was. The punishment and the final threat. Although he had started out by trying to avoid the straightforward Parent approach of immediate punishment, the alternative with which the manager ended was equally Parent. He was expecting Ted to adopt a Child role—in particular, the Child role where the Child admits its guilt. Then the manager's Parent could "forgive" Ted's Child and issue its warning. Unfortunately, Ted's Child chose another role. It chose to lie, as many a Child will do when it suspects it will be punished for the truth. The entire scenario illustrated a rather sophisticated form of NIGYSOB.

How much better things might have turned out had the manager been able to start the conversation without *expecting* any particular response of Ted. In searching for an Adult approach, the manager might have recognized that Ted's behavior (going to the movies during the most productive part of the day) was inconsistent. To Ted, the manager might have said, "I happened to see you going to the movies yesterday afternoon, Ted, which struck me as unusual. If anything's wrong and I can be of any help, I'd like to try." Ted, relieved to have someone he could talk to about his problems, might well have answered, "Gosh, all this pressure I've been under lately has really been getting me down. I just *had* to do something about it." Ted and his manager might then have gone on to deal constructively with the problem of the pressure Ted felt, perhaps finding a way to diminish it.

Gaining Autonomy over Your Expectations

Expecting things is a typical occupation of the Child (which can then become depressed or disillusioned when its expectations are not met) and the Parent (which may become annoyed or angry). The Adult knows that the only things which can realistically be expected to occur are those with a probability of one hundred per cent—a probability rarely, if ever, ascribed to events involving human beings. We often set ourselves up to become upset by remaining in our past, playing old tapes, and expecting things to occur which in fact have a very low probability of happening.

One way of learning how much our expectations may be adversely influencing us is to notice how often we get angry at people *for what they do.* (Or what they *don't* do.) Or how often we get hooked (angry, depressed, disillusioned) by events which occur. If we get caught in either of these traps very often, our expectations are probably getting the best of us.

An excellent method we can use to neutralize our expectations is to ask ourselves these two questions:

1. If there is something I would like to occur, and if by some chance it does not, will I react Parent or Child?
2. Is this what I want?

Most of our expectations of other people are part of relationship contracts we either have or want to have with those people. The contracts say that certain things should happen, and we are inclined to want to hold people to our own personalized, often vague, understanding of the contract. We expect such-and-such of the other person. We are, in a sense, projecting onto him our own internalized idea of how he should be. This is usually a playback of our own Parent data and rarely bears any relationship to what the other person really *is.* When we relieve ourselves of the burden of our expectations, we relieve the other person of the pressure to sign a secret contract. When we recognize that he is not in this world to live up to our expectations, and when we decide we will not go around feeling bad (angry, frustrated, hurt, betrayed) if he does not live up to them, we open the door to an Adult relationship. Our best bet from a management point of view is to help *his* Adult to see *him*, not to hook *ourselves* into irrelevant and troublesome feelings.

Neutralizing our expectations is often not as easy as it sounds. Sometimes we may completely think through a way of dealing with someone in our Adult, only to hear our Parent (or Child) speaking the well-thought-out words! The *words* are Adult; the *voice* is Parent. The transaction is ruined! Take this situation, for example.

Jeff, supervisor of the drafting section of an engineering firm, had chosen Wayne for a particularly difficult assignment. He needed some complicated drawings done very quickly, and he needed them done well. Although he had some reservations about choosing Wayne (Wayne could be sloppy at times), he also knew that Wayne could do the best job in the section—when he wanted to. Jeff had gone out of his way to impress upon Wayne the importance of this particular project, and after a long conversation, he finally felt safe in giving Wayne the assignment.

Now two days later, Wayne has submitted the drawings. They are unusually sloppy. Jeff is furious! But he is trying to develop his managerial skills and does not want to show his anger. He knows that running off at the mouth rarely solves anything. He calls Wayne into his office, trying to think of an Adult way to start the conversation. He decides simply to call Wayne's attention to the fact of the sloppiness. No Parent statements. No recriminations. No sounding disappointed. Just an Adult observation of fact.

Jeff says to himself, "I'll tell him, 'Wayne, I see your sloppiness hasn't improved.' " A smile of satisfaction comes over his face. That's the way to start out. He won't be hooked! He stops abruptly.

"No, that won't do. Sloppiness is probably a Parent word. I'll say, 'Wayne, I notice your work hasn't improved.' "

Jeff pauses for a moment to digest what he has decided. It seems okay, but something still bugs him. He shifts uncomfortably in his chair. "No. That won't do, either. *Improved* also sounds Parent. Maybe I better say, 'Wayne, I notice you weren't as neat as you said you'd be.' "

He pauses again, *this time* to mull over the idea. It's beginning to look like he's got it. Finally, he says to himself, "Good! *That's* what I'll say."

He settles back and waits for Wayne to arrive. Suddenly,

he has a flash! "Wait! If I say, 'as neat as you *said you'd be,'* it might sound like I'm annoyed because he didn't keep his side of the bargain! Like I've got some sort of secret contract with him!"

With an inaudible sign of frustration, he says to himself, "How in the world do I just stick to the facts?" After a minute or two more of thinking, Jeff finally decides, "I know what. I'll say, 'Wayne, I notice this work is not as neat as you've done before.' (*Pause.*) That's as neutral a statement as I can think of, damn it!"

Wayne walks into the office. Jeff glares at him and says, "Wayne, I notice this work is not as neat as you've done before," his voice dripping with sarcasm.

Wayne backs off. No doubt about it, he's going to catch hell!

Often, the secret to neutralizing our expectations is not so much in choosing Adult-sounding words, but rather in dealing directly with the source of our own bad feelings. It is very much like working through the bad feelings that hook us into games. Had Jeff asked himself how he was making himself feel bad, he would have immediately discovered the secret contract to which he was trying to hold Wayne (*You* must behave properly in order to make *me* look [feel] good!). As it turns out, Jeff believes that the way Wayne and other people behave "reflects" on him. (This attitude is not unusual in our society. It is, in fact, the source of many of our secret contracts.) Jeff has set himself up to feel good when people behave well, and to feel bad when they don't. He *expects* them to behave well. Whether or not their behavior actually reflects on him (in the eyes of his boss, for instance) does not matter. Until Jeff recognizes what is happening inside himself—how he sets himself up to feel angry—all the Adult-sounding words in the world will not help him come on Adult. Only when he realizes that how he feels does not have to be related to how other people behave—that he is, in a sense, the "boss" of his own feelings—will he gain autonomy over what happens inside himself and effectively neutralize his own expectations.

Creating an Atmosphere of Trust

One of the most important aspects of the relationship between any two people is the degree of trust existing between them. In business management, the willingness of the employees to trust the manager will frequently determine the extent to which the manager can manage effectively. In helping people gain autonomy over their lives (change themselves), trust can often be the single most critical factor. A person thinking of changing something about himself simply *will not do so* in the presence of someone he does not trust. The risk is too great. He will need to concentrate so intensely on himself that he will feel completely exposed, defenseless. He will need to be protected when he deals with himself, not threatened.

In order for a manager to communicate to others that he can be trusted, he must recognize whether he can, in fact, trust himself. If I trust myself and I trust another person, my actions automatically imply the possibility of an I'm OK—You're OK relationship between us. If I do not trust myself (if I have to keep myself in check; if I'm afraid of what I might do if I permit myself to feel, live, enjoy life, or do what *I* want; if I'm wary of my hidden impulses, ashamed of my basic desires, bothered by the "bad" thoughts which keep running through my head), it will be hard for me to trust others, and that may undermine the possibilities of developing an I'm OK—You're OK system between us.

A New Code of Honesty

Barry, a conscientious young supervisor, could tell that Charlie had not been doing a good job lately. He thought something might be bothering Charlie, and wanted to help. One morning, he decided to approach the subject casually. "How's everything coming, Charlie?"

"Okay," Charlie answered offhand.

Barry could *tell* Charlie was avoiding something. Something must be wrong! How could he find out? "Any problems?" he asked.

"Not really," was the reply.

That wasn't at all satisfactory. He would have to press harder, he decided. "Are you *sure* things are going all right?"

"Yes."

Barry paused. What else could he say? His voice trailed off plaintively. "Well, let me know if I can be of any help. . . ."

"Okay."

Barry slowly walked away, his resources exhausted, knowing no more than when he had begun.

This effort could have been more rewarding. Barry was interested in Charlie and wanted to help. But somehow they were both sucked into a game of "Please Tell Me—No I Won't," and Charlie was not being honest with him. How did it happen?

The problem was in Barry's approach. He had made the mistake of deciding, all by himself, that he was going to help Charlie. By not giving Charlie a voice in this decision, he had set up an I'm OK—You're *not* OK system. From that point on, the only thing that mattered to Barry was getting the information he needed. The harder it became, the harder he pressed. The harder he pressed, the more Charlie resisted. The transactions became directed at Barry's increasingly urgent need for data, not Charlie's possible need for help. A game quickly developed because Barry had posed many unanswered questions for Charlie—why Barry needed the information, who he wanted to help, and why he thought he could help. Charlie had no reason to accept a contract of honesty just to satisfy his supervisor's unexplained curiosity!

Rather than take this approach, Barry could have made himself available to Charlie, and let it go at that. In speaking, he could have stuck to Adult statements of fact dealing with the reality of the present—preferably focused on *himself*, not Charlie. In establishing an atmosphere of trust, it is often better to focus on one's own share in the transaction, letting the other person assume responsibility for speaking about *his* share. This establishes an I'm OK—You're OK system.

Instead of asking oblique questions, Barry might have said, "Charlie, something seems to be bothering you lately, and I'd like to help if I can." Charlie might have been surprised to learn that someone knew he was bothered, and gratified to know someone cared. He might have replied, "Gee, I'm glad you mentioned it. I've really been worried lately." He might then have gone on to tell the supervisor about his problems.

On the other hand, Charlie might still have denied he was

troubled or he might have turned down the offer of help. He might have replied, "Thanks anyway, but everything's okay." If he had, Barry would nonetheless have had a large reserve of sentences to fall back on, *so long as he continued to make Adult observations about himself*. He could have said, for instance, "Charlie, it really bothers me to see you this way." He could have continued, "I don't know why I'm disturbed, but it would make me feel a lot better if we could talk about this." Or "I guess I feel I have to solve everyone's problems, or I'm not doing my job."

While Charlie might have been too defensive to open up this time around, this approach would have made clear that Barry was an honest man, willing to talk openly about himself. It would also have made clear that he was available to help, should Charlie need him.

Tony, assistant manager of a branch office of a large metropolitan bank, walked into the office of his new boss. Tony had a problem that he was not sure how to handle—the type of problem he had been accustomed to talking over with his previous boss. He wasn't sure how much he could confide in his new boss, but his problem could wait no longer, and for better or worse, the time had come to break the ice.

As Tony walked into the office, the manager greeted him jovially.

MANAGER: Say Tony. What kind of look is that to have on your face! Come on, now. Wipe that frown away and put on a smile.

TONY: Well, I'd like to, but I've got a problem to talk to you about.

MANAGER: Okay. That's what I'm here for. To help with the problems. I want you to feel free to lay it on the line.

Tony was beginning to have misgivings, but he plunged ahead, anyway.

TONY: I hate to bother you with this. It's about Sam. He's been with us here for almost twenty years. He's been drinking heavily lately, and I'm afraid it may start to affect his work. I've talked to him about it, but it doesn't seem to have done much good. He's getting close to retirement and it would be a shame if anything should happen. I just don't know what to do.

There was a short pause. The manager broke the silence.

MANAGER: Has anything happened to affect his work, so far?

TONY: No.

The manager appeared to consider the problem for a while. Then he smiled, nervously.

MANAGER: I think you'll have to play it pretty much by ear, Tony. Not knowing Sam, there really isn't too much I can help you with.

TONY: Well, I was wondering if you've ever run into the same type of situation.

MANAGER: I can't say that I have. But I'm sure Sam doesn't want to lose his job. Now, how about it? Is there anything else I can help you with?

TONY: Not really. It's just that Sam's an old friend.

MANAGER: Tony, you're just making a mountain out of a molehill. Now, cheer up! Put your smile back on and go out there and knock 'em dead!

Tony got up slowly and walked out of the office. The manager had done his best to help Tony feel better, to "cheer him up." But it hadn't worked. People do not smile because they are told to or because they think they are supposed to. They smile when they are happy. And they cannot be happy when they are worried. Rather than gaining Tony's confidence, the manager had succeeded in conveying the secret message that Tony should keep these troublesome problems to himself. "Don't bother me" fairly screamed out each time the manager opened his mouth. Tony would know better the next time.

This scene deserved a happier ending. As Tony walked in, the manager could have said, "You look worried." (An Adult observation at the feeling level.) After hearing Tony's problem, he could have said to himself, "This sure sounds like something I don't want to get involved in. I haven't the faintest idea what to do. My first reaction is to push it back on Tony. I guess my Child is running scared, trying to deny the problem. If I ever want Tony to have confidence in me, to trust me, I can't turn him away. The best thing I can do is to be honest with him."

To Tony he might have said, "I can see why you're worried. This is something I don't know much about, and it's sort of delicate. I'm afraid I'll just botch things up rather than be any help. However, something's probably bothering Sam, and maybe if we all got together and talked about it, it might help. At least we can let Sam know we understand." This conversation might not have helped Tony solve his problem, but it could have gone far in establishing an honest relationship between Tony and his new boss.

Many bosses simply do not know how to be honest with their subordinates. Even though they want the loyalty and trust which come from an honest, open relationship, they let their poor, fearful Child dictate their management techniques. Often they are hung up by Parent tapes about the *role* they play (being a boss) as well as the *roles* their subordinates play. Once we project ourselves, or someone else, into a role, all the requirements of that role loom up in front of us, and we prevent ourselves from becoming aware of the reality at hand. In the case of Tony and his boss, the boss was not aware of how to fulfill his role, as *he* saw it (solving Tony's problems). And his Child had learned long ago to panic under such conditions. ("I get scared when I can't do what's expected of me *by* me.") In working toward an open relationship, in getting someone to trust you, it is important to avoid assuming the burden of a preconceived role. When you do not expect such things of yourself or the other person, you can stop your Parent and Child from sending out secret messages and demanding secret solutions. You can also make honest Adult observations about how you perceive the other person and about where you yourself are in the context of the transactions.

In a sense, this is a new code of honesty. It involves accepting responsibility for one's own contribution to the feelings being generated in any system of transactions. It involves becoming aware of *how I myself contribute to what is going on*. It means recognizing the truth about my own feelings and being willing to reveal that truth to others. "I am afraid." "I don't feel capable." "I feel angry." "I feel threatened." "I am stuck." "I feel bad when I am near such-and-such a person, but that bad feeling is in *me*, not him." When we say such things, we are making Adult observations about how our Child is reacting to a situation. The Adult is much more capable of being honest than either the Parent or Child, each of which may at any time have ulterior motives for doing something.

Sometimes such straightforward statements are inappropriate in everyday conversation. People may not understand them, or they may not be able to accept them. These are times when less direct phrases like, "I feel a *little* angry," "I feel *almost* helpless," "I have *some* self-doubt," or "I'm a *little* afraid that," can be quite satisfactory, *so long as they are meant to reflect a basic feeling.*

Real honesty breeds honesty in return. It is basically a matter of identifying where you are and being explicit about it to others. It says, "I am human. Like all humans I have self-doubts, insecurities, and fears. Here I am, right now, feeling these things. I understand what it is like to be human and feel these things. You may tell me what you feel, and I will understand."

How the Child Undercuts Our Conscious Intentions

In establishing an atmosphere of trust through honesty, there is one major pitfall to beware of. It can come up quite suddenly, and be disastrous. Ralph, fifty-two-year-old manager of a large chemical plant, has been having trouble dealing with Todd, his head chemist. Todd is a fine chemist, but he is wishy-washy. He gets bogged down in details. He rarely completes a project on his own. He bugs Ralph with his spineless, cowardly attitude and his unwillingness to stand up to Ralph and act like a man. But most of all, Todd's mannerisms get on Ralph's nerves. Todd acts effeminate. He flutters his hands, talks in a high-pitched voice, and to Ralph's way of thinking, does not act the way *a man should act.*

Today, Ralph has decided to stop beating around the bush with Todd. He recognizes that part of the difficulty between them has been *his* responsibility—the result of his own preconceived notions about people—and he has decided to do something about it. He is going to use his new code of honesty and be open with Todd. He hopes that Todd will reciprocate.

Ralph calls Todd into his office and shuts the door behind him. He takes a deep breath, and with a serious look on his face, starts to speak. "Todd," he says, using all the courage he can muster, "I'm going to level with you."

There is a pregnant silence as Todd waits to hear the bad news. But Ralph gulps slightly and continues, "Whenever we get together, things just don't go well, and I think I've been contributing to the difficulty."

Another silence. Todd is amazed. This isn't at all like Ralph! Ralph goes on, trying to accept responsibility for how he contributes to their difficulties. "For some reason I always seem to get angry at you, Todd . . ."

Ralph hesitates. He isn't quite sure how to explain this. He gropes for the words, hesitates again, and continues, ". . . whenever you get that silly-looking effeminate grin on your face!"

Todd is stunned! "What's *wrong* with my grin?" he retorts.

And before Ralph can answer, he knows he has blown it. His good intentions have gone up in smoke. He started out wanting to take responsibility for his own anger, but somehow ended up shifting the blame back to Todd.

This is one of the most common examples of how the best laid plans can go awry. We often recognize how we contribute to a bad transaction and decide to do something about it, only to have our Child step in and subtly undercut our conscious intentions at the last minute. (I recognize when I feel bad, but then I find myself avoiding responsibility by placing the cause of that bad feeling *outside* of me—in some other person.)

"*I* get angry when *you* get that silly grin on your face."

or,

"*I* get frustrated because *you* won't work hard."

or

"*I* feel let down when *you* do a poor job."

or,

"*I* feel insecure because *you* don't make me feel secure."

The Child is particularly fearful of its bad feelings, and will set up elaborate defenses to avoid taking responsibility for them. In this case, its strategy is to fall back on an old, very seductive tape. *I* feel bad because of *you! You* are responsible for my bad feelings! *You* create them (in *me*)! If my Child succeeds in convincing me of this (even at the last minute), I will automatically set up an I'm OK—You're *not* OK system and blame you for my feelings—which will save me from having to admit them to myself. This may protect me from seeing myself, but it forces me to use *you* to do so, and will undermine my attempts to establish an atmosphere of trust with you.

When I do this, I am not being honest. The other person knows intuitively that my bad feeling is not in him and that he is not responsible for it. The fact is, I do something to *myself* to make me feel this way. I replay an old tape. The other person may remind me to play the tape (by what he says, or does, or doesn't say, or doesn't do), but it is *my tape*. I turn it on, and I am the only one who can turn it off.

When I can accept responsibility for my own contribution to a bad transaction, I am able to establish an atmosphere of honesty and trust that is hard for the other person to resist. A not OK, mistrustful person may take a while to respond. At the outset he may spend most of his energy trying to figure out what the catch is, but when he learns that there *isn't* any catch, and that he doesn't have to respond if he doesn't want to (that's OK, too, as I will have neutralized my expectations about him), he will usually come around.

This approach establishes a clear-cut I'm OK—You're OK system, and provides one of the best possible ways to stroke a person. People respond because it is their instinct to respond to unconditional strokes. They respond because, underneath it all, they must. The possibilities for using this kind of relationship to help people realize their full potential as productive human beings are virtually limitless.

10. Mastering In-Depth Management

Helping People See Themselves Clearly

One most formidable task of an executive is that of motivating the not OK people who work for him. While some people are more stuck than others, all erect substantial barriers to seeing themselves clearly. Perhaps the biggest obstacle is simply the not OK Child's stubborn insistence on rejecting reality data. Have you ever shuddered when confronted with a candid snapshot of yourself? Or when you heard your voice on a tape recorder? That little shudder we feel inside, that unwillingness to recognize ourselves, is brought on by our Child. Whenever we are in the grip of not OK feelings, we simply will not let ourselves see ourselves; and nurturing our own internalized view of what we are like, we will deny the need to change.

The greatest challenge to the skillful manager is that of getting information about a person past the not OK Child so that it can register accurately with the Adult. Many people *are* willing to change once they have a clear picture of themselves. But our customary ways of feeding data are often designed to hook the Child, not to by-pass it.

Howard, assistant manager of a retail department store, has had his job for eleven years. Passed over for promotion three times, he has seen four store managers come and go. He is up for promotion once again, but he isn't going to get it. Howard's boss has just called him into his office to give him some honest feedback on what's wrong.

As we join their conversation, Howard is slumped down dejectedly in his chair. He looks like the weight of the world is on his shoulders. His boss is speaking.

"Howard, the trouble with you is that you're just not a pusher. You let people walk all over you."

"What do you mean?" Howard replies, with a puzzled look on his face.

"Well, you just don't *assert* yourself enough," his boss continues, trying to get his point across. "You don't seem to *want* to get ahead.

"Oh," Howard says, with a glimmer of recognition. He thinks for a moment, then goes on. "But I really *do* want to get ahead. I just don't know what else to do."

"If you ask me," his boss answers, "you need to try *harder,* Howard, and show us you really mean what you say."

Howard takes a deep breath. This is his familiar dead end. He has been here a thousand times. He replies, slowly, "But I'm already trying as hard as I can . . ." His voice trailing off.

Howard's boss can see he hasn't gotten anywhere. He was trying to give Howard an honest picture of himself, but somehow wasn't succeeding.

This episode could have been much more productive had Howard's boss been able to recognize that all his comments, honest though they may have seemed to him, were *negative* observations produced by his Parent. They provided the kind of negative strokes that Howard's not OK Child has looked for all its life, strokes to which it *immediately* knew how to respond. Listen again to how they sound.

"You're not a pusher."
"You let people walk all over you."
"You don't assert yourself."
"You don't want to get ahead."
"You need to try harder."

Telling a not OK Child that it is not OK does not provide it with any useful information. (The Child already knows this.) It simply enables the Child to maintain the integrity of its already depressive life position. Howard's Child sets people up to tell him that he is not OK, and for the eleven years he has been on the job, Howard's bosses have willingly obliged.

Focus on the Reality of the Present

How, then, can we avoid the trap Howard's boss fell into and succeed in giving someone a clear picture of himself? The secret is to steer clear of Parent dialogues about what he *does wrong*, or how he *can improve*, and deal exclusively with verifiable reality data of the present—particularly, data about how we perceive the person at this very moment in time, *here and now*.

If Howard's boss had taken this approach, he might have said, "Howard, you look like the weight of the world is on your shoulders."

If Howard had asked, "What do you *mean?*" his boss might have said, "Well, I notice that you're slumped down in your chair."

Recognizing that he was slumped down, Howard might have replied, "Yes, I feel sort of dejected."

Their conversation might have continued, "What about?"

"It's just that I want to get ahead, but I always seem to get bogged down."

"I hear you saying you feel frustrated."

"I guess that's right."

"Part of you seems to want to get ahead, and part seems to be holding you back."

"Hmmm. You know. I never thought of it that way!"

Their conversation is not yet resolved, and on the surface it would appear not to have much direction, but it *is* beginning to give Howard a picture of himself.* If Howard's boss can continue to suppress his urge to give their conversation direction, if he can continue to keep his eyes and ears open to how Howard is coming on in the present, and if he can continue to feed this data back to Howard in as undiluted a fashion as possible, he may well succeed in his efforts to help Howard see himself.

The apparent aimlessness of this conversation is in a very real sense its strength. It is aimless only in the sense that it is not being directed or controlled by the Parent in the head of Howard's boss; and it is not being used by that Parent to try to *force* Howard (Parentally) to see its own one-sided, judgmental view of Howard's behavior. The less aimless and more directed approach originally selected by Howard's boss ("You're not a pusher," etc.), although efficient, was efficient only in the sense that his boss's Parent knew what words to use, used them quickly, and felt good about its own (Pa-

*What Howard decides to do about himself is a separate question. Techniques for helping him make this decision are discussed later in this Chapter. One thing is sure at this point, however. Having his boss *tell* him what to do will only confirm his not OK script. It won't help him change.

rental) grasp of the issue. It was totally inefficient in the sense that it communicated nothing at all that Howard's Adult might possibly hear!

As aimless and as time-consuming as focusing on the reality of the present may appear, it is an extremely effective method of hooking someone's Adult (and of keeping him *in* his Adult once he's there). Verifiable information about what is happening here and now is not nearly as easy to deny as either the memory of the past or speculation on the future, and will often succeed in getting past the not OK Child simply because it is too obvious to reject!

This approach is, in fact, the only approach having any chance whatsoever of altering Howard's behavior. The other alternatives are either to do nothing at all—to keep things the same, playing the old, useless games (which is how Howard's bosses have in the past prevented themselves from doing anything positive with Howard)—or to fire Howard (which has not been done in eleven years, and which many companies would be reluctant to do to any average, honest, well-intentioned employee).

In looking for reality data to feed back to a person, it is often helpful to concentrate on what that person is doing physically. Elmer, a forty-two-year-old geologist, commented to his supervisor one day, "I wonder why I can't concentrate on this project?" Suppressing his desire to provide a Parent answer to Elmer's question, the supervisor responded instead by remarking about how he perceived Elmer at that very moment. He said, "You look very disturbed, Elmer."

When Elmer replied, "No, I'm not really disturbed. I was just *wondering,* that's all . . . ," the supervisor knew he hadn't hooked Elmer's Adult. He also knew not to start a power struggle with Elmer's Child. ("Yes, you are." "No, I'm not.") He knew that if he won such a fight, it would only confirm Elmer's life script. He turned instead to the physical data at hand, and said calmly, "Your body seems to be tense, Elmer, and your hands are moving in an agitated fashion." There was a moment of silence as Elmer digested what he had heard. When he, too, became aware of what state he was in physically, he replied thoughtfully, "I guess I'm more disturbed than I realized."

When we replay our old not OK tapes, we frequently reflect physically our basic not OK feelings. We are often unaware of what we are doing while we are doing it. Helping someone become aware of what he does to himself when he is in the grip of not OK feelings can go far towards increasing his Adult awareness of how he continues to replay his old tapes in the present. Physical symptoms, such as tense muscles, dejected posture, and nervous hands and feet, provide the most obvious data available for observation, and will be least subject to denial by the not OK Child.

An interesting sidelight to this conversation concerns its start. People often convey a certain willingness to look at themselves through phrases like Elmer's "I wonder why I can concentrate?" Whenever someone wonders aloud about himself, or questions why he does things a certain way, he will probably be more receptive than usual to hearing things about himself. These occasions can present excellent opportunities for providing such a person with reality feedback. They are opportunities well worth taking, even if the initial signal is weak (as it was in Elmer's case, when his Child immediately stepped in to deny that a signal had indeed even been given, "I'm not disturbed, I was just *wondering. . . .*"), because the success of the reality feedback process hinges entirely on *the receptivity of the person involved.* If a person is receptive, he will hear you. If he is not, all the cajoling in the world will rarely open his ears. Although most of us might prefer to give such feedback when we ourselves have the urge, the most effective time to do so is not when we want to give it, but when the receiver has expressed even a tenuous willingness to *receive* it.

Choose Neutral Words

One of the biggest difficulties in giving this feedback is in selecting the words. They must be devoid of any Parent or Child implications, and must be able to convey the message that what is going on is merely the transfer of information from one computer to another.

Words like,

You look like . . . .
I notice that . . . .
I hear you saying . . . .
I am aware that . . . .
I perceive that you . . . .
I see you as . . . .

are particularly helpful in doing this. They are meant to provide someone with a mirror image of what he is, as well as with the implied understanding that it is OK to be that way. (If the person wants to change, this is where he will be starting from.)

Listen for Internal Dialogues

Another secret to giving reality feedback is to hear the internal dialogues that go on in other people's heads. A person sometimes may appear to be in both his Parent and his Child at the same time, or, occasionally, he may seem to be in one and then the other, switching back and forth between them faster than the eye can follow. If he *is* switching back and forth, his Parent and Child will often suggest what is happening by carrying on a dialogue with each other. This dialogue may be revealed in the words he speaks.

Fred, a thirty-two-year-old systems analyst, turned to his boss in utter exasperation, saying, "I know I should be doing a better job on this project, but I just don't want to!" Instead of taking offense at this outburst and reacting to Fred's Child in a way that would only confirm Fred's not OK life script (punishing Fred, firing him), Fred's boss decided to feed back to Fred what he heard him saying. He said, "I hear you having a fight inside yourself, Fred. Part of you [Parent] says you ought to do better, and part of you [Child] is rebelling." Fred's mouth dropped open. "Is *that* what you hear?" he said with surprise.

These internal dialogues, often a symptom of strong internal conflict, may be hard to hear when they are going on inside one's own head. A good listener, however, can frequently tune in on them if he is alert to Parent and Child implications in the words people speak. Bruce, a young engineer, muttered to himself after just having made a costly mistake, "Look what you did *now*, Bruce baby. You went and fouled things up good, this time. Didn't you?" His boss, rather than laughing at Bruce for talking to himself or trying to console him in the depths of his misery, observed, "I hear you punishing yourself in your head, Bruce." (T.A. translation: "I hear your Parent beating on your Child.") Bruce thought for a moment and then replied, "You know, I think you're right. My parents used to talk like that to me when I was a little boy. Here I am still doing it to myself!"

Many internal dialogues between the Parent and Child represent the age-old clash between what we think we *should* be (the projections our parents placed on us, which represented what *they* wanted us to be, which became a part of us as we absorbed them into our Parent) and what we *are!* They may also represent the clash between what we think we should be and what we would *like* to be! In either case, when the Parent in us says that we are perfect, that we don't make mistakes, that we have high standards of conduct, and that we are always willing to sacrifice, the Child in us knows that these things aren't nearly as true as they sound.

But the Child also knows not to talk back to the Parent—at least not openly. As a result, many troubled people go around carrying on these dialogues in their heads—scolding themselves, arguing with themselves, rebelling against themselves—engaged in a never ending struggle to reconcile the two parts of them which simply refuse to see things the same way.

Clarify Individual Responsibility

In giving someone reality feedback, it is often helpful to place full responsibility for what that person does to himself squarely on his shoulders. Joe, a thirty-eight-year-old assistant vice president of a large suburban bank, had been offered a promotion to full vice president. Instead of jumping for joy, as his boss thought he would, Joe hesitated to accept the promotion. He lost sleep for several days and started looking very worried. When his boss asked what was the matter, he said, "I want the money, but I don't want the responsibility."

In replying to this statement, his boss wanted to help Joe see how he had let his Child tangle himself up. He guessed that Joe's Child had never learned to deal with frustration, that it had never learned to decide for itself which of its "wants" provided the greatest yield. (Perhaps Joe's decisions as a youngster had all been made by his parents, and his real learning opportunities had been rare.) He also had a hunch that Joe's Child had developed some kind of catastrophic expectation about accepting responsibility and that perhaps it exaggerated the negative aspects of everything it disliked.

Whatever was going on, Joe's boss wanted to make sure that Joe had a picture of what he was doing to himself, and he wanted to imply that Joe was the only person who could do anything about it. He replied, "Joe, I hear you frustrating yourself." (He also might have said, "I see you upsetting yourself" or "I sense something unpleasant in your understanding of responsibility" or "I sense something about responsibility that frightens you" or "You seem to be scaring yourself.")

Joe, on hearing his boss's words, stood dumbfounded. "Is *that* what I'm doing to myself?" he said, incredulously. Then, after a long pause to collect his thoughts, he remarked quietly, "You know, I really appreciate your telling me this. I knew something was wrong, but I couldn't quite put my finger on it!"

Sometimes it is easier to help a person see what is happening inside him by ignoring the content of the words he speaks. Ralph, a twenty-eight-year-old attorney, had just given his senior partner an elaborate justification for why he needed help on a certain project. As he finished speaking, a sly smile flickered ever so briefly at the corner of his mouth. His senior partner responded, not to the content of his speech, but to his smile. In an understanding voice, he said, "I experience your feeling that you've put something over on me, Ralph."

Harry, a twenty-six-year-old accountant, had long been afraid to broach a particular subject with his boss. One day, when he felt he had summoned enough courage, he resolutely walked into his boss's office to give it a try. As he started to speak, he coughed, stammered, and put his hand to his mouth. His boss remarked gently, "You seem to be stopping yourself from talking, Harry."

Brad, a long-time career social worker, was explaining to his boss why he had never made it as a supervisor. During his explanation he unconsciously punctuated his sentences with short, nervous laughter. He finished, saying, "Supervising isn't as easy as you'd think. *(Chuckle.)* I was just never really cut out for it. *(Chuckle, chuckle.)*"

His boss, noticing the laughter, commented softly, "I hear you laughing at yourself, Brad. Could it be that you secretly didn't *want* to succeed as a supervisor?"

Ironic laughter is often used by the not OK Child to get its secret story across in the midst of all the programmed, surface rationale being spoken. Through its use, the manipulative, controlling Child (the one who writes the script) identifies itself as the real power in the person's life.

Any observable data can serve as appropriate material for

reality feedback, so long as it is happening *now*, in the present, and has a fair chance of being perceived by the other person's Adult. (If the person is very angry, or very fearful, *no* data will be appropriate.) Whenever possible, the data should reflect the spontaneous gestures, sentences, movements, and speech patterns which are characteristic of the Parent and Child, and which have occurred outside the person's Adult awareness. The feedback should be given as soon as possible after the data is observed, with no intent other than to increase the other person's insight into what is going on.

If the other person is not ready or willing to accept the data, he will make this clear by either categorically denying the data, or by acknowledging it (he may have been peripherally aware of it, anyway) by saying, "So what?" In either event, trying to force him to see a reality he does not want to see will only create an I'm OK—You're not OK system and will in no way ease the communication. A competent manager will assess a subordinate's capacity and willingness to change and permit the subordinate to change at his own pace and in his own way, within a time frame consistent with the goals of the organization. (People may change significantly, given six months or a year; but seldom will they change within only a month or two.) A manager concerned about his inability to find the right moment to give a subordinate reality feedback, or that there never seems to be an appropriate moment, might do well to obtain a specific contract with that subordinate about when that subordinate will be willing to hear (and when he will not be willing to hear).

Helping People Grow (Change Themselves)

In order to help people change themselves, a person must first neutralize his own expectations. (Not that he still will not expect things of people. But he will not get hooked when they do not do what he expects, and he will not lay his expectations on them inadvertently.) He must turn off his old Parent tapes about why people are like they are and disregard all the old slogans and witches' tales he may previously have believed about how to handle people in work situations. (Spare the rod and spoil the employee. Lazy people need to be pushed. Once a failure, always a failure.) He must recognize that it will be difficult to stay in his Adult for long periods of time, and he must prepare in advance for his Parent and Child to show through, planning to use only his friendly, fun-loving Child, and his warm, understanding Parent. (These will stroke the other person in positive ways.) He must work actively to achieve an I'm OK—You're OK system, a system in which others will be sure to trust him. Once another person's Child knows it can trust him, once it knows that he will neither take advantage of its vulnerability nor project onto it his own expectations of what it should do, it will then be more inclined to entertain thoughts of changing.

Someone interested in learning to help others change must also learn to recognize when he has his own attention—when he himself is clear, and when he is best in a position to observe reality accurately and describe it to someone else. He must be able to check himself out in advance. He must know when the data he is about to communicate may be colored by his own misperceptions and distorted by the process of passing through his own head before being returned to the other person. He must, in effect, know when his data is likely to be accurate and when it is not, and he must be willing to avoid giving it when it is not.

The Helping Process

Monty, manager of the billing department of a large utility company, had worked long and hard to give Alfred, one of his subordinates, a clear picture of his self-defeating behavior. After having convinced himself of his success, Monty sat back, waiting expectantly for Alfred to change. As week after week went by, and nothing happened, Monty became puzzled. Finally, he could no longer contain himself. He approached Alfred, asking, "Now that you've got such a clear understanding of the way you act, Alfred, why don't you *do* something about it?"

Taken by surprise, Alfred exclaimed, "What do you mean? I can't do anything about it! That's just the way I am!"

Many people go through life completely unaware of their ability to influence their own lives. They do not change because they do not *believe* they can. Their Parent data tells them they cannot and their life experience has been one in which people *did not* change. They are loaded with Parent rationale to back up their helpless scripts. ("I can't change because it's in my genes." [The gene theory.] "My 'unconscious' is in charge of my feelings." [I can't control my mind.] "I am the way I am, and if I changed I wouldn't be me." [The "who I am" theory.])

Even people not burdened by such hopeless Parent data have trouble changing. They don't know *what* to change. (They have no pattern of selecting things to work on.) They don't know *how* to change. (They don't know what to do once they decide.) And, frequently, they don't *want* to change. (They're already stroking themselves for what they're doing, no matter how dysfunctional it may be.)

Telling people to believe what they do not believe, telling them what to change and how, rarely produces positive results (unless the people themselves are willing to be influenced by your Parent data, or happen to agree with it). Pressing another person to change may merely force his Child to say whatever you want to hear, to release the pressure. If his basic life position is that he is not OK, and that he cannot do things, then telling him he *is* OK, or that he can do things, will never convince him—he has already accumulated a lifetime of data to disprove you. Yet stroking him, and being straight, can often lead him to question his data. By dealing objectively with the facts, without making him defend his position (he is, after all, entitled to his position), you may cause him to reconsider data from his past. When he bemoans his own ineptness, you may say things like, "Look, in my eyes you are a fine, capable person. I know you may see yourself differently." This may not change his thinking on the spot, but it may plant a seed of doubt, especially if you have laid a good groundwork of understanding and trust. He may think to himself, "Here is someone who understands me and he thinks I'm OK. Maybe I'm not as bad as I think."

The key to helping someone change is to get him to the point where he is willing to express the fact that he has some problem, and that he is willing to work on it. (A person needs a *reason* to change, and he must know that he is able to.) Pressure cannot get him to change in the sense that the pressure comes from your Parent and reflects your internalized need for him to change. However, your Adult need not stop expressing its own view of his real capacity to change. ("I believe you can change, if you want to. I know you believe differently.") Adult pressure of this sort represents the age-old clash between an OK life position (yours, in this case) and a not OK life position (his). It represents the difference between reality and nonreality. (Everyone who has an Adult computer, with the possible exception of a few people who have grave defects, has the capacity to gain autonomy and change.) In the long run, the Adult is a very potent force. You, the Adult, need never agree with his Child's depressive, unchangeable view of himself, and you are always there to remind him that his data about himself may in fact be both inaccurate and misleading.

In marriage counseling and clinical situations, the point where someone is willing to work on something is often reached when the person either hurts enough or the stress on the family system is severe enough that something simply must be done. In job situations the hurting and the stress factor may still be significant, but this same point may be reached as a result of group pressure (when the person finds out that he is the only one who is not changing), by his deciding that the other fellow's grass really *is* greener (when he sees that people who change get ahead and feel better), or by infusions of reality data from his boss or other interested persons as they help him examine his script, uncovering those self-defeating things he has done in the past but does not want to continue doing.

Identifying the Source of the Problem with Questions

Once someone has reached the point where he wants to work on something—when he has decided he *will* work on it—it is important to stick with him as he thinks it through, helping his Adult to examine his Parent and Child behavior and to identify which specific aspect of his script causes the difficulty and prevents him from doing what he wants to do. (It could be a Child decision of the "never again" variety, a Parent slogan inappropriately applied to current situations, or anything else taken into his script at an early age and never reexamined.) The process of talking about the problem also provides a means for helping him sort the problem out and parcel it into manageable proportions before making a contract on what to do about it. Questions provide the most effective means of accomplishing all this.

Earlier, in discussing methods of giving people a clearer

picture of themselves, we dealt entirely with one specific type of transaction—that of providing carefully selected data input for another person's Adult computer. ("I hear you saying . . . .") Yet there is another equally effective way of communicating with a computer. Not only do computers accept data input, they produce data output (in computer language, a *printout*).

Data output is usually obtained by presenting a computer with a specific request for information. This request typically is stated in the form of a question. There are, however, many ways of asking questions. Most computers house a considerable amount of data, and the appropriateness of the output obtained at any given time will be greatly influenced by the appropriateness of the question used to produce it.

Marty, age thirty-nine, was chosen six months ago to head the real estate department of a large suburban mortgage company. At the time he seemed a good choice for the job. He was hard working, personable, and an expert in his field.

Since then, however, Marty has turned from a nice guy into a tyrant. His department has become a virtual hotbed of insurrection, and Marty's suitability for the job has seriously been called into question.

Today, Marty has been involved in a heated argument with two of his employees, which ended abruptly when Marty flew into a rage and told both employees to go to hell. Frank, Marty's boss, has heard about the contretemps and has called Marty into his office. As we join them, Marty is sitting tensely in his chair. He knows he's in trouble. His facial muscles are tight and his jaw is jutting out defensively. Frank, who was responsible for promoting Marty in the first place, is at his wit's end. Frank is speaking, "Marty, what's the matter with you?"

Marty doesn't know. He replies, "I don't know."

Frank is thoroughly perplexed. He continues in a voice of utter exasperation, "I can't figure out what gets into you. Why do you do such things?"

Still unable to answer, Marty replies, "I just don't know!"

This conversation illustrates a common pattern of questioning which, though frequently employed, rarely produces data of any value. Rhetorical questions such as "What's the matter with you?" and "Why do you do such things?" almost always invite "I don't know" answers, serving only to direct the dialogue toward ever deepening frustration. Most people, in fact, do not know why they do what they do, and while such questions may hook their Adult, the questions themselves are usually futile—their Adult *does not know*.

How much more helpful this conversation would have been if Frank had first asked Marty whether or not he was interested in finding out what went wrong, and if he had then used questions to see if Marty's Adult was aware of what was happening in the present. If Frank had taken this approach, their conversation might have gone like this:

FRANK: Marty, things seem to be going wrong in your department. Would you like to see if we could find out what is happening?

MARTY *(Somewhat cautiously)*: Sure.

FRANK: Okay. Are you aware that your jaw is jutting out, and that your face muscles seem tense? *(He might also have said, "Do you notice how tensely you're sitting?" or "Did you hear how your voice sounded when you said, 'Sure.' ")*

MARTY: I wasn't aware of my jaw before, but now that you mention it, I am.

FRANK: Can you express what you are feeling right now?

MARTY: Yes, I'm feeling defensive.

These questions, unlike the rhetorical questions illustrated earlier, are questions which the Adult will almost always be able to answer, if only by saying "Yes" or "No." They do not require lengthy printouts, nor do they demand philosophical explanations of events. They ask, essentially, "Are you receiving data (about your Parent and Child), and, if so, are you willing to share it with me?" They establish the fact that two-way communication exists, that the Adult has been hooked and is willing to pursue the subject. If the conversation had reached this point successfully, Frank might have continued with questions of a different kind.

FRANK: What's this about feeling defensive?

MARTY: I've had trouble in my department, so I feel I need to defend myself!

FRANK: How will defending yourself help?

MARTY: It'll show I was justified in what I said.

FRANK: Why do you need to justify yourself?

MARTY: So you'll know I was right!

FRANK: What's this about "right" and "wrong"?

If we stop here for a moment, we can see that Frank has switched to questions like "What's this about?" "How will this help?", and "Why do you need . . . ?". These questions require more thought than the first few. They call for more than simple "Yes" or "No" answers, and are, in a sense, open-ended. They tend to follow the direction that Marty has chosen for the conversation, and they help him focus his thinking in a way that will enable his Adult to identify the basic Parent or Child motivation behind his actions.

This kind of questioning can be very useful in helping a person reduce the expression of his difficulty to a basic Parent or Child statement. Many Parent and Child tapes are so old that even though they still motivate us to automatically do the things we do, we only perceive them as vague, poorly defined, obscure impulses. Such questioning can help a person clarify for himself what is going on inside himself. Then, and only then, can he examine the facts about why he does what he does. Then, and only then, can he assess their appropriateness and decide what, if anything, he would like to do about them.

In Marty's case, we can recognize the cause of his present difficulty as a typical Parent polarity—that of putting things in a framework of right and wrong.* This, and other polarities (between good and bad, weak and strong, black and white, and so on), can be particularly troublesome. We can become so tied up in them that at times our attention, like Marty's, is directed at coming out on the right side or the

*Marty also appears to have cast Frank in the role of judge (with the ultimate power to decide right and wrong). Interesting enough, if Frank were to accept the role selected for him by Marty's Child (by getting hooked into the Right-Wrong game), nothing would be accomplished, other than the furthering of Marty's script. The learning situation would dissolve into thin air.

good side, rather than on finding out how we have contributed to a crossed transaction.

Frank, continuing from the point where we left off (when he had just asked, "What's this about 'right' and 'wrong'?"), might have pursued the conversation by exploring with Marty the origins and implications of Marty's Parent data about right and wrong (had Marty been willing). Or he might have chosen merely to provide Marty an alternate view of the subject—a different way of seeing the same situation—so that Marty's Adult would have additional facts at its disposal as it reassessed the matter. If Frank had chosen this second approach, he might have said, "You know, Marty, I view this situation somewhat differently. I really don't see transactions between people in terms of their rightness or wrongness. Things may go well, or they may not, and if they don't, it can be helpful to find out how it happened. That's all. . . ."

This approach is particularly appropriate where deeply ingrained Parent data is involved. People often need time to reassess such Parent data. A reassessment cannot always be done immediately, or even overnight. Although the words above might not bring about an immediate change in Marty's attitude, they may well give him something to think about.

If Frank had no special need to deal with the specific argument which had erupted between Marty and his employees that day, he might have ended the conversation there. He had hooked Marty's Adult, they had explored one source of difficulty for Marty—the right and wrong polarity which brought on his defensiveness and which quite possibly might have induced his earlier urge to NIGYSOB his employees (zapping them in some sort of defensive manner for being "wrong"). Starting with the reality of the present, Frank had been willing to let Marty lead the conversation, asking questions only for the purpose of helping Marty clarify where he was. Much had been learned. If this conversation were to serve as a pattern for future conversations between the two, there would be little doubt Marty would soon become an effective manager.

On the other hand, if Frank had needed for business reasons to deal with the subject of the heated argument, after first getting Marty's agreement to pursue the subject, he might have approached it like this:

FRANK: Now, Marty, what was this argument you had today all about?

MARTY: Well, those two fellows weren't doing the job they should be doing.

FRANK: So?

MARTY: So I took them aside and told them so!

FRANK: And?

MARTY: And they had the nerve to say I didn't know what I was talking about!

FRANK *(Pausing)*: Did you?

MARTY: You're darn right! I've caught them loafing around here half a dozen times in the past few days!

FRANK: How's the quality of their work? What about the quantity?

MARTY *(Pausing)*: Well, I don't know. No one's complained lately. It seems to be pretty good.

FRANK *(Stopping the conversation at this point)*: Okay, Marty. I hear you saying that you're not comfortable unless the people around you seem to be busy—that you're operating from some [Parent] data that says people who don't look busy are loafing, and that loafing's *bad*. When you catch someone loafing, you feel you must scold him.

The secret to uncovering the basic Parent or Child motivation behind Marty's behavior is merely to listen to the words he uses. The words reveal all. If he is willing to continue talking, sooner or later they will come out. In order to stay with him, however, one must resist being taken in by the apparent validity of his Parent or Child statements. When Marty said, "They had the nerve to say I didn't know what I was talking about!", it would have been futile to reply, "I don't blame you for getting angry, Marty!", going on to play Ain't It Awful with him, or jointly scolding the other two employees. Regardless of how plausible his Parent data may sound, treating it as anything but the apparent source of Marty's own confusion will be self-defeating.

Finding a Contract

Being able to identify what someone does to create difficulties for himself is of little value unless that person is willing to make a contract with himself not to do it any more. Few people come to such contracts easily. Making a contract usually means giving up something, and what must usually be given up is a very familiar feeling or habit. This familiar feeling or habit will often be experienced as comfortable, even enjoyable. It will typically appear more comfortable or enjoyable than what we anticipate changing to. In addition, when we are in the midst of repetitive script behavior, we are already getting stroked, or we are stroking ourselves, for doing what we are doing. (Remember, even getting a kick is getting a stroke.) Thus, in contracting to change, a person often is faced with the seemingly unpleasant task of choosing against one facet of his own self-interest—comfort.

Someone faced with this choice will need a very strong reason to change. He will really have to want to change. He will have to be willing to give up something very important from his past. Chuck, a NIGYSOBing attorney, wanted to feel good enough as he went through life to avoid having to systematically zap others to relieve his bad feelings. He wanted to feel good, generally. In order to do so, he had to be willing to give up the temporary feeling of elation he received whenever he put someone down. Nancy, a Kick Me player, wanted to stop setting herself up for kicks, but had first to decide that she was willing to sacrifice her familiar feeling of helplessness and give up the special comfort she felt in crawling into her own shell and not succeeding. Perry, a young systems analyst, wanted to stop overeating. He knew it made him sluggish. In order to do so, however, he had first to be willing to relinquish the comfortable, satisfied feeling that came over him after a meal, whenever he had succeeded in completely stuffing himself.

In helping someone reach a contract, it is often useful to help him determine what it is he will be giving up, and to clarify whether or not he in fact wants to make a contract to do this. People will be more inclined to give up things that are no longer important to them than they will be to give up something with continued significance in their lives. An old Parent tape which was never ingrained too strongly is easier to let go than a script feeling which has become really familiar and very comfortable. Unfortunately, the two are sometimes related. In the previous example, for instance, Marty might well have been inclined to give up his automatic reliance on his right-wrong polarity, if that were all that was involved. However, if this polarity were closely tied to the feelings that came over him in defending the "right" side of a position and zapping the person on the "wrong" side, and if these feelings were important to him, his reluctance to give up the feelings might cause him to hold on to the polarity.

For a person to change, he must make a contract to change. Someone interested in helping him change can do so most effectively by helping him find a contract he is willing to accept. Once he has defined and accepted a contract that he can live with, the most effective way to help him keep his own contract involves asking the "How do you prevent yourself. . . ?" questions described earlier. This approach will help him increase his autonomy and, in effect, keep tabs on his contract for himself.

Getting the Most Out of People

In organizing and managing systems of people, it is important to define the purpose of bringing the people together. A clear definition of the goals of the organization, of the *context,* is indispensable to the efficient running of the system. People work together best not only when they operate from the two-part position I'm OK—You're OK, but when they are also in accord with the goals of the organization, when their true stance is the three-part position, I'm OK—You're OK—*and the context is OK!* Whenever there is conflict with the over-all goals of the organization, even if the people themselves seem OK to one another, the system itself will not be OK.

An adequate statement of the goals of the organization will not only include the general purpose for the existence of the system (for schools, teaching children; for companies, earning profits; and so on), but will also state the conditions under which those goals will be achieved. In particular, it will attend to the manner in which people will be treated in attaining those goals. A clear statement about a system must include data about how that system will be run.

A system organized to get the most out of people is one in which people are encouraged to use both their natural Child and their Adult computers. These two essential parts of a person's makeup are the ones most often held in check, discouraged, ignored, or beaten into submission by the Parent of whoever is in charge of the system. They are the two elements most threatening to a controlling Parent. Many a boss envisions himself losing power and giving up control of his organization by permitting the Adult and Child in his subordinates to emerge. In a sense his perception is accurate. He *is* giving up power and control, but it is only the power and control which in the past his Parent has maintained through the use of manipulations and secret contracts. It is not the strength and insight still available to him through his own OK Child and his Adult. If he operates very much from his Parent, however, he will often see this as giving up *total* power and control, and he may be reluctant to do it. The dilemma faced by many a manager is that to get the most out of his people he must first be willing to give up his old Parental power, risk losing his control (which his Adult and Child were never involved in, anyway), and abrogate all his old secret contracts. Although this often appears risky, it is usually a risk well worth taking.

Management techniques which in the long run most successfully optimize production are those which permit employees to exist as *people,* not as pawns, or as only part people (as only Parent or only Child, as when secret contracts exist), or as human machines. Such techniques involve establishing a system of OKness in which people perform well because they feel good about themselves, because they feel good about what they are doing, and because they receive good, positive strokes for doing what they are doing. Such techniques involve defining the context and keeping a fit between the interests of the people in the system and the goals of the organization. In large organizations, this involves a process of communication which must go on fairly constantly from the top down. Many people who are responsible for operating systems have had only one kind of system as their role model—the traditional family system in which they were raised. In this system, transactions are frequently based on very limited kinds of Parent-Child relationships. Goals are seldom explicit and typically muddled. (People marry for all sorts of unclear reasons.) Organization systems patterned after family systems often reflect the same confusions as family life.

In all systems, however, people develop best (whether children or adults) when they are deliberately given situations in which they can make their own choices—where they understand the context and have a stake in the outcome (where their ideas contribute to results) and where they are permitted to experiment and share ideas without being subject to judgment. Such conditions permit them to develop their Adult and to reduce their reliance on Parent-Child (tell-me-how-to-do-it) transactions. Such conditions provide, as part of the learning process, explicit permission to fail. Mistakes are not used as invitations to censure, punish, or judge or as invitations to feel bad. They are used only to provide new data about what not to do. In a very real sense, permission to fail is permission to grow. It is as important to building strong organizations as it is to building strong children and healthy adults.

Source Notes

Chapter 2. Getting a Feel for People

1. W. Penfield, *Memory Mechanism* (A.M.A. Archives of Neurology and Psychiatry, 1952), p. 67.
2. Thomas A. Harris, *I'm OK—You're OK* (New York: Harper & Row, 1967), p. 18.
3. *Ibid.*, p. 19.
4. *Ibid.*, p. 36.
5. Eric Berne, *Games People Play* (New York: Grove Press, 1964), p. 25.
6. Thomas A. Harris, *op. cit.*, p. 41.

Chapter 3. Catching Up with the Experts

1. Thomas A. Harris, *I'm OK—You're OK* (New York: Harper & Row, 1967), p. 42.
2. *Ibid.*, pp. 48-49.
3. Eric Berne, *Principles of Group Treatment* (New York: Oxford University Press, 1966), p. 264.
4. *Ibid.*, p. 269.

Chapter 4. Extending Your Perspective

1. Thomas A. Harris, *I'm OK—You're OK* (New York: Harper & Row, 1967), p. 116.
2. Eric Berne, *Games People Play* (New York: Grove Press, 1964), p. 40.
3. Thomas A. Harris, *op. cit.*, p. 117.
4. Eric Berne, *op. cit.*, p. 60.
5. Eric Berne, *Transactional Analysis in Psychotherapy* (New York: Grove Press, 1961), p. 214.

The choice of the three typical "business" scripts discussed in this chapter was greatly influenced by *The Managerial Grid*, by Robert R. Blake, Ph.D., and Jane S. Mouton, Ph.D. (Houston: Gulf Publishing Company, 1964).

Index